Feminist Technosciences

Rebecca Herzig and Banu Subramaniam, Series Editors

Bad
Dog

**PIT BULL POLITICS AND
MULTISPECIES JUSTICE**

HARLAN WEAVER

UNIVERSITY OF WASHINGTON PRESS

Seattle

Bad Dog was made possible in part by the University of Washington Press Authors Fund.

Interior design by Thomas Eykemans
Composed in Chaparral, typeface designed by Carol Twombly
Cover design by Katrina Noble
Cover illustration: Jaclyn Clark, Unsplash.

25 24 23 22 21   5 4 3 2 1

Printed and bound in the United States of America

UNIVERSITY OF WASHINGTON PRESS
uwapress.uw.edu

LIBRARY OF CONGRESS CATALOGING-IN-PUBLICATION DATA
Names: Weaver, Harlan, author.
Title: Bad dog : pit bull politics and multispecies justice / Harlan Weaver.
Description: Seattle : University of Washington Press, [2021] | Series: Feminist technosciences | Includes index.
Identifiers: LCCN 2020020395 (print) | LCCN 2020020396 (ebook) | ISBN 9780295748016 (hardcover) | ISBN 9780295748023 (paperback) | ISBN 9780295748030 (ebook)
Subjects: LCSH: Pit bull terriers—Social aspects. | Designer dogs. | Intersectionality (Sociology)
Classification: LCC SF429.P58 W43 2020 (print) | LCC SF429.P58 (ebook) | DDC 636.755/9—dc23
LC record available at https://lccn.loc.gov/2020020395
LC ebook record available at https://lccn.loc.gov/2020020396

The paper used in this publication is acid free and meets the minimum requirements of American National Standard for Information Sciences—Permanence of Paper for Printed Library Materials, ANSI Z39.48–1984.∞

For Charles Weaver, 1940–2012

.

Contents

Acknowledgments

This book owes its existence to an extended network, human and non-human, without whom this thinking, much less this writing, would not have been possible. First and foremost, I want to thank my incredible interlocutors, whose ideas shape all aspects of this book. I am also deeply grateful for the continued mentorship of Donna Haraway, whose encouragement and continued investment in shared thinking and conversations have nourished not just this book but my life. I am also deeply indebted to Carla Freccero and Karen Barad for their continued mentorship, which has extended well beyond my PhD. This book was also made possible by the mentorship and supportive thinking-with of an amazing group of folks working in and near animal studies across a range of spaces, including but not limited to Susan McHugh, Myra Hird, Brigitte Fielder, Clement Loo, Margo DeMello, Ken Shapiro, Alexandra Horowitz, Robert Jones, Sarah Hann, Gunnar Eggertsson, Eliza Ruiz Izaguirre, Juno Parreñas, Mel Chen, Katharine Mershon, Elizabeth Selena Zinda, Dana Luciano, Banu Subramaniam, Angie Willey, Neel Ahuja, Eduardo Kohn, Michael Lundblad, Ann-Sofie Löngren, Tora Holmberg, Jacob Bull, Ane Gabrielsen, Jami Weinstein, Eliza Steinbock, David Redmalm, Colin Dayan, Claire Jean Kim, Kimberly Tallbear, Sandra Koelle, Mara Miele, Daniel Solomon, Cleo Woelfle-Erskine, Donald Cleary, July Cole, Logan O'Laughlin, Tyler Wall, Katja Guenther, Deboleena Roy, KT Thompson, Natasha Myers, Jacob Goodman, Gabriel Rosenberg, Alice Bendinelli, Ashton Wesner, Amelia Hicks, and Astrid Schrader; I hope all of you see threads of our conversations in this writing!

Additional colleagues with whom I have shared academic and, often, queer affiliations have also sustained me in myriad ways in the process of writing this book. For their early mentorship of my undergraduate work in feminist Science and Technology Studies at Wesleyan University, I am deeply grateful to Joe Rouse, Jennifer Tucker, Christina Crosby, and Natasha Korda. For their mentorship, colleagueship, and comradeship, I owe an enormous debt to many folks with whom I connected through UC Santa Cruz, including but not limited to Eva Hayward, Gerwin Gallob, Kami Chisholm, Rebecca Herzig, Karen DeVries, Lucian O'Connor, Adam Hefty, Lisette Tatiana Olivares, Lindsay Kelley, Natalie Loveless, Trevor Sangrey, Johanna Rothe, Annika Walke, Roya Rastegar, Kalindi Vora, Jenny Reardon, Warren Sack, Nancy Chen, Anne Spalliero, Melanie Lee Godinho, Sheila Peuse, Noah Tamarkin, Sarah Smith-Silverman, Jacob Metcalf, Jessica O'Reilly, Lulu Meza, Scout Calvert, Sara Orning, Ruth Müller, Martha Kenney, Alexis Shotwell, Barbara Epstein, Neferti Tadiar, Jenny Reardon, Irene Gustafson, María Puig de la Bellacasa, Sarah Bracke, Joe Dumit, Neda Atanasoski, and Ulrika Dahl. I continue to be profoundly grateful for the connections I made during postdoctoral work at UC Berkeley, and I want to extend my gratitude first and foremost to Cori Hayden, without whose mentorship this book would not have happened; for their conversations and thinking-with, I am deeply grateful to Veronica Sanz, Charis Thompson, Nicholas D'Avella, Doris Liebetseder, Nolwenn Büller, Marissa Mika, Samuel Weiss-Evans, and Veronica Sanz. Patricio Boyer, Trish Tillburg, and Mel González at Davidson College continue to be sources of support and inspiration, and I owe special thanks to Katie Horowitz, the zucchini to my fennel. Similarly, I am deeply grateful to the amazing people and organizations at Kansas State University who have helped me thrive, including Kathleen Antonioli, Lisa Tatonetti, Michele Janette, Christie Launius, Susan Rensing, Angela Hubler, Valerie Padilla-Carroll, Kimberly Garver, Amber Neely, Joyce Wu, Jess Falcone, Heather McCrae, Mariya Vaughan, Tanya González, Kimberly Garver, Kimathi Choma, Bryan Samuel, Brandon Haddock, Clara Kientz, Marion Schweitzer, the Gender Women and Sexuality Studies Department's intellectual circle, the K-State LGBTQ* FSA, and K-State Affinity Group Leadership. Special thanks go to my K-State colleague-twin, Rachel Levitt, whose friendship and sheer brilliance have nourished me in more ways than I can count. Finally, friends and colleagues localized through what might be more aptly termed trans* affiliations have also been critical to my work in this book, and I am so deeply thankful to Susan Stryker, Laura Horak, Cáel Keegan, and Eliza Steinbock in this regard.

I am also deeply grateful for the opportunities I have had to share the thinking from this book through invited talks. I owe thanks to the University of Chicago's Animal Studies working group, and particularly to Katharine Mershon and Bill Hutchison, in this regard. Montana State University also provided me a wonderful opportunity to develop some interventions key to this book, and I am particularly grateful to Karen DeVries, Sara Rushing, and Kristen Intemann. The University of Kansas's Hall Center for the Humanities gave me invaluable feedback on this writing, and I am beholden to Katie Batza, Stacey Vanderhurst, Brian Donovan, Akiko Takeyama, An Sasala, and Kara Kendall-Morwick in particular. Finally, I am indebted to the wonderful folks at UC Davis for their feedback on this thinking, particularly Wendy Ho and Kathleen Fredrickson, in conjunction with Rana Jaleel.

While there are only two of them, the images in this book have been central to my writing and thinking. In particular, I am profoundly grateful to Lili Chin, whose illustrations have been formative to my own understandings of dogs for many years, and who generously allowed me to use one of my favorites of her works, *Doggie Language*, in this book. The American Antiquarian Society's making available of Josiah Nott and George Gliddon's *Types of Mankind* was invaluable. I also owe thanks to Shelter Animals Count for providing me with key data. Related to the material work that has gone into the book, I am indebted to the folks at the University of Washington Press. A special shout-out goes to Larin McLaughlin, who made me believe in this book in the first place; I am also deeply grateful to Erika Bűky, Hanni Jalil, Julie Van Pelt, Anne Mathews, and Julie Fergus. Finally, and crucially, I thank the anonymous reviewers whose careful reading and nuanced feedback profoundly shaped this writing.

This book would literally not have been possible without the generous support of a variety of funders. First among these is U.S. National Science Foundation, whose grant funded the postdoctoral research for the bulk of my fieldwork for this book (proposal #1230494); I am particularly indebted to Kelly Moore in her role as program officer. I also owe Cori Hayden and the Center for Science, Technology, Medicine, and Society at UC Berkeley a debt of gratitude for not only facilitating the NSF grant but also provisioning me with additional funding in the following year. I thank Tora Holmberg in particular for facilitating the sponsorship of two fellowships at the Centre for Gender Research in Uppsala. Finally, my first chapter owes its existence to the support of a Faculty Enhancement Award and later small grants from the College of Arts and Sciences Dean's Office at Kansas State, and I am profoundly grateful to Kansas State in helping make this book a reality.

Academia can be a profoundly isolating world, and there are a number of folks outside it to whom I am deeply grateful for their friendship and support over the years this writing spanned. Many friends in the San Francisco Bay Area (some of whom have since moved elsewhere) made this book possible, among them Sandra Koelle, A. Anthony, Amera Rizk, Durt, Alan Ray, Jason Kuhafkan, Kinshasa Bennett, Samuel Whiteswan-Perkins, Natalie Chandler, Gretchen Till, Rossella Barry, El Durant, Aaron Potash, Maki Kasai, Morgan Pulleyblank, Travis Miller, Miles Lyons, Raquel Gutiérrez, and Max Henry Repka. I am also deeply grateful to the trans support groups sponsored by both API Wellness in San Francisco and the Pacific Center in Berkeley, which sustained me in more ways than I can count. I am deeply grateful to Jonas Levin and Erica Foster for their wonderful queer/trans welcome to Kansas and continued friendship. I thank my friends in Bay Area dog worlds whose sustained conversations and interest in this thinking have not only profoundly shaped my analysis in this book but also my life: I am indebted to Mara Velez, Kiem Sie, Ana Poe, Randi Woods, and Samara Love for not only their careful interventions but also their caring friendship. In a related vein, I am deeply grateful to the Helping Shelter Animals group on Facebook, which has been critical to my thinking regarding the no-kill movement.

Finally, I thank those among my closest affiliations who have shaped and continue to shape my life in profound ways. Haley, you are sorely missed. Annie, you have been a wonder and a challenge, and I am grateful for every day we have together. Tucker, you are the best cat I have ever known, and I forgive you for being untrainable when it comes to your morning demands. Katherine Miller, you are the best best friend in the world, and I am very glad to know you and to have known you for these past twenty-nine(!) years. Dad, I still miss you terribly and I wish you were here to read this. Danny, you are a wonderful brother, and I'm so thankful. Mom, thank you so much for all your support and love these many years; I hope this book gives you something to share with the Oakland Women's Literary Society.

Bad Dog

Introduction

Cynthia: And I think if you walk around [city X] now, you see a lot more people with pit bulls who look like regular people who belong in [city X]'s neighborhoods, you know? . . . You don't see the ghetto image, which is what used to be the case with pit bulls most of the time.

—PSEUDONYMOUS INTERVIEW BY AUTHOR, JULY 2017

What it means to be a "pit bull" began to change in the United States at the start of the twenty-first century. What had been widely regarded as the categorical "bad dog" started to shift into a being deserving of care and concern, one who had a place in city life and the family home. This shift tracks with another related change in the politics of dog worlds: a sharp rise in and increasing attachment to the importance of "rescuing" animals and incorporating them into family homes.

I use quotation marks around terms in these sentences for several reasons, the first because the "pit bull" is more an idea than a specific type of being. It is generally taken to refer to a squat, muscular, short-haired dog with forward-flopping ears, anywhere between 30 and 150 pounds in weight—hardly a breed per se. Dogs called pit bulls very rarely have papers documenting their lineage as the "American Pit Bull Terrier" recognized by the American Kennel Club. The term *pit bull* references a vague sense of a type of dog whose reputation, dating from the early 1980s, precedes it, giving it what one advocacy organization terms a "bad rap."[1] However, throughout the early 2000s and 2010s, advocates pushed for the increasing acceptance of pit bulls, fiercely criticizing and arguably changing widespread notions that specific characteristics, such as aggression, are innate to a particular kind of dog. Destabilizing the term *pit bull* itself, these labors lead me to put not only "pit bull" but also "bad dog" in quotation marks.

Entwined with these changes was a rise in practices of "rescue," a term that generally refers not to the practice of finding dogs lost in the wilds or extracting them from burning buildings but to taking in strays and dogs surrendered by owners, usually to municipal animal shelters. With the rise of "rescue" practices came related identities, with people becoming "rescuers," and organizations (particularly privately run nonprofit agencies) becoming "rescues." The salvation connoted in these namings reveals how changing practices in animal welfare have entailed transformations in identities. And, as remarks like the epigraph demonstrate, wherein the "ghetto" maps a very different space than that occupied by "regular people," these changes connect to and even emerge through dynamics involving racialization as well as gender, class, sexuality, nation, ability, and colonialism.

This writing combines ethnographic fieldwork—participant observation in the daily workings of the animal shelter that was my fieldwork site; semistructured interviews conducted with interlocutors connected with my fieldwork site, like my conversation with Cynthia; more casual conversations that were not recorded and are reconstructed to the best of my ability; autoethnographic reflections—musings on my own actions, relatings, and thinking; and a range of materials from popular culture and news coverage. As is common in ethnographic work, I have changed the names of my interlocutors, although I have retained details of their race, class, and gender. Cynthia is a white, fortysomething, upper-middle-class straight woman who volunteered regularly at my fieldwork site. And while research protocols dictate that I not disclose exact locations, my work took place in a fairly urban area of California and in an animal shelter that, like many of its kind today, hosted many pit bull–type dogs. Run by paid staff and unpaid volunteers, this shelter was a municipal, publicly funded, and publicly accessible space. I mention this fact because the shelter's very publicness made it "open admission," meaning that it took in all animals within its geographical remit. At the shelter, in addition to interviewing staff and volunteers, I walked and cared for the many dogs in its possession and facilitated "playgroups"—that is, groups wherein shelter residents were encouraged to play with each other. My formal fieldwork, covering roughly a year between 2012 and 2013 and a shorter period in 2017, along with autoethnographic insights dating from 2003—the beginning of my own companionship with several pit bull–type dogs—coincides with burgeoning advocacy for both pit bull–type dogs and rescue dogs in the U.S., giving me a unique perspective on the shifts I name with "pit bull," "bad dog," and "rescue."

The rise of the no-kill movement in animal-related activism inflects the work undertaken by staff and volunteers at my fieldwork site, including Cynthia's. "No kill" dates from roughly the mid-1990s, when Richard Avanzino, head of the San Francisco Society for Prevention of Cruelty to Animals (SPCA), introduced a model of animal sheltering oriented primarily towards adoption, as a counter to the widespread practice of euthanizing animals who ended up at the "pound." Animal advocates put forward a philosophy that no animal should be euthanized. This philosophy was widely embraced and enacted by privately run organizations but has recently gained traction in other areas too. For example, in January 2020, California governor Gavin Newsom incorporated into the proposed state budget a $50 million grant to make all of the state's shelters, including those that are open admission, no kill.[2] The politics of no kill are highly contentious, and I deliberately undertook my fieldwork at a shelter where euthanasia, while not by any means routine, did take place. Moves such as Newsom's would not be possible in the first place if not for the work of advocates on behalf of the most numerous canine shelter residents: the pit bull–type dogs Cynthia mentions.

A July 1987 cover of *Sports Illustrated* makes both visceral and visible the "bad rap" with which pit bull–type dogs have struggled in the U.S. Featuring a brindled dog with teeth bared, the cover proclaims in capital letters, "BEWARE OF THIS DOG," with a subheading, also all caps, "THE PIT BULL TERRIER."[3] Such practices of representation echo widespread efforts beginning in the 1980s to ban the dogs themselves through "breed-specific legislation," or BSL. These measures continue, albeit unevenly, to be put forward today.

The synonymizing of "pit bull" with "bad dog" took the form of commentaries that urged caution and posited that "the pit bull" was by nature possessed with a "will to kill," prone to bite without warning, liable to "turn" from a seemingly benign pet into a vicious beast inclined to attack both humans and other animals.[4] However, such narratives were increasingly challenged in the late 1990s and early 2000s. When I adopted my first pit bull–type dog, Haley, in 2003, a white-faced dog with a seal-colored body whose ears had been closely cropped by her first owners, roughly two-thirds of the people we met viewed her with automatic suspicion and distrust, while the other third tended to proffer alternative narratives along the lines of "It's how you raise them." Towards the end of Haley's life, this balance changed, with probably about 60 percent expressing the latter view.

This move from understanding pit bull–type dogs according to "nurture" rather than "nature" reflects the labor of scores of advocates who challenged BSL not only in legal arenas but also through practices of representation, seeking out opportunities to demonstrate that the dogs were, very publicly and visibly, "good." And while these advocates engaged a more complex positioning than the simple trope of "It's how you raise them" might indicate, such nuances were lost on a larger public.

A key tipping point in pit bull politics—and here I borrow the language of the essayist, cultural commentator, and pit bull advocate Malcolm Gladwell—came in 2007, when Michael Vick, a National Football League (NFL) quarterback and an African American, was charged with involvement in dogfighting.[5] As I detail in chapter 3, many people in the U.S. went into a frenzy, with animal advocates in particular excoriating Vick and even burning him in effigy.[6] As the charges against Vick became more detailed, with allegations surfacing of abuse, beating, neglect, and killing of pit bull–type dogs by electrocution and drowning, a groundswell of public support on behalf of the remaining dogs at Vick's Bad Newz Kennels—dubbed "Vicktims"—led to their being kenneled in animal shelters rather than euthanized. They were eventually assessed by experts in dog behavior and released to several rescue organizations.[7] This shift—what Megan Glick terms the dogs' "humanization"—in which they were perceived and described through anthropocentric terms such as *murder*, contributed to and in many ways tipped the balance of cultural perceptions of pit bull–type dogs.[8] The former Vicktims became "Vicktory" dogs performing labors in the limelight: many were certified as "Canine Good Citizens," offering emotional support in loci such as hospitals. This work marked the individual dogs as "good" in a manner that arguably extended to other dogs placed in the category of "pit bull."[9]

Key to the shifts in public perception of the Vick dogs, along with pit bull–type dogs in general, were changing connections to racialization and gender. It was not just Vick's NFL stardom that made his case prominent, but more specifically his gender and race. Black and brown masculinities in the U.S. have long been stereotyped as innately violent and aggressive. This perception of Black masculinity has resulted in moves like that of George Zimmerman, who murdered the unarmed seventeen-year-old African American Trayvon Martin and justified the killing by claiming fear of an attack. Vick's own Black masculinity is and was key to both the humanization of his dogs and their later redemption, for their status as innocent victims emerged through perceptions of the threat Vick posed to them. Conversely, advocates routinely dehumanized Vick by arguing that he "should be put down."[10]

And here I return to Cynthia's remarks, for the racialization involved in pit bull politics goes beyond ties to specific bodies and people. Cynthia's reference to the "ghetto" evokes a space that, to paraphrase the geographer David Delaney, race makes.[11] And the "ghetto" emerges as a racialized space not just through histories of redlining—denying services such as bank loans and insurance to residents of areas predominantly occupied by nonwhite people—and related politics of urbanization, but also through the contrast Cynthia invokes with "regular people"—that is, people who are assumed to be white. Indeed, when the majority of the Vick dogs moved from rescue organizations into loving family homes— placements well documented in television appearances, books, and a blog—they were effectively segregated from Blackness by being placed into domestic spaces presumed to be "good" and, therefore, tacitly white. In this regard, shifts in both the Vick dogs' lives and broader perceptions of pit bull–type dogs hinge on changes in their relationship to racialization. These workings of racialization map how whiteness, not just Blackness and brownness, comes to be crafted in and through relationships among humans, nonhuman animals, and place.

Interspecies Intersectionality

Connections between racialization and perceptions of pit bull–type dogs inform an analytic that undergirds this book: interspecies intersectionality, or the ways that relationships between humans and nonhuman animals not only reflect but in fact actively shape experiences of race, gender, species, breed, sexuality, and nation. The term *intersectionality* was coined by the feminist and legal theorist Kimberlé Crenshaw in 1989. Writing about the tendency for courts to fail to understand Blackness and womanhood as working together in discrimination cases, Crenshaw argues for the need to challenge logics that hold Blackness as tacitly male and femininity as tacitly white. She adduces the example of Black women suing General Motors for employment-based discrimination in 1970. The company had laid off all Black women under a last-hired, first-fired policy during a recession but had retained both white women and Black men in the workforce. The plaintiffs lost their case because they were read as either Black or female; while Black folks and women were considered protected classes and therefore able to claim harm under antidiscrimination laws, the law disallowed Black women as a protected class.[12] Crenshaw characterizes both these flawed logics and a counter to their approach through the metaphor of the traffic intersection:

> Consider an analogy to traffic in an intersection, coming and going in all four directions. Discrimination, like traffic through an intersection, may flow in one direction, and it may flow in another. If an accident happens in an intersection, it can be caused by cars traveling from any number of directions and, sometimes, from all of them. Similarly, if a Black woman is harmed because she is in the intersection, her injury could result from sex discrimination or race discrimination.[13]

For Crenshaw, "providing legal relief only when Black women show that their claims are based on race or on sex is analogous to calling an ambulance for the victim only after the driver responsible for the injuries is identified." While Black women "sometimes experience discrimination in ways similar to white women's experiences," and "sometimes they share very similar experiences with Black men," and often they experience discrimination on the basis of both race and sex, Crenshaw's metaphor points to how, "sometimes, they experience discrimination as Black women—not the sum of race and sex discrimination, but as Black women."[14] Here Crenshaw challenges the additive model in which racism and misogyny join in discrimination, for this effect is a whole not greater than, but different from, the sum of its parts, and it is these joined movements of multiple discriminations that yield *intersectionality* as a descriptor of forms of oppression that work together in ways that render them inextricable from each other. Crenshaw's formulation extends beyond legal contexts to the cultural and political: much like the courts, feminist theorizations rest on an assumption of femininity as tacitly white, while antiracist work tends to center the experiences of Black men. For Crenshaw, intersectionality counters not just legal but also political and academic positions that erase the specificity of Black women's experiences.

Like many revolutionary ideas, Crenshaw's theorization of intersectionality was contentious. Some critics claimed that she continued in the tradition of early Black feminisms—most notably the work of the Combahee River Collective and the poet and theorist Audre Lorde—in a manner that merely crystallized those earlier interventions.[15] Others argued that Crenshaw's theorizing did not attend enough to the dynamics of power. Patricia Hill Collins invoked a "matrix of domination" to diagram the forces of power and oppression at the intersections identified in Crenshaw's work.[16] Perhaps most relevant to this writing, intersectionality began to be claimed by mainly white feminists as a tool to address the very erasures Crenshaw detailed in her elaboration. Many Black feminist scholars in particular took exception to this move as an appropriation of the theory by its targets, particularly in academic loci such as women's studies departments. Such claims are evident in a satirical *McSweeney's* piece titled "I Googled 'Intersectionality,' so Now I'm Totally Woke." Demonstrating that the adoption of language—terms such as *intersectionality* and *woke*—does not necessarily entail efforts to understand key issues, the *McSweeney's* piece communicates both the potential emptiness of references to intersectionality in particular circles—mostly those of well-meaning white folks—and the worries that such usage is, in fact, more an appropriation of than an engagement with the experiences the theory addresses.[17]

Given the fact that this writing could be read as enacting just such an appropriation—engaging intersectionality in thinking with nonhuman animals—I now turn to debates about the concept's travel, as detailed by Jennifer Nash in reference to what she terms the "intersectionality wars." Nash, who focuses on academic writing rather than popular culture, troubles the language of appropriation, which also surfaces in terminology such as *colonization* and *theft*. Understanding intersectionality as appropriated, for Nash, produces intersectionality as standing in for both Black feminism and Black women, "both of which are sites of magical value and incessantly devalued." In other words, Nash argues that assertions of the appropriation of intersectionality effectively conflate intersectionality with both Black feminisms and Black women and, crucially, do not reflect but rather create both as victimized and emptied of value. Further, such claims fail to demonstrate how the movement of the analytic is not simply the routine circulation of an intellectual idea. And then there is the fact that to claim one's work as intersectional is to ascribe a value to it that rests on the assumption that *intersectional* equals *good*, which Nash contests.[18] For Nash, then, the intellectual travel of intersectionality itself is not inherently bad, and to label it as such reduces it to a form of property, foreclosing the potentiality of the analytic to extend into and challenge ways of doing and thinking beyond the bounds of the descriptors *Black feminisms* and *Black women*.[19]

In addition, Nash posits that critiques of intersectionality have been and continue to be deflected in ways that fail to engage their substance. A short list devised by Devon Carbado of "standard criticisms" of intersectionality illustrates Nash's point: this listing includes issues with its invocation of identity as opposed to processes; its seeming "freezing" of aspects of selfhood in a way that does not account for "the dynamic and contingent processes of identity formation"; and its focus on subjects—persons who can, for example, make appeals to the law—in a way that makes it difficult to identify connections between, for example, race and place. For Nash, the very fact of such a listing not only dismisses these critiques through its summary-style approach, bundling critiques together as if they were variations of the same in a manner that fails to engage their substance, but it also maintains the proprietary logic she challenges by framing them as incursions from which intersectionality needs to be "protected" and even "rescued." For Nash, this move to protect intersectionality from perceived incursions in fact produces rather than exposes the imaginary figure of "the critic" as a danger. And, for Nash, the move away from the property logic and the deflections of intersectionality's critics she hopes to initiate through her analysis takes the form of a question: "What would happen if we—black feminists—considered intersectionality's critics as figures who lovingly address us, who generatively bring (rather than destructively take), and who offer their participation in black feminism's long-standing world-making project?"[20]

While I do not seek to critique intersectionality here, I most certainly aim to engage and expand on it through my pairing of the terms *interspecies* and *intersectionality*. And I hope to contribute to the kind of world envisioned by the many Black feminist and queer of color scholars with whom this book thinks. To begin, I circle back to a point made by Nash in an earlier piece in which she troubles intersectionality's relationship to identity in thinking through how some subjects mobilize or "choose not to mobilize . . . particular aspects of their identity in particular circumstances."[21] Invested in questions of power, Nash's query raises issues related to both passing and privilege; as a theorist in both queer and trans* studies, I too am interested in these dynamics.[22] For example, the life experiences of a Black transwoman arguably index a different relationship to both identity and related oppressions than those of a straight cisgender Black woman, revealing how even Crenshaw's central figure, burdened by multiple oppressions, in fact occupies a tacitly straight and cis position in Collin's "matrix of dominations." I am interested in thinking about intersectionality in terms of domination, passing, and unearned advantages, or privileges, in a manner that extends beyond the intersections of gender and race and into factors such as sexuality and gender identity. To return to the metaphor of the traffic intersection, privilege might entail simply being at a point where fewer streets or paths come together, having the choice to drive where only a select few are allowed, or not having an accident in the first place.[23]

Critically, traffic intersections are also spaces of movement. Thus, while some of the critiques Nash names in the "wars" trouble intersectionality as understanding identities as static, Crenshaw's metaphor of traffic is inherently dynamic. In this thinking I echo an approach taken by the feminist and queer of color theorist Jasbir Puar.[24] In addition, in thinking with movement I am interested not just in different movements that might collide in intersections, but in movements through, with, and together. Here I draw from the work of the trans* studies scholar and legal theorist Sarah Lamble, who quotes Gail Mason's writings on interpersonal violence in noting that "categories of gender, race and/or sexuality do not just intersect with each other. . . . Rather, they are the 'vehicles of articulation' for each other." For Lamble, perceptions of one facet of identity deeply shape those of another: "When a boy is accused of being a fag it is not only his sexuality that is in question, but also his masculinity: He is perceived as being not man enough."[25] To build on the thinking of Lamble and Mason, I am interested in intersectionality as the conceptual name for identifying the inextricable and dynamic interrelatings of power and oppressions that shape what can be referred to as identities but are also understood as experiences.

While my definition may appear rather vague, and perhaps travels far from the fabled traffic intersection, I hope that the addition of the term *interspecies* sharpens the logic. Jasbir Puar and Julie Livingston's definition of *interspecies* refers "to relationships *between* different forms of biosocial life and their political effects."[26] They emphasize *inter*, a prefix derived from Latin with meanings including "between," "mutually," and "together." And the betweenness they emphasize is not simply the relationships of beings of different species but rather biosocial life, a phrasing that indexes living beings who come to be (that is, become beings) through both biological processes—those of fleshly material—and social processes—systems and logics that shape and give meaning to those beings. Further, the compounding inherent in the term *biosocial* posits such processes as inextricable: it is not the additive formation *biological plus social*.

Then there are the "political effects" of these relatings, that is, the way that *interspecies* characterizes relationships between life forms that inflect and reach out into a larger world. For example, understandings of COVID-19, which decimated the world in 2020, emerged through biosocial processes involving scientists in labs; geographies; racist, Western-normative ascriptions of "backwardness" in the East Asian live-animal markets from which the virus supposedly originated; and fears of "contamination" through which peoples from East Asia were seen as threats whose movements must be controlled and censored.[27] Finally, Puar and Livingston are interested in *relationships*, or *relatings*, that engender these political effects: the base unit of this sense of *interspecies* is not the encounter of one life form with another but rather the *relationship between* life forms. This orientation mobilizes my own thinking, for I am invested in thinking through and analyzing how specific forms of relating between biosocial beings shape experiences of power, oppression, and even identities.

To convey a sense of what I mean by *interspecies intersectionality*, I return to Cynthia's reference to a shift in relatings, whereby "pit bulls" once localized in the place-relationship of the "ghetto" are now visibly engaged in relationships with "regular people," that is, people not residing in the distinctively nonwhite space of the "ghetto" but who "belong" in the cityscape where Cynthia herself resides. With these latter relatings and the use of *regular*, Cynthia clearly sees a reflection of both herself and her own sense of belonging. Further, the workings of racialization inform her understanding of both the "pit bulls" associated with the "ghetto" and those now paired with "regular" (that is, white and middle-class) people and neighborhoods. Critically, I am not inferring that the interrelationship of white middle-class humans and pit bull–type dogs is itself an instance of interspecies intersectionality; rather, in the spirit of Crenshaw's original formulation, I use interspecies intersectionality as an analytic to help identify the workings of power, oppression, and experiences of identity that precede and emerge through these interrelatings. And in examining these connectivities, I am not positing that individual dogs are Black or, for that matter, white, for theirs are not experiences of racial subjection or privilege in the sense of human experiences of racialization. Dogs do not inherit the histories of a transatlantic slave trade or the realities of contemporary practices of profiling, and they do not "have" race in the ways that Cynthia might be understood to have whiteness or someone like Vick to have Blackness. Rather, they are racialized through contacts and connectivities. In this regard, interspecies intersectionality facilitates understandings of the biosocial workings and political stakes of the experiences, identities, and ways of being that emerge through human and nonhuman animal interrelatings as processes connected to but not concretized in formations of identity.

Intersectionality is generally understood to apply to humans in particular, those "subjects" who can make appeals to the law. The extension of the analytic to incorporate nonhuman animals might be taken as a form of violence, given that the very idea of the "human" emerged through and continues to be shaped by both racism and colonialism. Some readers might struggle with the pairing of *interspecies* and *intersectional* because of the many ways that humanity has been denied to Indigenous peoples and people of color, not to mention LGBTQ folks, migrants, and people with disabilities. Further, the very term *species* emerges out of a contested history in which slavery proponents argued that people of African descent were a different species from those of European (and particularly Northern European) descent. While I delve into these issues in chapter 2, what I suggest here in response to this concern is that the pairing of interspecies and intersectional attempts not to elide but rather to inherit these violences. Put differently, the oppressions named by the analytic of intersectionality are in many ways subtended by a sense of the "human" that has been crafted through determinations of the nonhuman, subhuman, and, crucially, animal, such that understandings of the nonhuman and, particularly, "the animal" are, in fact, omnipresent in the very processes of racialization and colonization that are identified through intersectionality. Through interspecies intersectionality I hope to name and analyze not just how interspecies relatings reveal and produce particular formations of discrimination, power, and oppression—racialization and colonization, as well as misogyny and heteronormativity—but also how the "human" as a contested formation informs these relatings.

In Cynthia's reference, the "ghetto" reveals a sense of race that inheres not in specific people or "subjects," but rather in a place. In this regard, some might argue that the language of *assemblage*, introduced by Puar in contrast to intersectionality, might be of more use. Puar's understanding of *assemblage* tracks the work of racialization, colonization, and heteronormativity through movements that extend beyond the boundaries of bodies, through an interrelated array of "actors" that "de-privilege the human body as a discrete organic thing," that bring into question the idea of the "subject" of law and the state, and that work through "affect"—a term that describes how feelings can travel between beings and shape bodily movements prior to their concretization in the language of emotions. Critically, Puar's *assemblage* reworks identity, for in it, "categories— race, gender, sexuality—are considered events, actions, and encounters between bodies, rather than simply entities and attributes of subjects."[28] To return to the COVID-19 example, the Othering of humans of East Asian descent through targeted attacks, when read through the analytic of *assemblage*, can be understood as a process wherein racialization emerged not between or within bounded bodies, but through entwined movements of beings, viral and otherwise, whose encounters upset the idea that a body has physical boundaries. And the fact that the COVID-19 virus acquired geographical and racial identities—President Donald Trump characterized it as a "Chinese disease"—underscores how approaches that focus on movements and encounters can facilitate understandings of how aspects of sociality, such as racialization, emerge in ways that exceed the bodies, identities, and subjectivities of specific people.[29] However, while my writing certainly takes up a way of thinking that echoes *assemblage*-style thinking, I deliberately orient this book through the analytic of interspecies intersectionality.

My reasons for this choice lie in the complicated racial politics of the academic fields in which *assemblage* approaches hold strong, as well as those of animal studies, animal activism, and dog worlds. First, while scholars in Puar's lineage certainly take up the concept of *assemblage* in ways centrally concerned with race, migration, and nationalism, the term itself emerges from a body of poststructuralist thought in which the writings of the French philosophers Gilles Deleuze and Félix Guattari loom large, and in which a sense of the "posthuman" is invoked as part of a move away from bodies that often reads as if race in particular were no longer a concern.[30] Moreover, both animal activism and animal studies are widely perceived as either unconcerned with or deeply problematic with regard to the dynamics of racialization.[31] My use of *intersectionality* thus highlights the importance of both gender and race to this writing. Racialization in particular is central to both pit bull politics and dog rescue, for remarks like Cynthia's express a way of thinking that is widespread in these spaces. With *interspecies intersectionality* I center rather than potentially marginalize the confluence of race, gender, sexuality, and species. Further, my use of *interspecies* brings with it an attention to movements, encounters, and relatings, a sensibility that inflects intersectionality with an understanding in keeping with Puar's *assemblage*. Finally, I am a fan of alliteration, and I feel a certain joy in the repetition of *inter*, not to mention the emphatic relationality of not one but two *inter*s in the phrase.

Thinking Queerly

While my invocation of interspecies intersectionality is centered in the twinings of race, gender, breed, and species, this book is also deeply queer. This queerness surfaces in the workings of sexuality in and through the interrelatings I name. For example, the "regular" people Cynthia references are not only tacitly white and middle class, but also straight. Queerness often works as "irregularity," an interruption of a what is held to be normal or "regular." And *normal* encompasses a combination of factors: sex assigned at birth correlating to gendered ways of dressing, moving, and speaking, which in turn fit with a partner whose sex assignment and mannerisms are of the "opposite" category, with the combined goal of producing children through sexual intimacy. *Queer* emerges when there are gaps, mismatches, or ellipses, when these factors fail to "line up." Here I am paraphrasing the work of the queer theorist Eve Kosofsky Sedgwick, who elucidates not only how queerness emerges in those moments where, say, someone's sex assignment as male does not "match" their preference for dresses and skirts, but also how these clusterings both reflect and actively shape ideas of "normal" and "norms."[32] By *norms* I mean that which is tacitly held to be a default or "regular" and the standard by which difference or deviance is assessed. The norms Sedgwick interrogates are those associated with heterosexuality, or what is also called *heteronormativity*. These norms inflect gender and sexuality as racial and colonial projects. Any drugstore's makeup aisle demonstrates a vision of white femininity as a form of aspirational beauty. More crucially, a Filipina transwoman is much more likely to be arrested on the presumption of being a sex worker—a charge known in trans communities as "walking while trans"—than a white transwoman. The gender and sexuality of people of color is frequently marked as deviating from a specifically white and Western norm.[33] Examples include the policing of Indigenous men's hair, with respect to what are now called mohawks, along with braids and pompadours; these signs of resistance to Western- and Anglo-specific norms are often read as failures of masculinity.[34] My use of the analytic *interspecies intersectionality* interrogates the entwinings of gender presentation and sexuality with gender, race, colonialism, and species.

This book is also queer in its interrogation of and investment in changing understandings about practices of relating. For example, the transformations in pit bulls that Cynthia identifies happen through shifting attachments to and placements in both homes and families. The severing of the Vick dogs' ties with Vick himself hinged on their "redemption" not just through placement in spaces of "rescue," but also through their later positioning in family homes.[35] These homes, marked as "good" through the complicated weave of pit bull politics and rescue work, are white in a structural sense: in the words of the queer of color and comparative literature scholar Chandan Reddy, larger ideas of home and family in the U.S. have been "defined over and against people of color." Reddy argues that the "American standard of living" and the connected concept of the family wage that arose in the late nineteenth century were elucidated by organized labor as pertaining to those who were citizens, male, and white—a definition produced in relation to and against "the 'unorganized' and 'informal' segments of labor, which were female, non-citizen, and non-White."[36] And because "the family wage in the United States defined the 'home,'" the space of the home itself came to be conceived as "exclusively White and American."[37]

This history carries forward to the present. Reddy and I are engaging a sense of whiteness that exceeds literal bodies: my claim is not about the specific people who adopted the Vick dogs, but rather about their positioning in a landscape of racialized norms. Further, the policing of heteronormativity extends well beyond gender presentation through a white-supremacist ideal of family formations. As the political theorist Cathy Cohen notes, policies rooted in fears of "overpopulation" that encourage the use of dangerous forms of birth control and sterilization of people of color reveal a heteronormativity focused not just on policing overtly lesbian and gay practices but also on regulating the sexualities of the many who fall outside the norm of the white, heterosexual, nuclear patriarchal family formation.[38] According to notions of white-supremacist heteronormativity, the "goodness" of the Vick dogs' new homes inheres in a specific kind of family formation.

Movements

The central arguments of *Bad Dog* take the form of four key moves. The first of these is my use of the analytic of interspecies intersectionality to identify and expose troubling connections in the dog worlds on which this book focuses and to disrupt these connections by bringing into question the norms and ideals on which they rest. Chapter 1 takes up this project by analyzing the practices and identities of contemporary advocacy efforts that work through narratives of rescue. Troubling the moralism of no-kill approaches, I disrupt the "saviorist storyings" that produce "rescue" dogs and human "rescuers," focusing on the dogs' own understandings, which are often occluded by these sticky signifiers. For example, I challenge the common assumption that the ideal ending of rescue and adoption narratives is a "forever home" with a white picket fence. Dogs who move into these spaces in fact often experience a great deal of boredom and deprivation, a fairly impoverished way of relating that contrasts markedly with the lives of dogs who live with, for example, houseless people. Through exposing and challenging these assumptions, I identify the troubling norms of home and family reinforced by saviorist storyings and draw attention to the structural violences of racism and colonialism on which they rest.

My second main argument takes up a mode of thinking rooted in ways of relating specific to dogs as nonhuman animals, a move toward understanding focused through and localized in what I term a *sensibility*. This move, detailed in chapter 2, counters a larger episteme—the landscape of the logics that make something knowable in the first place—that prizes an ideal of rationality rooted in the Enlightenment-era figure of the "rational man." The emergence of this figure was made possible by locating irrationality in the bodies of colonized peoples, enslaved peoples, people with disabilities, and, to a lesser degree, women; further, these "others" were marked as irrational on the grounds that their very bodies made them "slaves to passion," unable to think in the manner demanded by the dawning Age of Reason. And lest anyone argue that this type of knowledge politics is a thing of the past, a quick look to the many ways that knowledge claims are dismissed today because someone is deemed "too emotional" should disabuse them of this notion. Building on the work of theorists and writers in animal studies, I take up *sensibility* as a way to counter this knowledge politics by understanding thinking itself through a deeply sensory register, one rooted in bodily experiences and ways of knowing that are shared by and move between humans and nonhuman animals. An extension of this sensibility into a larger awareness of the structural violences associated with interspecies intersectionality helps me elucidate a knowledge politics that might translate into a different way of building worlds.

My third main argument, the focus of chapter 3, extends the disruptions of interspecies intersectionality, sensibility, and awareness into ways of being—that is, ontologies. Examining interspecies relatings encompasses not just knowledge practices but questions of who humans and nonhuman animals are and who they become. For example, my own experiences as a queer white settler middle-class transperson accompanied by a pit bull–type dog are illuminating, for when I was at my most liminal in my medical and hormonal transition, I often went for walks with Haley, and people did not, for lack of a better descriptor, mess with me. Our experiences together made me realize that "my" gender in fact was made possible by and emerged through our relating. The entwinings and emergences of facets of what I have clumsily called identity are dynamic ways of being that come out of, in this case, a human-dog relationship. Naming these relatings "becomings in kind," I localize some of their more troubling emergences in order to interrupt them.

The confluence of interspecies intersectionality, becoming in kind, sensibility, and awareness leads me, in chapter 4, to *Bad Dog*'s larger overall argument and back to its work as a fundamentally queer book. Looking at connectivities in human-dog and dog-dog relatings, I locate contacts, encounters, and emergences that, in spite of their placement within deeply normative frameworks—the family home, the animal shelter—reveal ways of thinking and being that promisingly stray from the norms of animal shelter and rescue work. These relatings, which surface through the deeply sensory attentions of sensibility and awareness, yield alternative modes of building understandings, counters to the logics of "rational man" and his episteme, and forms of mutualistic being and becoming that are markedly different from the routine violences and politics I critique throughout the book. I name these connectivities *queer affiliations*: queer for the ways they reveal forms of what Mel Chen terms "improper intimacy," and affiliations because they act as joinings, even momentary ones, that are not and cannot be collated into the descriptors *kinship* and *family*.[39] These queer affiliations demonstrate how queerness seeds not just critique but also the promise of change, for they delineate alternative ways of thinking, being, and understanding that emerge in and in spite of the often rather depressing political landscape of dog rescue and sheltering. In these queer affiliations I find hope for changes in human-dog politics that promise a path toward multispecies justice.[40]

Logics and Understandings

The queer affiliations I elucidate at the close of *Bad Dog* highlight ways of thinking that commingle being and doing, entwining affect and understanding in a deeply bodily move that counters the "rational" episteme and normative violences of a family-oriented politics of relating. However, queer affiliations also interrupt animal-related politics, for they challenge common logics that hold in the intersections of animal advocacy and human politics. Following Cynthia's invocation of dogs and "ghettoes," she asserted, regarding pit bulls, "They're not all in [West City Y] anymore," and "I think the more they do show up in other neighborhoods with different kinds of people, the more it starts to break down the stigma." Building on this narrative, she notes that these changes work "the same way that integration does," and that "it's much less likely you're gonna hate all Black people if your next-door neighbor is Black and they're great."[41]

Cynthia's phrasing invokes a parallel between the experiences of nonhuman animals and of marginalized humans; the pit bulls removed from the "ghetto" challenge discrimination in the same way as Black people moving into predominantly white neighborhoods. And her words reflect a common trope in animal activisms: deploying the language of race to describe the marginalizations of nonhuman animals, that is, invoking a "like race" logic. Indeed, Cynthia's is a mild example when compared to those invoked by PETA (People for the Ethical Treatment of Animals) in their "Meat Equals Slavery" campaign.[42] In such rhetorical moves, also reflected in works like Marjorie Spiegel's *The Dreaded Comparison: Human and Animal Slavery*, nonhuman animal advocates deploy a substitutive logic by claiming that nonhuman animals are, themselves, enslaved.[43] Commandeering the moral and emotional charge of injustice attached to slavery and transferring it to the bodies of nonhuman animals, these types of moves erase the experiences of actual enslaved humans, an enslavement inextricable from Blackness. And unlike interspecies intersectionality, which focuses on connectivities that emerge through relatings and engender racializations, such approaches instead put nonhuman animals in the place of marginalized humans—thereby replacing humans in the margins of Patricia Hill Collins's "gridding" of power and oppression—and then claiming that such marginalization pertains only to nonhuman animals.

With the queer affiliations that emerge in this book I hope not only to counter the "like race" logics common to animal advocacy (and LGBTQ advocacy!) but also explore alternatives to activisms that pit nonhuman animals against marginalized humans. Referencing the five-year-old crisis of lead-contaminated drinking water in the majority Black community of Flint, Michigan, in April 2019, Twitter commentator @Maddie_Jones 515 posed the following questions: "Do white people know that dogs in Flint don't have clean water either? Have we tried that approach?"[44] Jones's questions problematize the differential offering of attention and care toward nonhuman animals and marginalized humans in the contemporary U.S. These questions resonate with numerous other political challenges in the same vein, such as a 2018 cartoon by Lalo Alcaraz featuring a dog in a cage, with a white, blonde-haired woman sporting an American flag tank top crying, "Oh my God! This cruelty must stop!" Behind her is a stack of cages containing crying and shaking brown children.[45] Pointing to the Trump administration's policy of separating migrant children from their families and housing them in concentration camps, the cartoon asks viewers to question how care and concern are frequently directed less toward marginalized humans than toward dogs.[46] These examples and many others not only challenge "like race" logics, for they ironically position nonhuman animals above marginalized humans in the hierarchy of needs, but they also pose these positions as competing. However, in the allocation of care toward either nonhuman animals or marginalized humans one can witness what I will name, in dialogue with the scholar Lori Gruen, a logic of "zero sum" thinking; the needs of one or the other surface in these representations, but never both at once.[47]

That such disparities in the treatment of humans and nonhuman animals exist is undeniable when we compare resources allocated to the residents of Flint with the labor that is undertaken on a regular basis by, say, dog rescue organizations filling planes with Chihuahuas from the southernmost U.S. states to move them to more northern areas where they are more likely to be adopted.[48] Indeed, dogs gathered in places ranging from Mexico to Taiwan easily acquire what are called "pet passports" to facilitate their travel to the U.S., even as thousands of human migrants starve, undergo torture, and die in efforts to obtain visas or asylum.[49] However, critiques that elevate marginalized humans above nonhuman animals offer a false choice of either/or, ignoring and even denying both the ways that humans and nonhuman animals experience marginalization together and the fact that this differential care may not actually be good for the animals in question: dogs that formerly roamed freely in villages and small towns may benefit from medical interventions and regular food sources, but they often struggle with sometimes severe behavioral issues upon entering lives of confinement in their new "forever homes."[50]

The ideas of "pit bull," "rescue," and "bad dog" are localized in the friction between the "like race" and "zero sum" conceptualizations of the politics of nonhuman animals and marginalized humans. This friction is perhaps all the more pronounced when one considers the notions of justice that subtend each approach. "Like race" animal advocacy takes up a narrative of freedom that erases the pervasive unfreedom of the very humans it cites, while "zero sum" approaches detect injustice in comparative profferings of care, such that nonhuman animals can be regarded as stealing a justice that should, instead, be allocated to marginalized humans. Through the myriad interruptions and disruptions I elucidate with the application of interspecies intersectionality, sensibility, awareness, and becomings in kind, I posit queer affiliations that promise not only ways to think, do, and become differently but also ways to move toward a sense of justice that joins together the concerns and needs of marginalized humans and nonhuman animals. And in the ways that queer affiliations push a different means to understand and think and do differently, in their countering of the logics and norms *Bad Dog* troubles, and in their potential to join the issues faced by both marginalized humans and nonhuman animals—that is, in their togetherness—I find hope.

1

Gimme Shelter

Saviorist Storying, Animal "Rescue,"
and Interspecies Intersectionality

Early in my fieldwork for this book, I was out for a walk with my dogs when I ran into Gretchen, a queer white woman of about forty who has worked in animal advocacy for a number of years. A gruff person whose impulses to sympathy tend towards the marginalized—houseless pet owners, queer communities ravaged by AIDS—Gretchen was both frustrated and flabbergasted as she shared the following story. Her neighbors—a white, straight-married, upper-middle-class couple—had found a Chihuahua wandering in the streets the day before. They had brought the dog home, not wanting to consign it to the euthanasia they were sure awaited it at the shelter. At some point during its stay, the dog cowered when the husband swept the floor. They had turned up at Gretchen's house early that morning, convinced that the dog was part of a domestic violence situation, that it had been deliberately set loose by the victim of said violence for its protection, and therefore that it couldn't be returned to its original neighborhood—a neighborhood occupied mostly by poor folks of color and poor white folks with a small number of gentrifiers—and couldn't be taken to a shelter either, because the original abuser (imagined as a man of color) might then claim it and use it for leverage. Refusing to disclose the exact location where they had found the dog, they implored Gretchen to take it to a "rescue" where it might find a "good home."[1]

As Gretchen and I walked our dogs together through a grassy field, we marveled at the leaps of imagination involved in this tale. However, we also worried about the fact that Gretchen now had possession of a healthy dog whose glossy coat and affiliative demeanor led both of us to think that it already had a home, one that Gretchen might never be able to locate.

Numerous entwined factors shaped the travel of this dog. The first of these is the no-kill movement in animal advocacy, in relationship to municipal animal shelters in particular. Emerging in the U.S. in the 1990s, the movement aimed to change common approaches in animal shelters or "pounds," where strays were often routinely killed rather than adopted out. Between 1984 and 1994 Richard Avanzino, president of the San Francisco Society for the Prevention of Cruelty to Animals (SPCA), transformed the organization into one of the first animal shelters that eschewed euthanasia. Gregory Castle, CEO emeritus of the Best Friends Animal Sanctuary, a Utah animal sanctuary founded in 1984 as "the flag-ship for the no kill movement"—whose existence is arguably the reason the terms *animal sanctuary* and *no kill* are widely regarded today as synonymous—credits the success of Avanzino's work to the creation of a "template for achieving a no-kill community by implementing a set of thinking-outside-the-box programs and policies that prioritized lifesaving," including "high-volume adoptions, targeted spay/neuter programs, volunteer and community engagement, a foster home net-work, quality medical care and more."[2] Other key figures are Lynda Foro, whose grassroots organizing helped solidify a network of organizations and activists in the mid-1990s, and Nathan Winograd, whose 2007 book *Redemption: The Myth of Pet Overpopulation and the No Kill Revolution in America*, in conjunction with his work for the San Francisco SPCA and a number of other organizations, helped solidify support for the movement among a public previously unfamiliar with such matters.[3]

The above history is necessarily truncated—not to mention contested—but the key principle of no kill leaves little room for nuance among its adherents. Thus, while Foro, writing in 2001 for Maddie's Fund—a nonprofit organization that funds a wide range of programs and research related to no-kill advocacy—describes the movement as com-prising "caregivers and organizations" that share the "common goal . . . to save animals' lives when there is a quality alternative to killing," later iterations are more trenchant.[4] Indeed, books like Winograd's reveal a quasi-evangelical shift, putting forward a "story of animal sheltering in the United States [as] a movement that was born of compassion and then lost its way," one that argues that no-kill advocates are "heroes" of a "revolution" that "says we can and must stop the killing."[5]

With the rise of no-kill activism in the 1990s and 2000s came a concomitant shift in perceptions of shelters. Visitors to my fieldwork site often ascribe "villainy"—the moral counterpart to Winograd's heroism—to what many in the movement now call "kill shelters," or animal shelters where euthanasia is practiced.[6] Indeed, Gretchen's neighbors' choice not to take the dog they found to the local shelter reflects a fairly widespread view—despite the fact that, for people who have lost animals, such a shelter is one of the few places to look for them. Alternative terminology that I encountered during my fieldwork challenges this view: "open intake" and "open admission" refer to shelters that do practice euthanasia, are generally funded by cities and counties, and are therefore legally mandated to take in all of the animals that come to their doors (as was the case with my fieldwork site).

To complicate matters, data regarding just how many organizations exist, of what type, and how they may have changed over time are nonexistent. As the ASPCA notes, "currently, no government institution or animal organization is responsible for tabulating national statistics" for animal shelters and rescues, although work by a coalition named "Shelter Animals Count" (SAC) is attempting to rectify the problem through a voluntary-participation database, inaugurated in 2010, that incorporates the range of organizations—classified as animal rescues and shelters operating with or without government contracts, and government animal services—involved in animal welfare work.[7] This lack of data is further muddled by classification problems, with a veritable hodgepodge of organizations claiming the status of shelter or rescue. Many of them are funded by both municipalities and private sources, such as "friends of" charities. Because of this confusion, I use the terminology that was most commonly deployed among my interlocutors, with *shelter* referring to an open-admission site with a government contract and *rescue* meaning a privately run, nonprofit facility based on the no-kill model.

Some key details underscore the differences between rescues and shelters and the relationship between the two types of organization. The first is the direction of movement: most rescues "pull" animals from shelters, usually for free. As they are privately run, they can be selective in their choices. Further, in my experience it is rare for a rescue to take a dog directly from an individual. The traffic of "pulling" animals arises largely from legal provisions whereby a shelter and the city or county that runs it become the legal owners of a stray animal after a certain number of days. This is not the case for most rescues, although, as Gretchen's neighbors reveal, misconceptions about rescue intake processes abound.

The kinds of dogs that travel in and through shelters and rescues also differ. While shelters are open to all comers, some rescues focus on the more heart-wrenching cases, taking on dogs with documented histories of neglect and abuse and related, costly medical needs; others focus on specific breeds; still others simply take in smaller (read: cuter and more easily adoptable) dogs in greater numbers. As privately run entities, rescues can and do charge a wide range of fees for adoptions (sometimes upwards of $500), while shelters generally limit the cost to $50–$125 and sometimes offer free adoptions with the help of sources such as Maddie's Fund.[8]

Criteria for potential adopters vary wildly. While many shelters require only proof of home ownership or leases with provisions explicitly allowing for pets (and even this requirement is not universal), rescues often require more onerous provisions, such as access to a backyard with six-foot fencing, no cats, and assurances that animals won't be left alone for longer than six hours. One interlocutor described to me in disbelief how a wealthy acquaintance was turned away because the heated pool in her backyard posed a perceived risk, even though no animals were permitted outside unsupervised.[9]

Many who work at shelters today describe a great deal of acrimony resulting from no-kill proponents who come from rescue-based activism intent on changing practices in open-admission shelters. Nathan, a white queer man and shelter worker aged around thirty, was not the only one of my interlocutors to speak of "the shelter battles" in describing his work.[10] This language reflects not only Nathan's individual frustrations in dealing with no-kill activists but also a perception widespread among my interlocutors that no-kill and open-admission policies are impossible to reconcile while staying alert to the needs of the animals involved.

A different but related fault line in dog worlds concerns the dynamics of dog breeding, as evidenced in a common slogan and bumper sticker: "Adopt, don't shop." This line positions shelters and rescues together against those who buy and sell dogs: breeders and purchasers of purebred dogs, those who sell dogs from their homes that may or may not meet breed standards, and those who sell dogs in pet stores. Advocates of adoption take the position that adoption fees, unlike proceeds from a breeder's sales, go toward "funding an organization, saving a life, and sometimes even [keeping] money out of the hands of people who are more concerned about making a profit off the lives of animals [than] considering their health and welfare."[11] And while opposition to the sale of dogs tends to focus on "puppy mills"—breeding programs that generally produce dogs for pet stores and the like, and which are widely criticized for poor sanitary conditions, overbreeding, and faulty veterinary care, in part due to lack of industry regulations—I have witnessed shelter-adoption advocates accuse individuals who have purchased dogs from breeders of choosing the product of a for-profit industry over dogs whose lives may be lost to shelter euthanasia.[12] Competitive dog sports such as agility (an event in which dogs runs through an obstacle course, modeled loosely on stadium show jumping for horses) were long restricted to purebred dogs. A 2015 decision by the American Kennel Club (AKC) to create a separate category of competition for non-purebred dogs, while welcomed, was also greeted quite critically: Julia Lane, writing for *Bark: The Dog Culture Magazine*, describes it as a "separate but equal" designation, language that underscores how histories of racialization in the U.S. figure large in dog worlds.[13] And while adoption advocacy makes allies of shelters and rescues, it also demonstrates how no-kill thinking infuses most aspects of dog worlds, given that the model introduced by Avanzino and others is premised on high levels of adoption.

Gretchen's story emerges from a particular space—the fairly urban area of California where I did my fieldwork. As in most of the United States, the geography and demographics of the area have been shaped by histories of redlining and environmental racism, with historically wealthy areas generally populated mainly by wealthy white people, and areas closer to manufacturing bases and industrial pollution inhabited largely by people of color. And, as in most urban centers in California today, affordable housing is increasingly scarce; many former residents have been priced out of the region, and evictions and exorbitant rent increases are a daily threat. In this climate, rental housing where animals are accepted is generally more expensive, more decrepit, and scarce. As a result, poor folks, and especially poor people of color, are being forced out of the region in droves, and many are unable to take their animals with them. Further, like virtually all of the United States, the site of my fieldwork occupies stolen land, and Indigenous peoples make up a great number of those who have been pushed out of the area through both settler colonialism and gentrification.

A final element in the story of Gretchen's neighbors is a shift in consumer cultures in the United States that is reflected in pet ownership. Pets and their food and accouterments are increasingly big business. The industry generated $53.3 billion in the U.S. in 2012, the year I began my fieldwork, and an estimated $75.38 billion in 2019.[14] The growth of this industry is evident not just in sales of expensive dog beds and pet GPS trackers, but also in an increasing range of high-end services for pets, with dog hotels, day spas, and dog-inclusive vacations now supplementing the more run-of-the-mill, if also increasingly expensive, dog day-care centers and walking services. The growth of this industry tracks with numbers from 2019 indicating the highest degree of income inequality since the Census Bureau started tabulating it in the 1950s.[15] Veterinary insurance for pets, once uncommon, is now not only widely available but offered as an employment benefit by one in three Fortune 500 companies as they seek to increase their appeal to twenty- and thirtysomething employees, who are also now increasingly permitted to bring their dogs to work. The same cannot be said of those in the ever-growing "gig economy," such as Uber drivers and Instacart shoppers.[16]

The growth of the pet industry reveals not only an expanding range of increasingly expensive product and services but also the entrenchment of a particular culture of pet care as a norm. Those who see dog hotels and day cares as cumbersome but necessary expenses are increasingly inclined to see a less affluent person's decision to leave a dog out in a yard all day as evidence of "neglect" rather than economic necessity when, for example, irately describing such situations to local animal control officers over the phone.[17]

The rise of no kill, the shelter battles, gentrification, and a booming pet care culture conjoin in what may now seem an overdetermined fashion in the story of Gretchen's neighbors. Their actions, while outlandish and unethical, make perverse sense in the context of this landscape and the histories accreted into it. Their rush to saviorism represents a twisted yet direct mapping of these many tensions. Their story is also fantastical in a way that beggars belief—when I shared it with interlocutors, I tended to preface it with along the lines of "I couldn't make this up if I tried." And yet I find it revelatory: it *interrupts* these histories by laying bare the deeply racialized and gendered anxieties that move through and shape them. In what follows, I use interspecies intersectionality to analyze how saviorism not only shapes narratives of rescue but also reveals the formative work of structures such as neoliberalism and colonialism to such narratives.

Interspecies Intersectionality in Rescue

The deeply racialized imaginary at the heart of Gretchen's story underscores the ways that race, gender, and species are not merely reflected but actively crafted. Her white neighbors cast themselves as the saviors of a dog with a breed history easily traceable to Mexico from the imagined violence of an imagined Black man. It is tempting to frame their actions, in parallel with Gayatri Spivak's writings, as white people saving brown dogs from Black men.[18] In the whiteness that emerges in and through this saviorism, threatening Black (and brown) masculinities are remedied by the removal of the triangulated third party, a dog whose innocence stands in for that of the (again imagined) violated brown woman. This is a whiteness made possible through the body of the dog, through the geographies of that evocative plea for a "good home," a whiteness that hinges on an interspecies relating that is, in fact, a theft.

Race is a key facet of identity both reflected in and produced by the cultures of rescue. For example, Jennifer, a white woman in her thirties who works in dog training and behavior and who has a gift for summarizing complex issues into sound bites, was almost casual in noting to me that the world of animal rescue is "lily white."[19] Another interlocutor, Sandra, an African American woman in her thirties, described an argument she had with the leader of a prominent rescue organization that engages in a great deal of outreach work in low-income neighborhoods made up almost entirely of people of color. Never one to hold her tongue, Sandra pointed out to the upper-class white woman that the organization pretty much entirely lacked "people who look like me," a problem exacerbated by the geographical focus of the organization's outreach work.[20] Sandra's criticism, while accurate, was less than welcome, and, as she recently noted to me, the problem has yet to be remedied.[21]

While I have yet to locate any research on the racial or ethnic makeup of rescue organizations or, for that matter, shelter volunteers, Jennifer's and Sandra's observations hold true in my own experience and in organizations I have tracked more broadly through the internet. These spaces also tend to be quite tokenistic in foregrounding any and all people of color who participate as volunteers. Jane, a Chinese American interlocutor, described to me multiple instances of this obliviousness and related tokenism. When trash was thrown at her near the venue of an animal training event, the white friend who was with her at the time, and who was not targeted, couldn't understand what the incident had to do with race. Jane told me she decided to stop volunteering at one prominent rescue organization after a holiday party not long after the 2016 election. The white, straight, middle-class leader had approached the only other person of color in the room, a Latinx woman in her thirties, clasped her hands, looked warmly into her eyes, and asked, "How are *your* people doing?" For Jane, this moment was so profoundly Othering that she could not return to what she otherwise found to be important and empowering work.[22] The Latinx volunteer continued to feature prominently in the organization's online media for several months, until she too withdrew.

Indirect and anecdotal evidence from rescue organizations reveals similar racialized dynamics. For example, on a blog titled *Redemption Dogs*, the author, "Nicoledogs," argues that "we need to talk about racism, prejudice and dog rescue." Specifically, she points to problems of discrimination in adoptions encountered in her "10 plus years in rescue." These include widespread "refusal to adopt to families based on their ethnicity," justified by reasoning she paraphrases: "Don't Chinese people eat dogs?," "Oh they will just feed the dog curry," and "You can't trust immigrant families with dogs!" This logic further extended to "'Oh! We have an application from a Jewish family, we'll charge them more, they've got money.'"[23]

Nicole's writing also demarcates whiteness as a tacit norm: "When I told my friend Rodney, who is a person of color out of California, about this article he said: 'I didn't know that was a thing but now I think about it I never see pictures of anyone who isn't Caucasian adopting a dog. Certainly no stories.' Are people of color simply not adopting or are they opting to go to breeders because rescues give them such a hard time?"[24] This dynamic extends to assumptions ingrained in rescue practices:

Nicole notes that while "so many of the dogs that come into rescue come from poor areas [where] race is always implied, . . . no one ever thinks to give dogs who look abused or neglected a second opinion—no matter where they came from, whoever owned them was a bad person."[25] Her writing underscores how practices of rescue lean on a sense of whiteness as the norm, with "of color" always a designation connoting bad owners and likely abusers.

In many ways this whiteness simply reflects ongoing social dynamics, but it is also actively shaped through the bodies of animals. Whiteness is the default tied to the "good home" of an adoption photo, and it represents a safe haven for dogs who might otherwise wind up being added to some imagined form of "curry." It is whiteness that emerges as a space of supposed sympathy to the plight of "your people." It is white privilege that makes Jane's companion unable to identify racially targeted violence.

Not only these organizations' leadership, membership, and adoption practices but also their logics and framings demonstrate a whiteness at an epistemic level—that is, through knowledge production and ways of thinking. Names of rescue organizations such as "Their Lives Matter" and "Black Labs Matter" coopt the language and work of a social movement— Black Lives Matter—meant to counter the ways that Black humans are rendered disposable by the state.[26] The name "All Paws Matter" plays on white activists' counterclaims that "All Lives Matter"—claims that further erase Black deaths—in a way that seems to find such an erasure funny.[27] "Doggie Protective Services," a rescue that specializes in small dogs, has a name evocative of Child Protective Services, a state system widely criticized for its disproportionate targeting of Black, brown, and Indigenous families and communities.[28] All of these efforts take up and value canine life in a way that erases the lives and concerns of marginalized humans. Such moves are common in animal-related activism, as is evident in the title of Marjorie Spiegel's *The Dreaded Comparison: Human and Animal Slavery*. In their erasures not only of people of color but also of the identities and political work of people of color through the appropriation of language endemic to antiracist efforts, these organizations and their traffic in the bodies of dogs replace concerns specific to people of color with those of a white-normative logic of rescue.

A common theme throughout animal rescue in the U.S. is imprisonment. For example, many visitors to my fieldwork site commented on how a shelter is, to them, a prison. Rescues with names like "Saving Death Row Dogs" further index the pervasiveness of this language and logic.[29] Indeed, the invocation of the shelter as a prison or "death row" seeks to identify animal confinement and euthanasia as unjust by invoking a space where humans experience, to quote the legal theorist Dean Spade, "overwhelming racialized and gendered violence."[30] Yet this language is most often employed by well-meaning white people who are largely unaware of the racial, sexual, nationalist (with respect to ICE detention facilities), and gendered dynamics of the injustice enacted in today's practices of incarceration. While it attempts to evoke sympathy for shelter dogs, this language effectively appropriates the affective charge of injustice attached to spaces like "death row" while simultaneously erasing any connections to the specific *kinds* of humans whose lives, bodies, and communities are destroyed by carceral violence. Further, both prison references and racially appropriative rescue names reflect the affective privilege of whiteness, cisness, and straightness—that is, the privilege of not *having* to notice or care about, say, racialized and transphobic violence and injustice, a buffering from specific kinds of human suffering that acts as a tacit norm. Through the bodies of dogs who are rescued from "prisons" and "death row," and who become those animals whose lives also "matter," emerge human "rescuers" of those animals who are by definition disconnected from the lives and discourses of people of color.

In the world of animal rescue I examine here, race works in conjunction or intersection with additional key facets of identity, one of which is ability. Stories, images, and videos of dogs who are presented as now being able to play and live just like other dogs through the use of specially designed wheels or prosthetics circulate widely. But these stories betray what thinkers in disability studies term a "super crip" fetish: that is, they reveal salacious and almost pornographic exceptionalizations of disabled bodies.[31] These stories represent disabilities as problems easily solved with a little technology and ingenuity, with a lone hero centered in a narrative oriented toward the "overcoming" of access-related obstacles. In a December 2018 Petco commercial, a young boy shovels snow to earn money for a bike but ends up taking apart the bike to build a wheel to replace the missing hind leg of the dog his family adopted during the holidays. Now boy and dog—obviously a rescue by the evidence of its missing leg—can play together at the same pace![32] In some of these stories, the dog is paired with a human with disabilities: this is represented as some kind of perfect matchmaking gesture, with their disabilities becoming a bond and a component of their mutually shaped identities. Such stories erase the larger problem of what Susan Wendell, among others, terms the "social construction of disability," because these interventions involve reshaping bodies to fit into hostile worlds, rather than pushing those worlds themselves to reshape and, at the least, do less violence to nonnormative bodies.[33] These narratives also reify particular understandings of "normal" embodiment, wherein dogs, and occasionally humans connected to them (most of whom are white), emerge as closer to normal in and through the relationship of rescue.

An additional aspect of identity central to animal rescue in the contemporary U.S. is that of socioeconomic status. Because prosthetic dog wheels usually cost between $200 and $500, turning a disabled dog into a "normal" dog requires significant financial resources.[34] Some of the more popular types of rescue stories depend on ample disposable income, such as the popular example of the white gay male couple whose house has been entirely remodeled with high ledges and ramps for the use of their more than twenty rescue cats.[35] It bears repeating here that basic adoption requirements typically assume a level of economic and class privilege: especially for adoptions involving "bully breed" dogs, many shelters and rescues require proof of home ownership or leases specifically allowing such a dog, along with requirements such as six-foot-high fences around yards and guarantees that an animal won't be left alone for longer than six hours.[36] While class and financial status, unlike factors such as race and ability, is more a precondition than a dynamic shaped through these worlds, it is pervasive in ideas and ideals of rescue. Many of my interlocutors echoed one person's fantasy that if they were to win a large sum of money in the lottery, they would open "the biggest and best animal rescue ever."[37]

Geographies of the "Rescue" Imaginary

In examining contemporary discourses of rescue through the lens of interspecies intersectionalities, my intention is to paint a picture of not just my fieldwork site but a larger world, an imaginary, extending across much of the U.S., consisting of approaches to and thinking with the practices and dynamics of rescue. In this section I turn my attention to the ways that geographies inform my analysis.

In the movement of animals that is endemic to rescue, race emerges in critical ways. Gretchen's story of the "rescued" Chihuahua is representative: it depicts the movement of a dog from an outside space, urban or wild, into the space of an institution—the shelter—or a home. The same dynamic is evident in narratives of dogfighting busts, where images of skeletal dogs lying on patches of dirt and chained to overturned steel drums, contrast with glossy-coated canines in the loving arms of mostly white family members. These are narratives of bodies that move and travel, bodies that undergo physical changes through geographic transitions. (Because dogs are typically seized as evidence before media access is permitted, the photos accompanying such news stories often come from elsewhere: a photo that has become the stock image for such busts in the U.S. was actually taken in the Philippines.)[38]

Then there are the more local imaginaries of rescue, which are evident in posts on Nextdoor.com wherein someone takes in a dog (or dogs) running free (or "wild") and does their best to return the dog to their presumed home of origin, into another home or a rescue, or, as a last resort, the local shelter. This type of geographical movement—from outside to inside—is also key to most stories of individual shelter and rescue dogs: a dog is picked up as a stray by an animal control officer (ACO), ends up in a shelter before being pulled by a rescue, and then lands in a "forever" (or "furever") home.

Importantly, the hazy notions of the outside wild or urban spaces of these movements, imagined or real, gain solidity through their contrast with the institutional and domestic spaces. For example, dogs or puppies may be depicted squatting on rooftops as floodwater rises around them, being coaxed into crates to be delivered away from starving on the streets, or being abandoned outside in a box in wintry (or sweltering) weather. On their own, these images have overtones of the wild and unsafe, especially when accompanying captions allege human neglect, abuse, or abandonment. They appear even more untamed and frightening when juxtaposed with "after" pictures in which a happily leashed dog poses, glossy-coated, next to their new owner. These images build on David Delaney's argument that race makes space: it is true of the home as well as the wild.[39] Less frequently evoked are the shelters that often act as way stations on these journeys. Their dismal institutional concreteness is occasionally softened with stuffed toys and warm blankets, also a marked contrast to the extremes of the outside, but shelters are frequently identified as loci of incarceration, violence, and death.[40] In all of these stories, the domestic space of a home (where dogs will likely spend most of their waking hours alone) becomes a locus of warmth and comfort, positioned as the ideal temporal, geographical, and affective endpoint to a dog's journey.

The "forever" home is not racially neutral. Consider the experience of my interlocutor Marta, a Mexican American woman in her twenties who works as a professional dog trainer and lives with her parents, grandparents, and a younger sibling. When Marta went to adopt her current dog, the shelter required that all family members be present, but that was impossible for the elderly members of her household.[41] While the shelter ultimately made an exception to the requirement on the basis of her occupation, such policies demonstrate how the homes that provide the imaginary geographical and temporal endpoint of most rescue narratives are presumed to be nuclear in their kinship arrangements, a family formation that reflects white, Anglo, and Western norms.

Connections among home, family, and temporality in this imaginary augment my critique. For example, organizations such as Pit Bulls Are Family recuperate dogs into a domestic that counters their popular associations with men of color and dogfighting.[42] In the many "Home for the Holidays" rescue and shelter events held in the U.S. in November and December, dogs' placements are tied to a temporal and Christian narrative centered on the family, as demonstrated by pretty much every Hallmark movie ever.[43] This mostly Christian holiday thinking is perhaps obviously straight, even though there was clearly something a bit odd going on in terms of sex and biology in that manger. And, even when straight folks are not at the center of the story, the ideology at work is more "gay as in happy" than "queer as in fuck you," with adoption websites featuring loving photos depicting mostly white gay and lesbian folks with ample financial resources, not raging flaming queers whose gender deviance and illegibility as kin units exclude them from normative happy-family stories.[44]

This hetero- and homonormativity extends into other aspects of the rescue and shelter worlds. For example, many rescues use local gay pride parades as opportunities to promote both their organizations and adoptable dogs. Most of the organizations I have seen engage in these practices are run by straight people. As eloquently demonstrated in many works, including Kami Chisholm's outstanding film *Pride Denied*, gay pride has certainly lost its appeal for more radical or even left-leaning queers in light of its overwhelming corporatization (or pinkwashing), homonationalism (use as a prominent representation of a country's liberal policies in a manner that covers up other practices such as Indigenous erasure and genocide), and homonormativity (assimilation into lifestyles reflecting straight family values). Rescue organizations' promotions at such events read as more of an appropriation than an honoring of queer struggles and lives.[45]

Finally, the presence and policing of individual LGBT people within rescue organizations demonstrates the work of norms related to gender and sexuality. For example, the following notable instance was relayed to me by several interlocutors: a lead volunteer in a prominent organization transitioned from identifying as female to identifying as male and was soon disinvited from his public role because the organization's leaders asserted that the transition had made him overly prone to anger—although he had reportedly always been a fairly abrasive person and was in fact less so following his transition.[46] This transphobic action was undertaken by the same organization that had proudly marched in the local gay pride parade for over ten years, participating in a space ostensibly claimed to showcase queer acceptance in spite of its own expulsion of a transperson.

Ontologies of Rescue

This analytical tour of the imaginary of rescue leans on a rather diffuse understanding of *rescue*. This imaginary emerges through telling stories, or *storying*. Rescue links and gives purpose to the move of no kill and the conceptions of good and bad organizations, homes, people, and places that shape the examples in this chapter. Put another way, rescue engages storying through movement. Because of this, I expand my definition of rescue here beyond the physical spaces of organizations and the traffic of dogs' bodies to include the storying that gives this movement a telos. This movement is both literal—these stories travel from my interlocutors and cultural sites to me and, now, to you—and emotional, in that I am moved by these stories and compelled to share them with you. And while this latter sense of movement is certainly evident throughout the stories presented above, as with Gretchen's frustration with her neighbors, my own anger at her neighbors, and my urge to share her story and our frustration with you, nowhere is it more apparent than in the suppositions of abuse commonly understood as the justification for rescue.

"Most dogs, according to most people, have been abused," notes Sharon, a white lesbian in her forties who works as a behaviorist.[47] Sharon, one of the first people to be registered as a professional dog trainer in the U.S., has extensive experience with the "hard cases" of dog behavior and is frequently consulted when, for example, a dog inflicts a serious bite on another dog or a human in a household.[48] A quick search of the internet certainly reveals a plethora of horrific stories—dogs found in trash bags or garbage chutes, or living in their own waste in puppy mills—accompanied by calls for compassion, donations for veterinary care, and restitution in the form of criminal charges. However, as Sharon suggests, *allegations* of abuse far outnumber these cases. I have met hundreds of people who claim that their rescue dog was abused, but only a handful of them base these assertions in more than speculation. Further, the reasons given are often inferences similar to those drawn by Gretchen's neighbors, in which a fairly normal dog behavior—fear of long, stick-like objects, fear of men, or fear of people wearing hats or big coats—is translated into a narrative of past violence. Here I want to highlight how the imaginary of rescue yields and bolsters these pervasive narratives of presumed abuse.

Suppositions of abuse give a particular emotional reach to rescue's storyings. Paraphrasing another conversation I had with Gretchen, *rescue* could, and in Gretchen's opinion, *should* be taken to mean practices akin to running into a burning building to save the lives of humans and animals, yet most of the time it indexes the process of adopting an animal from a group stationed in front of the local Petsmart.[49] In this sense, rescue's storying conveys a particular meaning, that of salvation, which exceeds the scope of the actual practices involved.[50] Rescue's storying is more accurately understood as "saviorist storying," wherein activities such as adopting dogs from organizations are covered over by the lure, the solicitation of feelings of salvation.

Rescue is a sticky signifier: a dog once painted with its brush is forever known as a rescue. This is perhaps most apparent in the Hallmark Channel's decision to air the *American Rescue Dog Show* beginning in 2018. The title describes dogs not by breed or mixtures thereof, but by the practices underlying their movements. This involves ontological shifts, for the identity of these dogs is transmuted: these are not mutts or strays, but "rescues." This ontological work extends to the humans involved, for the choice to rescue a dog involves humans laying claim to goodness through their actions; witness the righteousness of Gretchen's neighbors. Saviorist storying creates not only dogs who become "rescues" but also their human saviors.

The most obvious evidence of this crafting can be witnessed through the common slogan "Who rescued who?" (or sometimes the more grammatically finicky "Who rescued whom?"), usually emblazoned on a paw print–shaped background on the back of a car whose noseprinted windows attest to the presence of a canine companion.[51] Saviorist storying creates dogs as rescues and their human companions as good and compassionate people, people who often claim also to have been rescued through this act.

The Dangers of Saviorist Storying

The concerns that arise from the application of saviorist storying, as exemplified in my fieldwork site, are related to epistemology, or the making of knowledge. Here I examine how saviorist storyings accomplish epistemic labor in conveying specific kinds of understandings of dogs put forward by humans, as well as efforts to respond to these knowledges. The saviorist storyings I detail not only involve concerns identifiable through the analytic of interspecies intersectionality but also frequently act to overwrite, counter, or cover over competing ways of knowing, thereby both revealing and enacting a knowledge politics specific to these worlds.

The no-kill movement is a key element in dog rescue today. My interlocutor Nathan pointed out to me that it is also a very effective form of storying. Drawing analogies to contemporary politics, Nathan observes that the problem facing the U.S. Democratic Party today is that "in debate, the Democrats continue to primarily focus on policy. . . . But, what happens is that policy can be picked apart [and torn] into pieces." In contrast, "the Republicans have started stories . . . that people can grab onto and relate to," which are robust because "you can't pick apart a story the same way that you can pick apart policy." And for Nathan this is why "no kill is winning in the shelter battle," because "the policy stuff gets picked apart, and who doesn't want, you know, the story where you can save the poor animal, you know?"[52] Nathan's use of the second person here—not one but two "you know"s, along with the phrasing of "you can save"—both enacts and demonstrates how these saviorist storyings craft and interpolate a "you." That is, Nathan's wording demonstrates how the storying of no kill solicits sympathy from a second person, a "you," who is urged to become differently, to become someone who would save a dog, a savior, through that sympathy, and who, through that process, shifts in identity.

Nathan is far from alone in his criticisms of no kill and practices of saviorist storying. For instance, Jessica, a white lesbian in her thirties involved in the provision of low-cost veterinary care, noted how dogs are often turned over to her organization because of its long-term relationships with houseless clients: when those clients are confronted by structural-turned-material violences, such as the criminalization of poverty, that force them to part with their animals, they trust her organization to find the animals new homes. Jessica observes that when she attempts to give potential adopters details of a dog's history, including name and birthdate, they often "glaze over." Positing that "they don't want to have to deal with the fact that this dog has a history," Jessica locates her frustration in the saviorism of such adopters: "They want it to be a clean slate so they can create this mythology."[53]

In Jessica's frustrations we can witness dynamics identifiable through interspecies intersectionality. Saviorist storying strips so-called rescue dogs of not just their histories but also their identities and the ways these identities are connected to specific humans. A new story becomes possible through a transition in class (and, often, connections to race) through assimilation into a new and different life pattern. These erasures have serious consequences. For example, when new owners fail to anticipate the proclivities of a dog with a long history of being with its human most of the day (as is the case with many dogs surrendered by houseless folks), or who has lived outside, so that indoors and outdoors are decidedly new concepts, they often return the dog to Jessica's organization or, occasionally, even to the shelter.[54]

Teresa, a queer Latinx woman in her thirties who has worked with various animal rescues since her late teens, echoes Jessica's frustrations, saying, "I just don't even want to throw down with any like, fucking ladies with pink flip-flops that just adopted their pit bull. . . . Like, 'It's such a love,' and it's just like, lunging at the end of the leash." Teresa posits that these new owners will "completely just ignore any behavior that's being presented, you know? 'Cause they'll go, 'Oh, he was so abused!'" In this description, Teresa points to the ways that problem behaviors such as leash reactivity—barking and lunging at other dogs, humans, bicycles, etc.—are not just ignored by new owners of rescued dogs, pit bull types in particular, but also excused through saviorist storying. And for Teresa, the sticking point—and here I return to rescue as a sticky signifier of rescue as a dog's identity—is that "they'll throw that story on top of any dog."[55] In Teresa's view, the problem is not just that the storying of rescue leads to people's disregarding what can be or become serious behaviors if left unaddressed, but that this storying covers such behaviors like a metaphorical blanket, dismissing them entirely in favor of an understanding rooted in salvation.

Further, Teresa's remarkable linguistic condensation of "ladies in pink flip-flops"—the honorific of *ladies*, which is usually (and certainly historically) applied mostly to white straight women, coupled with an impractical and gendered shoe choice—exemplifies how saviorist storyings' overcodings connect to and reinforce a tacitly innocent, white, and straight femininity. I name innocence here because a lack of knowledge about dog behavior becomes permissible, at least in the eyes of the women Teresa criticizes, in the context of storyings. Whiteness conjoined with femininity means that rescued dogs' problem behaviors are generally read by others as less than dangerous and certainly not grounds for intervening. By contrast, a dog behaving similarly with a woman of color at the other end of the leash will likely elicit comments from white cisgender men that the woman "needs to get that dog under control." This has happened to a number of my interlocutors even though they wear clothing prominently denoting their professional work as dog trainers.[56] Any attempt to excuse the behavior on the grounds that the dog was "a rescue" (which none of these interlocutors would do, given their own objections to such storying) would do nothing to deflect criticism.

Teresa's comment also reveals that there is a tacit whiteness and femininity to the *logic* of saviorist storying. Lacking knowledge becomes acceptable, unmeaning, even innocent, when ladies in pink flip-flops are at the other end of the leash. When this is not the case, even a wealth of knowledge and expertise tend to be met with disapprobation. Further, Teresa's metaphor of "throwing a story on top of any dog" highlights how saviorist storying covers over, blankets, the alternative knowledges that she gestures toward with the identification of "any behavior that's being presented." Knowledge rooted in reading dogs' bodies and actions—their behaviors—is replaced through saviorist storying with affectively charged, tacitly racialized and gendered, and worryingly empty under- standings of dogs centered in the imaginary of "rescue" and "abuse." Indeed, as Teresa notes, this "throwing on top of" functions "to the detriment of the animal . . . 'cause they just make excuses and don't address problems."[57]

Teresa's concern underscores a troubling epistemic lack that emerges through many saviorist storyings, for the knowledge of dog behaviors that is blanketed over and therefore erased is knowledge particularly relevant to public health concerns. This epistemic concern is evident in Nathan's description of his own burnout as a shelter worker: "A lot of it stems from a really extreme frustration that we've had a lot of really, really nice dogs decline so significantly that it was questionable whether they should even [be adopted] out. And that at the same time, it's a con- stant stream of people trying to save dogs that are like, really aggressive." Nathan notes that "we've seen dogs sit for six months, and then they go on the euth list, and then, like, five adopters show up within twenty-four hours." For Nathan, the timing of this saviorist storying is everything: "If you pull a dog the day it was on the euth list, then the dog was gonna be euthanized, and you saved the dog. If you pull a dog that's only been there for a week, then yeah, you rescued a dog from the shelter. It's not as good of a story."[58] By motivating adoptions with an affective salvationist urgency that overcodes more expert understandings of dogs' lives and behaviors, saviorist storying ultimately harms far more dogs than it saves.

Other interlocutors echo Nathan's frustration. For example, Sara, a biracial—African American and white—shelter worker in her twenties, argues, "I think that if a dog isn't safe, it doesn't need to be out there. Euthanize." Like many of my interlocutors, she shifts speech patterns, moving to a series of direct questions posed to me, her listener, that I understood to be more broadly aimed at the larger public with whom she interacted in her job: "Why are rescues—or whoever—trying to save the ones that are gonna cause damage? If they're gonna hurt another animal, kill another animal, hurt a person? Why do we want to put that one out into the world when there are so many good ones that really are dying because of lack of space?" A lifelong vegetarian whose birthday wishes usually involve requests to send money to refugees in locations such as Darfur, Sara responds to her own questions with a blunt statement of her position: "I don't think they all need to be saved."[59]

Sara's opposition to saviorist storying is based in the logic of numbers, space, and time. Dogs dying for lack of space are identified as dogs in need of help. Echoing Nathan's observations about dogs' decline during long-term confinement, Sara posits that only "solid" dogs should be going out, "not the—you know, not because . . . 'It has one more day before it's gonna be euthanized!'"[60] Like Nathan, Sara pushes for a timing of adoptions based on accountability to a larger public, rather than on saving dogs from imminent euthanasia. In both their accounts, safety trumps salvation as the central concern or care needed in this type of work.

Sara's questions highlight the affective overtones that many of my interlocutors identify as problematic in the work of rescue. Veronica, a Latinx shelter worker in her forties with a wealth of knowledge gleaned from years of working with behaviorally challenging dogs, stories the rescue practices she often witnesses in a similar manner: "There's this um, structure of no structure, so 'I gotta get this dog out, I gotta get this dog out, so I'm gonna pull him and then take him to a medical facility and board them there, or you know, stash them somewhere.'"[61] Her reference to "this structure of no structure" underscores how, according to the policy-grounded views shared by most of my interlocutors, no kill is lacking in logic. The pulling or adoption of dogs is seen as being driven by emotion to the exclusion of reason.

Diane, a fellow white queer academic who is ethnographically involved with a feral cat rescue, shared similar concerns, noting how some of the people involved in private rescue operations that she works with are on the verge of having their houses repossessed but still focus all of their energies and economic resources on getting "this next group of cats into homes."[62] My interlocutors identify a problem in which affective urgency leads self-styled rescuers to high-stakes decisions without attention to longer-term concerns. A feeling of urgency trumps what Veronica and others consider to be more careful responsibility to the animals and, arguably, the humans doing the supposed saving.

What Is a Life?

Many of my interlocutors expressed concern that the saviorist storying that influences actions, practices, and identities in rescue often fails to address a significant question: what *is* a life? Rowena, a white straight working-class woman in her sixties, self-employed as a dog walker, told me how she had recently tried to find a shelter that was both no kill and open intake, meaning that it accepted all animals that arrived in its jurisdiction. Describing one such shelter, she noted, "They said they've had some dogs that have been there a couple years," and that the dogs "go on sleepovers on the weekends away with people." She sighed and looked at me: "I just don't know." Then both of us paused. I offered my own distillation of our conversation up to that point: "Well, it's like you said earlier. That's not a life." She responded, "Right, it isn't."[63]

Spaces focused on rescue and no-kill policies often consign dogs and humans to one of two interconnected fates, neither of them ideal. The first is an empty life with little to no interaction, in which dogs develop behavioral problems due to long-term kenneling and do not get adopted out, ever. For example, Kayla, a white straight middle-class shelter worker in her sixties, put it to me: "Animal sanctuaries, . . . I'm sure that there are some of them that are small and, like, feasible to maintain, but a lot of them, I think, . . . become an animal hoarding type situation, or a warehousing situation." She added, "If you have a dog living in a crate for three years in a row, in its own waste? . . . It's not humane."[64] Kayla's concern about inhumane warehousing situations is echoed by Veronica, who notes, "I just want to make sure that we've done everything we can to keep the dog sane, and then at a certain point we have to look at a dog and go, 'This isn't right.'"[65] These critiques challenge saviorist storying. Given the isolation of most shelter and sanctuary dogs—almost all shelters and sanctuaries prohibit contact between dogs to prevent bites and disease transmission—and the challenges of caring for them in the long term, not killing animals can mean they spend years deprived of contact, eventually debilitating them to the point that they cannot thrive outside the institutions that claim to shelter them.

The second fate that emerges from the conjunction of saviorist storying and no-kill politics is placement of dogs in inappropriate homes, with potentially disastrous consequences. Kayla told me a story of a recently widowed, seventy-two-year-old white woman who went to a local rescue, telling them, "I want a dog that I can walk around. I'm gonna start walking." The rescue "adopted her a fucking seventy-plus-pound dog that they have multiple prior bites on, that they themselves described as animal aggressive and not good with men," who promptly "went after another dog and *dragged* her, and broke her ribs, and got loose, and mauled another dog!" When the dog was ultimately deemed dangerous by the city, Kayla counseled the woman to return him to the rescue, which the woman refused to do for fear that the dog would be euthanized. Indeed, this was all too common in Kayla's experience: "There's tons of people like that with dogs like that. Tons! Tons! I'm like, 'Maybe you should return this dog.' They're like, 'No! Then they'll kill it!'"[66] The woman kept the dog and ended up hiring multiple trainers and, eventually, a dog walker who could take the dog out safely.

When this woman had first adopted the dog, the rescue had simply given her a muzzle and told her to be careful when walking the dog. Kayla read this as a fairly deliberate obfuscation of a serious behavioral issue. Teresa echoes this concern in noting the propensity for rescues, and, in some cases, shelters, to deliberately withhold knowledge about dogs or to fail to exercise due diligence regarding behavioral issues. For example, Teresa had a friend who adopted a dog from a rescue and discovered the dog had acute separation anxiety. It could not be left alone for more than a minute at a time without engaging in extremely destructive behavior. Teresa postulated that the rescue had deliberately lied about the dog, "you know, 'cause they don't want the dog to not get adopted, and they don't want the dog to get euthanized, and so they cover it up."[67] In my shelter fieldwork, I saw this type of covering up far too often: even when dogs bit volunteers or other dogs, hard enough to break the skin, incidents were rarely reported, meaning that shelter staff and volunteers involved in adoptions were often deliberately kept unaware of worrisome behaviors.[68] Commitments to saviorist storying thus frequently cover over and hide important information about dogs.

In other cases, dogs' problematic histories may be made quite overt but discounted through saviorist storying. Rossella, an Italian American woman in her forties who works in a behavioral team at a shelter, shared with me her worries that her shelter had, in recent months, adopted out dogs who are "known biters, to households—not to rescues, to households." For Rossella, the concern is that "those households are now stuck with a dog that has a bite history, which should come with a whole lot of warning labels, but they're in that adoption bubble, there's those glowing, sparkling lights, and they sign away their lives, and sign eighteen waivers, and they don't care." In Rossella's telling, saviorist storying leads the new owners to choose not to see that their dog comes with literal warning labels. Rossella attempts to articulate the thinking of these adopters: "And the shelter probably just doesn't know the dog, right, because there's that whole, 'It's how they've been raised' thing, right? So, the shelter just doesn't understand them, it's just not the right situation for them."[69] The expert knowledge of shelter staff and even the dog's history of biting are occluded, and the dog's movement to a domestic, usually family-type space is imagined as erasing earlier problem behaviors and actions (a supposition that, sadly, only rarely bears out).[70] This type of overcoding through saviorist storying is haunted for many of my interlocutors, for they worry that this type of denial may result in mismanagement of a known problem, posing larger dangers to the human and canine public.

In asking "What *is* a life?," it is crucial to think through those moments when the owners of a rescue dog decide that, in fact, the dog's world is too small—that its interactions with other creatures, both human and nonhuman animals, have become too restricted, the dog poses too much danger, and that this is not the life they want their dog to have. After sharing her story with me, Kayla noted that in many such cases, adopters themselves end up euthanizing the dog for behavioral reasons.[71]

This brings us back to Veronica's remark, "We have to look at a dog and go, 'This isn't right.'" Veronica raised this point in the context of what she termed "the judgment conversation," referring to judgments directed at owners. She gave the example of a hundred-plus-pound dog with severe separation anxiety who, despite being medicated and receiving thousands of dollars' worth of training, had recently posed a violent threat to a family member. Responding to the views of the owners' friends, who were quite angry about the decision to euthanize and told them to simply "find another home" for the dog, she exclaimed: "There are not enough fifty-year-old, healthy women on farms with no strangers that ever come through and no other dogs. . . . That fantasy is bullshit!" She then shifted to the second person when discussing the family's decision to euthanize: "And to have to go through . . . the judgment of everybody, and everybody's telling you that you're doing something wrong? When you in your heart know that you just saved that dog's life by ending his life?"[72]

The stigma and shaming involved in decisions to euthanize, or even to simply return a dog to a shelter or rescue because of behavioral issues, are intense. This shaming comes from all corners—not only the friends and family who levy accusations of murder, tell owners they haven't done enough, or make impossible suggestions involving single (frequently also imagined as lesbian) women and farms, but also some shelter workers. Describing her frustration with burnt-out shelter workers hooked on the "saving mentality" who were inclined to see only the worst in humans, Kayla outlines a hypothetical interaction between a shelter worker and an owner surrendering a dog: "You belittle them and you try and convince them to keep their dog, and you shame them [and] you tell them that you're gonna kill their animal."[73] To add to the burden, most veterinarians refuse to perform behavioral euthanasia because the dog involved is usually quite sound in body. In all these situations, saviorist storying overcodes and refuses the knowledge involved in careful and responsible decision-making, claiming instead that any life is worth any effort, even as the lives of the humans and dogs affected deteriorate to the point of becoming unlivable.

Neoliberal and Colonial Shapings

In the issue of shame lies a key actor that shapes the conditions of possibility for saviorist storying's emergence in the first place: neoliberalism.[74] In the tales related by Veronica and Kayla, active shaming in the name of no kill attempts to make the financial and emotional costs faced by adopters into strictly private matters. When dogs pose threats that extend to the larger public, as with the dog adopted by the older woman in Kayla's story, owners are encouraged to keep them in homes, and to keep private the hurt and suffering fostered by a broken system rather than to recognize and address it as a public problem. The shaming by shelter workers that Kayla notes happens not just when dogs are returned because of behavioral issues, but also in cases where folks are priced out of their homes and new rentals either forbid all pets or specifically exclude bully-breed dogs. The larger social problem of a lack of pet-friendly housing is occluded here through the shaming accomplished by saviorist storying.

Neoliberalism also haunts these worlds in many other ways, including the creation of the rescue industry itself. The problems identified by my interlocutors stem, at least in part, from a landscape in which under-funded public shelters, as well as rescues, depend on private contributions of money and labor. Naomi, a white, straight middle-class shelter worker in her thirties, noted that even shelters are increasingly trying to position themselves as no kill because "that's how you're going to get your community to support you" through both volunteer labor and financial donations.[75] Private funding increasingly drives the choices and practices of the rescue industry. Data from Shelter Animals Count (SAC) back up this insight, for of the organizations participating—estimated to be roughly 50 percent of those in the U.S. today—self-described rescues have grown from 37 in the 1980s to 137 in the 1990s to 535 in between 2000 and 2009 to 1,215 in the 2010s.[76] Although these data track only organizations involved in SAC, they correlate with a Google Ngram Viewer search that reveals an uptick in the use of the phrase *animal rescue* in published works beginning in the early 1990s, with about a threefold increase by 2008, the last year for which data have been collected.[77] This industry has an astonishing lack of oversight, as Kayla's tale of the seventy-two-year-old woman suggests. Indeed, those private funders, in the main, are so caught up in saviorist storying that they are unable to see the real dogs and incredible harms, private and public, it covers over and erases, and it is the formal job of exactly no one to correct that problem.

With respect to the same story, Kayla comments, that, from the standpoint of the rescue involved, "on paper, it's a successful pull, and it's a successful adoption." There is no tracking of longer-term harms (or, for that matter, successes) in either shelter or rescue adoptions, just the short-term numbers that are provided to various funders as proof of successful work. Indeed, numbers drive much of the industry. As Kayla put it to me, most rescues are interested mainly in "retail-ready" dogs, meaning dogs of a variety of sizes, whose looks make them easily adoptable, rather than the pit-bull and Chihuahua types that make up the majority of shelter populations.[78] Rescue has become an industry where numbers and saviorist storying trump concerns about harms. The involvement of capitalism here is evoked by Paisley, a white working-class woman in her twenties employed as a trainer in a chain pet store, who complained to me that local rescues were, in her words, "flipping dogs," sometimes pulling dogs from a shelter (which is free for them) and then driving to store parking lots in posh areas and holding adoption fairs on the same day, charging a $400–$500 fee per adoption.[79]

Saviorist storying's epistemic overcoding plays a large role in these practices. For example, Sara expressed deep concern about representatives from rescues coming into the shelter where she worked and pulling dogs "without having any clue what they're like, at all . . . not one question asked." When I asked her how common this practice was, she replied: "I'd say a majority of rescues," involving both "little rescues and . . . really well-known ones." She commented: "I think it sets a lot of dogs and people up for failure." Sara pointed out that many rescues would then place a dog directly "into a foster home [that] wouldn't even know if [the dog is] good with their animals."[80] The urgency of saviorist storying, coupled with a focus on numbers, demonstrates how a neoliberalist rescue industry causes a great deal of harm to both individuals who adopt dogs with behavioral problems and a public whose safety has been compromised by the public relations imperative never to kill.

The numbers game also ties in with affect in the politics of life and death. Many of my interlocutors criticized rescues for "outsourcing" euthanasia. Rossella noted that a number of well-known rescues in the area were notorious for returning problem dogs to her shelter for them to be euthanized there.[81] Gretchen pointed out that, for years, a prominent local no-kill organization located near an open-admission shelter would simply walk dogs across the parking lot in order for them to be euthanized.[82] Shelters are concerned with their own numbers: Jessica noted that shelters occasionally refused to release a dog to a rescue because they viewed it as highly adoptable and wanted to claim the "happy trails" ending of a successful adoption for themselves and boost their own "live release" rate.[83] Both types of organizations were and are invested in avoiding the stigma of death, sometimes at great cost to the living.

What is at stake here is not simply making money, as with rescues that pull dogs for free and then adopt them out, clean-slated and "saved," but the production of another kind of value: the affect or feeling of saviorism itself.[84] Saviorist storying invests the bodies of dogs and humans with the added value of salvation in all of its emotional, sparkly glory. During my one fieldwork visit in assisting a low-cost or free veterinary clinic that catered to all comers, but was focused mostly on houseless humans and their pets, I noted afterwards a heady, almost addictive feeling from having helped humans and dogs, a feeling that even my own critical thinking regarding my whiteness and class status did not seem to dim.[85] The saviorist storyings of shelter and rescue make a powerful opiate that obscures the harms of neoliberalism and related structural violences.

However, neoliberalism is only part of the problem. The sense of emotional satisfaction that lends saviorist storying its charge and allure emerges from a specific history: colonization. Most relevant to this issue is settler colonialism, a key component of which is its "civilizing mission." The promise of salvation plays out on a spiritual level in the form of Christianity and on a material level in the transformation of the colonized into the "civilized." Colonization has occurred through the transfer of worship practices to Christian churches and the concomitant erasure of Indigenous cosmologies and ways of knowing across the globe. This "salvation" in the name of Christianity both undergirds and parallels the labor and claims specific to rescued dogs taken from the streets or the shelter—spaces of supposedly certain death—into the domestic space of the family home. Saviorist storying literally would not make sense without this narrative of settler colonialism and Christianity.

Settler colonialism also makes possible and shapes geographies and ways of relating. It worked and continues to work through the forcible movement of colonized peoples out of land stolen by settlers and into the domestic space of "proper" homes. This movement facilitates the imposition of kin formations that violently erase other ways of relating. This aspect of "civilizing," evident in the histories of American Indian boarding schools in the U.S. that claimed to "kill the Indian and save the man," has imposed specific notions of home and family.[86] Many scholars in Indigenous studies, among them Mark Rifkin and Scott Lauria Morgensen, have addressed this history. Rifkin notes that the "civilizing" practices of American Indian boarding schools involved a forcible molding into white, heteronormative, and cisnormative family formations.[87] As Rifkin observes, "The effort to 'civilize' American Indians and the attendant repudiation of indigenous traditions can be understood as significantly contributing to the institutionalization of the 'heterosexual imaginary,' in Chrys Ingraham's evocative phrase, helping build a network of interlocking state-sanctioned policies and ideologies that positioned monogamous hetero couple-hood and the privatized single-family household as official national ideals by the late nineteenth century."[88]

The civilization that continues to accompany supposed salvation and land theft is a process wherein *family* denotes, quite strictly, a nuclear family, and *home* a private household by definition separate from public life. This sense of home and family is central to the moniker of the forever (or furever) home, for it is the same understanding that makes a space into a home in the first place. Further, it emerged through the workings of a labor movement that defined the American family home, in the words of Chandan Reddy, "over and against people of color."[89] And it is straying from this space of home that marks dogs as "at large" and therefore subject to the laws of the settler state. Thus settler colonialism's mappings of land, and particularly of home, in conjunction with the work of racialization, give rise to the spatiality that determines whether a dog is perceived to be in need of rescue.[90]

My analysis of saviorist storying attempts to denaturalize it, to make what seems familiar and normal instead troublesome and even strange. And yet, because these logics and patterns are so formative to these worlds—just try to rethink home and family outside of the settler and white-normative model!—they are difficult to disrupt, alter, or change. This is because they become real, reified, material through the living bodies of humans and dogs: that is, this storying materializes in the many emergences of identity and relationships that play out in the rescue and shelter worlds. And yet it must be disrupted in order to effectively restructure the worlds I describe and begin building different worlds, worlds that might make more human and animal lives more livable.

Interrupting Saviorist Storyings

In pointing to the need for interruptions, I want to turn back to the conversation I described with Rowena, where I did that cool thing of moving into a kind of present moment and left you thinking that she and I had stopped in agreement that a life spent in confinement is not a life at all. However, we didn't leave things there. When she said "No, it isn't," I asked: "Or *is* it a life?" to which she responded: "Or is it? Yeah, they can't tell us! Exactly. . . . But you know, if they could talk, then they wouldn't be man's best friend."[91] Despite my reliance on storying, the central figures in my narratives cannot speak: we cannot ask a dog whether they agree with any of the humans who claim to represent their interests. Yet dogs themselves do point the way toward an interruption of sorts.

In her own practice working with humans and dogs, Sharon, the dog trainer who commented on pervasive assumptions of abuse, actually encourages storying as a way to build different and even new understandings. She notes that if her clients "can create a backstory that is or is not true doesn't matter, then it gives them something to hang their hat on, . . . so they . . . love their stories, and I actually encourage them to come up with their stories, and we talk about the fact that their dog probably wasn't abused." For Sharon, this push away from the focus on the horrors of presumed abuse (the storying that gets "thrown on top of" dogs, in Teresa's words) and toward a more realistic imagining of their dogs' pasts can be productive: "I find that what happens is that if they go, 'This dog had a deprived puppyhood' or whatever, that actually . . . if I perceive my dog as having a deprived puppyhood, then I may not expect as much of him as I would have had he not done that. In some cases this is a really good thing."[92]

Here, Sharon argues for a kind of storying that produces a distinct kind of knowing and builds a more empathetic relationship between humans and dogs. For Sharon, such understandings accomplish relational work, helping "people accept the dog they have and work with the dog they have, not the dog they wanted."[93] This move interrupts saviorist storying by attempting not to speak for or over dogs so much as to, in the words of the feminist theorist Maria Puig de la Bellacasa, think-with them: that is, instead of working through the filter of the sparkling lights of saviorist storying, it constitutes an attempt to produce knowledge attuned to, in concert with, and derived from the concerns, needs, and histories of dogs themselves.[94]

The form of storying Sharon encourages is an alternative way of knowing, in which dogs' bodies, histories, and perspectives ground the narrative rather than disappear through the telling of tales. Such ways of knowing are everywhere in my interlocutors' critiques: one of the best ways to cast shade in dog worlds is to say that a person or organization doesn't really "know" dogs. I explore these complicated and competing knowledge claims in detail in my next chapter and so comment only briefly here. I had a lot of fun sharing Gretchen's story with my interlocutors because it is both so outlandish and yet also so neatly encapsulates all of the problematic elements of these worlds. When I shared it with Kayla, we both had a great but cynical laugh. It is normal for dogs to hate objects and figures like vacuum cleaners, brooms, and strange men, because they are just plain weird and scary from the dogs' point of view. Just a little bit of thinking-with dogs, attempting to story through their bodies and perspectives, can go a long way in challenging assumptions of abuse and, therefore, disrupting saviorist storying.

Although trying to think from the perspective of a deprived puppy in order to understand its reaction to vacuum cleaners and large sticks may not seem to push against either a neoliberalist "rescue-industrial complex" or settler-colonial and racist dynamics of land allocation and understandings of family and home, this type of thinking-with is quite disruptive. This is because the lives of most dogs in so-called ideal adoptive situations are, imagined from their perspective, rather terrible. Imagine spending most of your day alone (or with a cat friend, in which case, you are mostly alone, with another animal deliberately trying to mess with you about 20 percent of the time). And when you do get to go out, say, to a dog park, you end up hanging around a bunch of strangers who are basically two-year-olds with knives. Very few of you have the skills necessary to navigate the complexities of social interactions, all of which happen in small, enclosed spaces where everyone ends up getting too excited until things tip, and then bam! No more dog park for you. Dogs who live with houseless folks often live far better social lives than those cooped up behind white picket fences in the suburbs: the geographical reordering of a life lived outside—even in the context of the criminalization of poverty and houselessness by many municipalities—often provides a much better social life for the humans involved as well. In this sense, storying that takes dogs' perspectives as central works against the fairytale ending of the "forever home." Put another way, attempts to think-with dogs and tell *their* stories interrupt the idealization of home and family in saviorist storying.

Attempts to think-with dogs can transmute ideas not just of the family and home but also of two additional spaces often invoked in saviorist storying: the shelter and the prison. Here I am thinking-with the American studies scholar Brigitte Fielder, who writes beautifully about nineteenth-century abolitionists' use of animal metaphors as a way to garner empathy for enslaved humans. Taking seriously dogs' perspectives on spaces of confinement bears directly on approaches to human confinement.[95] For instance, I spoke with María, a Latinx upper-middle-class woman in her thirties with a background in critical race and ethnic studies, who now works primarily as a dog trainer. She observed that, when appropriately qualified, prison metaphors can do great work in reorienting people's perceptions of both shelters and prisons: "It's like, the dogs who are in shelters are kind of like the drug offenders in prison. . . . They really shouldn't be there."[96] Instead of taking the narrow view that invocations of prison in shelter talk enact an appropriation that decenters and even erases the needs of humans in captivity, as I do at the beginning of this chapter, if one follows María's thinking, one might instead take prison comparisons as inept attempts to convey the injustice of enforcing settler mappings of space and territory—home versus "wild" or "at large" and therefore in need of containment—through the enclosure of dogs. Such thinking entails a practice of enforcing particular divisions and designations of space that enacts violences on both humans and nonhuman animals.[97]

Indeed, one can easily connect thinking like María's to the arguments Michelle Alexander makes in *The New Jim Crow* to highlight the many injustices—most of them entwined with racism, misogyny, colonialism, nationalism, homophobia, and transphobia—to which imprisoned humans are subject.[98] Further, acknowledgment of the largely ignored but huge problem that dogs are often "saved" only when their mental health is already irreparably damaged can serve as a means to bring attention to the injustice of both dog and human solitary confinement. Attention to this issue can be leveraged into not only challenging saviorist storying in dog worlds but also confronting human mental health issues, including widespread ableist understandings that occlude many impairments that are neither physical nor visible.

I want to close this chapter with consideration of a simple yet revolutionary approach, put forward succinctly by Kayla: "We need to be doing more work preventing shelter animals from happening."[99] Such an approach might stop saviorist storying before it starts, interrupting the siren song of rescue. Preventing many a dog from deteriorating over a long shelter stay and thus becoming "bad," however, requires a different kind of imagining. Some of the tangible manifestations of work that prevents shelter animals from happening include or could include low-cost and free veterinary clinics that go to encampments of houseless folks and provide free transit for animals to and from spay and neuter appointments; animal shelters that act as contact points for the family members of houseless folks, providing an address for licenses and a means for human family members and social service workers to keep in touch with both humans and their nonhuman animals; animal shelters that act as spaces where folks with limited resources can turn when, say, they require emergency surgery and need someone to look after their pets but cannot secure that help for free; animal shelters that offer free training and behavioral resources, including to folks who acquired dogs (and other animals) from other loci; free dog training tips and veterinary care offered as part of street fairs and related community events so that dogs don't end up being surrendered; efforts to make available affordable housing where pets are allowed; and shelters that take in both humans and animals affected by domestic violence, which, crucially, disrupt the weaponization of human-animal bonds in such situations. All of these examples demonstrate a shift toward a preventative and community-oriented approach in addressing problems that arise through human-animal bonds. Such an approach addresses problems holistically, working to keep humans and animals together, particularly when those humans are marginalized. This shift can be radical: efforts to combine medical care for houseless animals with free medical care for humans—which I have yet to witness—would be not just disruptive but revolutionary. And in these approaches I find glimmerings of other-worldings that shine not with the false sparkles of saviorism but with a kaleidoscope of the different ways of imagining, thinking, and doing that emerge when we are pushed to think of the needs of marginalized humans and animals together, not separately. In these glimmerings, there is the promise of multispecies justice.

2

The Human, the Animal, the Episteme

Like many of my experiences in dog training, this is a moment
suffused with frustration. My dog, Annie, and I are walking the
sidewalks of our neighborhood. Or, more aptly, I am doing my
best to get Annie's attention as she desperately scans her sur-
roundings, the whites of her eyes visible all the way around her
irises, her body posture forward, with nary an ear flick indexing
attention to me, the being at the other end of her leash. I recite
to myself the mantra I picked up through multiple sessions with
trainers, a months-long seminar on dog behavior, a year of fieldwork at an animal shelter, and several months (so far) of working
under the tutelage of several experienced trainers at a dog day
care: "Remind her that she is a dog IN a body! IN a body!" I somehow manage to turn her around with a piece of cheese dangled in
front of her nose. We step towards the curb and I ask her to perform one of the many tricks she knows—this time, to sit, put her
front paws down on the asphalt below the curb, then hop them
back up to the concrete of the sidewalk. She performs this several
times quite admirably and I reward her with more Monterey Jack
(her favorite of the cheeses at my price point). We then shuffle over
to a broken chunk of sidewalk that has been replaced by dirt and
grass, where I solicit this behavior again. I then ask for a "look," a
"sit," some turns, and a nose-touch, and reward each with cheese.
We then continue on our walk, with stops like these so frequent
that to term our activity a "walk" perhaps entirely misses both our
path and goals in this outing.

—AUTHOR'S FIELD NOTES, JUNE 2013

This chapter explores several entwined questions, foremost among them being "What is it like to think-with dogs?" As the above excerpt from my field notes illustrates, a central thread in my attempts at understanding dogs is the labor of trying to build understandings out of a congeries of bodies, movements, affects, and vision—the somatics of María Puig de la Bellacasa's "thinking-with." Attempts at understanding are often efforts to "read" dogs' bodies, where reading entails identifying the emotions, or bodily affects, that dogs experience, often routed through the deceptively simple terminology of "dog body language." I include *affects* here because a key aspect of the feelings shaping these interactions lies in their exchange; Annie's hypervigilance in the interactions described above becomes my own.

Moves to "read" body language are frequently followed by interventions that attempt to engage dogs by encouraging them to think in and through their bodies: that is, to recognize their bodies and sensory experiences as potential sites for redirecting and even disrupting sequences of emotions. By working to remind Annie first of the surfaces under her feet—grass, concrete, and asphalt—and then by soliciting other bodily movements, I hope to break her fixation on potentially fearful encounters and disrupt our affective circling. In her case, this circling stems from the fear of seeing other dogs while she is on leash and has nowhere to run. My goal is to get her to think *with* and *through* her body: I want her to notice and *feel* the differences in the earth and the concrete under her feet so that she grounds herself in the sensations of her body. I want her to think *as* a body and embodied being, to become sense-ible, rather than simply move, lunge, bark, or, as one trainer put it to me, act "out of her body."[1]

In taking up questions of bodily thinking and thinking-with dogs, I am interested in exploring how claims to knowledge demarcate the most contentious aspect of both my fieldwork and the larger worlds of animal sheltering and rescue: competing claims as to who really *knows* dogs. These are the seeds of the most bitter ruptures I have witnessed, and they frequently indicate one person's distrust in another's ability to adequately care for the animals in their charge. One remark that has stuck with me for many years is an interlocutor's assertion regarding a widely disliked shelter volunteer: "He thinks he's the dog whisperer, but he's really the dog autistic."[2] I cannot think of anything more discrediting in dog and rescue worlds than assertions that someone really doesn't *know* dogs—or, separately but related, doesn't know what they're *doing* when it comes to dogs.

There are species-specific limitations and differences, such as sensory disparities, that inform these knowledge claims and demarcate the unevenness of the affective sharing I describe. For example, dogs do not wear shoes, so the difference between earth and concrete matters more to Annie than to me. Kaitlyn, a white straight middle-class interlocutor, observed that even with her careful attention to dog body language, she thought she was missing "50 percent of what was going on" in dog playgroups because of humans' limited capabilities to detect and discern smells.[3] Further, the conjunction of bodies, languages, affects, and reading can be deeply confusing; the distinction between humans' *knowing* dogs and knowing what they're *doing* with dogs points up some of this confusion, for processes of reading body language also extend to humans' efforts to make their own bodies readable to dogs.

I am invested in exploring an affective bodily knowing, more akin to knowing what would it *feel* like to think-with dogs. My work is certainly about identifying knowledge produced in close alliance, affiliation *with* dogs, rather than the more distant terminology of thinking *about* dogs. However, as the language of affect illustrates, there is a sensibility here as well. Humans literally do not register the world in the same way dogs do. We live in a sensory world where sight is highly prized (witness Supreme Court justice Potter Stewart's famous claim regarding identifying obscenity, "I know it when I see it"). I want to get at a feeling-with, to turn into the more haptic register of a world where feeling, as contact with concrete versus grass, matters epistemologically, taking up sensory experiences *as* knowledge practices. My thinking engages what Jakob von Uexküll famously termed the nonhuman animal *Umwelt*, that is, the ways that nonhuman animals inhabit distinct worlds from humans through disparate sensory experiences.[4] This type of sensory knowledge, or knowledge-as-sensibility, employs thinking-with as feeling, hapticity, or touch, along with hearing and different ways of seeing: that is, knowing in and through multiple sensory modes that push beyond the knowledge claims common to an anthropocentric episteme.

However I also want to foreground how the analytic of interspecies intersectionality applies to the knowledge claims and the related epistemic and ontological practices of these worlds, as indexed in the ableism of the comment labeling someone as a "dog autistic." Claims to thinking today are unavoidably shaped by the development of the so-called rational man, that prominent figure whose emergence in and through the colonization of the Americas, the transatlantic slave trade, and the Enlightenment (the "Age of Reason"), hinges on a denial of the body in favor of the mind. René Descartes's famous phrase "I think, therefore I am" demarcates a (much-contested) division of mind from body, with the body envisioned as a base element enslaved to passion and therefore devoid of reason. I use *enslaved* deliberately here, for key to the emergence of rational man was the creation of marginalized humans— enslaved Africans and African Americans, Indigenous peoples, women, those deemed "feeble-minded"—as nonhuman, inhuman, and animal. In order to move toward or into claiming knowledge through bodies, to answer the question "What is it like to think-with and think-as bodily knowledges?," it is imperative to ask, "Who gets to have a body?" and "Who has been consigned to be *only* a body?"

In asking these questions, I am reminded of an interchange I had with a copyeditor early in this project. I had referred to a dog, the subject of the verb and the action described in the sentence, as *who*; the copyeditor, following many decades of protocol, had replaced my *who* with *that*. This interchange illustrates at least some of the stakes in claims about bodies and rationality, for *who* usually references people, and specifically people who are understood to be subjects, able to claim social and legal recognition, while a *that* or an *it* is generally dehumanized or marked as nonhuman and does not get to be a subject beyond the confines of a sentence diagram. Throughout this book, dogs generally get to be *who* or *whom*, a usage that linguistically asserts their claims as actors legible to and capable of making claims in and on social worlds rather than passive beings in the multispecies worlds I describe. However, the legacy of rational man rests in the denial of rationality to his Others: that is, rational man becomes such by denying subjectivity to peoples and deeming them other-than-human, animal, or even subanimal; reducing them to *that*, *what*, or *it*; or even erasing them entirely through genocidal logics like those typified in the mission of American Indian boarding schools: "Kill the Indian, save the man."[5] Thus, in this chapter I also ask, "How can I claim a *who* for dogs *and* be responsible to the ways specific humans have been forcibly denied *who* and consigned to animality as bodies?" Put slightly differently, is it possible to be accountable to the denial of *who* to marginalized humans while claiming it for dogs? Further, the epistemic production of rational man and his animal and animalized Others— rational, man, thought versus body, Other, animal—materializes through historically specific productions of race, indigeneity, gender, and sexuality. Thus, engaging a sensibility of bodily thinking-with dogs must attend to the variances among specific histories as well as among present-day practices.

This chapter departs from the previous chapter in applying the analytic of interspecies intersectionality not to narrative but rather to the history and present of an episteme, what might be thought of as a landscape of knowledge and what it makes thinkable. Wrestling with what Donna Haraway would term the question of how to "inherit histories of violence," this chapter poses urgent questions about how to think together the inheritance that is the founding conditions and ongoing work of an episteme of rational man and his (frequently animal and animalized) Others with the philosophical project of attempting, now, to put forward knowledge claims across a species divide.[6] I draw extensively from philosophy, history, and politics before moving to mostly ethnographic and autoethnographic data. I move away from questions of narrative and ontology by pointing to ways of knowing and doing that inhere in sensoria, that emerge apart from and, in some cases, in spite of the storyings detailed in my previous chapter. However, much like my other chapters, this chapter poses a disruption, this time in the form of an epistemic intervention, rooted in understandings based in interspecies intersectionality and with the potential to improve understandings of the political and epistemological marginalization of both humans and nonhuman animals in our current worlds.

I begin with an exploration of the inauguration of rational man in order to identify the role of animality in the construction of his Others. I examine feminist standpoint theories as a potential guide toward my own epistemic interventions. I detail the confusing conglomeration of language, affect, knowledge, and bodies involved in worlds where humans and dogs relate before exploring philosophical interventions specific to nonhuman animals. Turning to specific practices of relating that are embodied in positive reinforcement–oriented (R+) training practices, I identify and describe a sensibility that emerges from thinking-with dogs. This helps me articulate a move to awareness that disrupts the episteme of rational man and challenges the logics of Othering and, or as, animality.

The Logic and Sciences of Rational Man

In her essay "Unsettling the Coloniality of Being/Power/Truth/Freedom: Towards the Human, after Man, Its Overrepresentation," the philosopher Sylvia Wynter traces the history of the production of the "ethnoclass of Man" in shifting epistemes and concomitantly emergent racial orders of being.[7] For Wynter, this genealogy begins with the Man crafted through "the Renaissance humanists' epochal redescription of the human outside the terms of the then-theocentric, 'sinful by nature' [conception] of the human," whose goal was no longer "mastery over Original Sin . . . , but rather of mastery over their own sensory, irrational nature."[8] That is, Renaissance humanists inaugurated a Man intelligible not through a relationship with sin and the church, but instead as a subject of the state. This inauguration of the "subject" at odds with "nature" is borne out in the Enlightenment mantra "I think, therefore I am," which the sociologist Anibal Quijano, anticipating Wynter, points to as a "mutation" through which "Eurocentric rationality" fixed "the body . . . as object of knowledge, outside of the environment of subject/reason."[9] In the view of both authors, the introduction of the subject/reason in opposition to the body/nature inaugurated the logic of race as it is understood today.

For Wynter, the introduction of rational man led to the reclassification of "the indigenous peoples of the New World . . . as 'irrational' . . . 'savage' Indians," a perception weaponized as a justification for colonization.[10] Quijano underscores this assertion: "From the Eurocentric perspective, certain races are condemned as inferior for not being rational subjects. They are objects of study and consequently bodies closer to nature. In a sense, they became dominable and exploitable. According to the myth of the state of nature and the chain of the civilizing process that culminates in European civilization, some races— blacks, American Indians, or yellows [sic]—are closer to nature than whites." In Quijano's thinking, this assertion of rationality and its measuring of proximity to "nature" hinged on the concomitant introduction of empire and capitalism. The world market for goods as well as for enslaved peoples introduced distinctions of place that became the geographies of race.[11] Per Quijano, the contradistinction of Spain and Portugal relative to the Americas was expanded to place Europe in contradistinction to Africa, Asia, and Oceania. Through Eurocentric rationality, these place designations came to describe kinds of peoples *as* races.[12] The transgender and animal studies scholar Che Gossett adds to this thinking the observation that Africa took on a special role in these developments, for it was (and often still is) "symbolized as outside of history, logos and telos, and therefore as primitive, barbaric and bestial."[13] Place designations as race designations produced particular peoples as irrational, Other, and animal.

Central to the production of rational man's Others was the rise of the sciences. Indeed, for Wynter and Quijano, the inauguration of rational man made possible a move from the divine as causal to nature as causal, with physical and eventually biological sciences arising to dissect the rules and internal workings of nature in order to master it.[14] Nineteenth-century debates about the term *species* starkly reveal how these sciences conflated animal and Other. For example, as Ladelle McWhorter illustrates in "Enemy of the Species," scientific discussions centered on polygenism versus monogenism involved polygenist arguments that "Negroes" and "Caucasians" were different species.[15] Bending the criteria introduced by George Louis-Leclerc, comte de Buffon, who posited that "two classes of a living entity can be considered distinct species if cross-breeding either (1) is impossible, (2) is sterile, or (3) produces offspring who are themselves sterile," slavery proponents such as the physician Josiah Nott argued in the mid-1800s that "'Mulattoes' (crosses between Negroes and Caucasians) were sterile hybrids like mules and . . . each successive generation of 'Mulattoes' is weaker and less able to procreate until, by the fourth, the line inevitably dies out."[16] Of course, the true causes for high mortality rates included the conditions of living under slavery and white supremacy in the 1800s—witness the deplorable experiments conducted by J. Marion Sims on enslaved women to remedy the pervasive problem of fistulas—but slavery proponents eschewed these patently social violences and seized, instead, on a by-nature argument.[17] The polygenetic approach was solidified in the 1854 compendium *Types of Mankind*, edited by Nott and the Egyptologist George Gliddon, which, "along with [Samuel] Morton's morphological studies was cited as scientific support in

From Josiah Nott and George Gliddon, *Types of Mankind* (Philadelphia:
J. B. Lippincott, 1854). Courtesy of
the American Antiquarian Society.

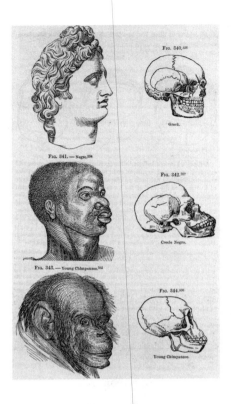

arguments for racial slavery and then for racial segregation through the
rest of the nineteenth century." Morton's arguments, asserting larger
skull sizes and therefore larger brains among Europeans, were famously
critiqued and shown to be inaccurate in the 1980s by Stephen J. Gould.[18]

One of the most famous images from Nott and Gliddon's book underscores how their stakes in species-level distinctions work through animality.[19] The "Negro" is positioned below the "Greek" and close to the
"Young Chimpanzee." The illustrations reinforce this hierarchical ordering, for the flared nostrils, prominent eyebrow ridge, and ridged neck
muscles of the "Negro" match those of the chimp. The image in fact *produces* the "Negro" as decidedly chimp-like, animal-like. By contrast, the
"Greek" entirely lacks these features. Claims of polygeny clearly crafted
a logic of race produced through a perceived continuity with animality.

While these debates changed shape with the publication of Charles
Darwin's 1859 *Origin of Species*, perhaps because Darwin was an abolition-
ist, they also shifted in substance, through the introduction of a narrative

of geographical and temporal progress toward "civilization." At the imaginary apex of this civilization stood a white human (admittedly shifting in definition through varying reforms to immigration laws). As Darwin himself notes: "For my own part I would as soon be descended from that heroic little monkey, who braved his dreaded enemy in order to save the life of his keeper; or from that old baboon, who, descending from the mountains, carried away in triumph his young comrade from a crowd of astonished dogs—as from a savage who delights to torture his enemies, offers up bloody sacrifices, practices infanticide without remorse, treats his wives like slaves, knows no decency, and is haunted by the grossest superstitions."[20] As Michael Lundblad argues in *The Birth of a Jungle*, while Darwinist thinking embraced monogeny as a concept, it still positioned many nonwhite humans *below* nonhuman animals in reference to progress toward "civilization."[21]

A key facet of these craftings of race is gender. As Quijano notes in describing pre-Darwinist thinking, "Women, especially the women of inferior races ('women of color'), remained stereotyped together with the rest of the bodies, and their place was all the more inferior for their race, so that they were considered much closer to nature or (as was the case with black slaves) directly within nature."[22] The philosopher and sociologist María Lugones posits that the inauguration of racial capitalism and European Enlightenment–style rationality produced a dual gender system. On the "light side," men and women were positioned dichotomously as strong and active, versus weak and passive. On the "dark side," "females" (not "women") excluded from white bourgeois femininity "were understood as animals in the deep sense of 'without gender,' sexually marked as female but without the characteristics of femininity."[23] Further, those who fell outside Western binarized gender systems entirely—those who were not easily understood as either male or female—were among the first to be set upon by the "dogs of war" deployed by conquistadors such as Vasco Núñez de Balboa.[24]

Darwinism augmented Lugones's dark/light dichotomy, for the sexual dimorphism that was key to his theory of natural selection was perceived as evidence of advanced evolution, and a conjunction of skewed sciences and the reading of cultural differences as bodily differences meant that "advancement" was registered as strongly evident only in white bodies, especially those tied to the culture of white domesticity.

Thus, after Darwin, the highly divergent gender presentations of white bourgeois culture were asserted as proof of more advanced evolution.[25]

Finally, Darwin also gave rise to a different kind of gendered policing in the form of eugenics, as worries that "human evolution had stalled" among those of European descent led to the perception that the "superiority" of Anglo-Americans was threatened by a "rising tide of inferiority." These fears were manifested in the form of state-sponsored sterilization of the "feeble-minded," Indigenous women, African American women, LGBT people (especially those residing in institutions), and Latinx women, which began in the mid-nineteenth century and continued into the late 1970s in the U.S.[26] The denial of rationality to Other bodies and concomitant assertion of their enslavement to "base passion" and "nature" inaugurated in the early sixteenth century continued through this logic of extermination, which itself produced race as a relationality that worked in and through gender, or denials thereof.

The production of man's Others thus worked (and arguably still works) through positing them as animal, proximate to animal, and subanimal.[27] To "think" in this context was not only to "be," but to be human; and to be human was to be white, male, able-bodied, neurotypical, cisgender, and straight. A lack of any these traits positioned one as an unthinking body, a part of nature in need of domination. And though I present a somewhat linear narrative of this crafting of man, race, and gender, the logics involved circulated and continue to circulate unevenly. Arguments for species-level differences through which some people were perceived as human and Others were decidedly not did not disappear with Darwinism or through eugenics, and the light and dark gender system Lugones details still holds in many ways.

The Animal/Other and the Political

Politics and political histories demonstrate how epistemic work of the kind outlined above is enacted through animals. For example, Indigenous peoples were and, often, still are connected to animals in the logic of colonization. Witness U.S. Army general Phillip Sheridan's statement regarding the buffalo massacres in the late 1800s: "Let them kill, skin, and sell until the buffalo is destroyed. . . . It is the only way to bring lasting peace and allow civilization to advance." The political scientist Claire

Jean Kim argues that Sheridan, along with his fellow settler colonizers, "understood well that the viability of independent Indian tribes depended on the survival of the buffalo."[28] Such policies, which forced many Indigenous peoples in prairie lands to starve, were joined with efforts to forcibly relocate them into government-approved formations of housing and ways of living, imposing settler-colonial heteropatriarchal family formations as norms, not to mention the concomitant kidnapping of children to be raised in state-run schools. This type of approach is also evident in Ole Gjerstad and Joelie Sanguya's *Qimmit: A Clash of Two Truths*, which documents the sled dog massacre by the Canadian Royal Mounted Police from the 1950s to the 1970s; this massacre deprived the Inuit in the eastern Arctic of not just a way of life and food gathering, but also a way of being. As with the peoples of the plains, it forced them into homes, family formations, and neoliberal capitalist consumption patterns presided over by the state.[29] Such political actions emerged from a logic wherein animal bodies, used as instruments in the attempted erasure of Indigenous peoples, were in fact joined to those peoples through those actions: to kill buffalo and sled dogs was to murder Indigenous peoples.

Less overtly genocidal maneuvers are also evident in political efforts linking animals to Othered peoples. For example, Kim explores the tensions of late 1800s California, when the labor of Chinese migrants became key to the building of the transcontinental railroad. Describing political cartoons from the late 1870s wherein "an apparently infinite number of grasshoppers with Chinese faces and queues swarm on Uncle Sam's farm as he and another white man try to beat them back," Kim argues that in such images, the animalization of the Chinese frames them as "unmitigated threats that must be exterminated." Kim also points to minstrel performances in which Chinese people were vilified with parodies of Chinese-accented English, coupled with suggestions that they ate cats and dogs.[30] These efforts reveal how humans were Othered through racialization by animalization and by the policing of animal husbandry and consumption.

Kim also shows how animality produces race as relational. For example, she points to an 1860s anti-Reconstruction political cartoon wherein a white man, specifically a Union candidate in favor of Black suffrage, has on his shoulders a Black man, on whose shoulders stands a Chinese man, who in turn bears a Native American man on his shoulders. On the ground, another white man holds an ape on a leash, exhorting the first white man to "put this Brother up." This ordering, which presents racial disparities on a spectrum with the white man on one end and the ape on the other (and rendering the Black man more "civilized" than the Chinese or the Native American), underscores the point that "race has been articulated in part as a metric of animality, as a classification system that orders human bodies according to how animal they are—and how human they are not—with all of the entailments that follow."[31]

Unsurprisingly, these varying productions of race through animality continue. Examples are virtually unlimited: they include the widespread circulation of political cartoons and memes depicting President Barack Obama and his family as ape-like, representing their faces with chimpanzee-like mouths and noses, and President Donald Trump's 2018 assertion that Latinx migrants to the U.S. "aren't people, these are animals."[32] Relational craftings of race persist in connections between specific kinds of humans and animalities, particularly in popular culture: Nagini, the snake belonging to Lord Voldemort in J. K. Rowling's Harry Potter series, appears as both a snake and a seductive woman of East Asian descent in Warner Brothers' *Fantastic Beasts* film franchise, while the hyenas in Disney's original 1994 *Lion King* and the 2019 live-action remake are marked as Black and brown through what Dan Hassler-Forest terms "their ethnically coded 'street' accents."[33] In fact, many animal-centered films engage this racial work. "Classics" such as Disney's 1941 *Dumbo* featured black crows as jazz singers, the leader of whom was named in the film *Jim*.[34] The indictment of the NFL quarterback Michael Vick on charges of dogfighting (discussed in the next chapter) engendered a media storm characterized by calls such as "Save a pit bull, euthanize a dog fighter," reflecting a surge in racism via animalization—note the term *euthanize*, not *murder*—as well as racialization rooted in perceptions about practices of animal husbandry.[35] Indigenous peoples continue to be targeted through animals, with traditional whale- and seal-hunting practices vital to native lifeways and cosmologies under fire from organizations like Greenpeace as recently as 2013, in spite of the fact that the greatest threat to both Native and marine mammal populations is not Indigenous practices but global climate change caused by Western capitalist consumer cultures.[36]

Finally, people of color continue to be targeted through the literal weaponization of nonhuman animals. The "bloodhound" formerly put to work tracking people escaping slavery has been transmuted into the police dog (usually a German Shepherd or Belgian Malinois) whose targets consist almost entirely of Black and brown people. A 2013 report found that "100 percent of the victims of police dog bites in Los Angeles in the first six months of that year were Black or Latino."[37] Dogs were used in a similar manner to attack Indigenous protesters of the U.S. government's violation of the sovereignty of the Standing Rock Sioux Tribe with the construction of Dakota Access Pipeline (DAPL) in 2016. In 2018, free-roaming white supremacist militias illegally corralled migrants into the U.S. (many of them asylum seekers) on the Texas-Mexico border using dogs.[38] Bénédicte Boisseron argues that in such cases "the dog bite not only dehumanizes but also, and more importantly, commodifies the human victim by making her fit for animal consumption." This practice animalizes in a particular way, for "species dominates race, making blackness an indicator of species rather than a racial marker."[39] To "blackness" I would add brownness, indigeneity, and noncitizen status. All these examples reveal how both the threat of and the actual bite produce the target as animal, not human, and, because of the racial basis for the initial targeting, produce people of color in particular as animal Others. Taken together, these many examples reveal not just politics as usual, but ways of thinking and modes of understanding—that is, the logic of a larger episteme that produces rational man's Others as flesh, body, and object, or animal.

Thinking Bodily and Standpoints

While there have been numerous challenges to the episteme I outline here, most salient to this writing is a body of thought emerging from feminist philosophers of science. Embracing the denigrated body as a source of knowledge, feminist standpoint theory prizes the locations of the Others of rational man as important loci from which to build not just alternative understandings, but better understandings. *From* is key, for in feminist standpoint theories, prepositions matter. Moving away from a binary of mind/body, feminist standpoint theories push for a different, nonbinary metaphorics in which locations matter, specifically the bodily locations from which knowledge claims emerge in relation to power.

To begin to understand standpoint theories, visualize a map on which the identities of people with power, such as humans who hold political authority, are positioned in the center. Then imagine the identities that one might inscribe as lying on the periphery of those positions of power, that is, those who are usually excluded from processes such as the crafting of and voting on legislation and the mapping of voting districts: for example, folks of color, LGBTQ* people, people with disabilities, poor people, women, migrants, Indigenous people, people who lack access to education, people in places where colonialism and racism work to erase them as human, and people who claim more than one of these facets of identity. In the context of the U.S., such a map places at the center those who are white, male, able-bodied, neurotypical, socioeconomically stable, U.S. citizens, Christian, English-speaking, and college-educated, with those who are Othered in various ways positioned on the outer edges of a starburst shape. And for standpoint theorists, this map of identities is also a map of bodies. Specifically, those on the margins of this mapping are those who have been denied the status of rational subject and instead positioned *only* as bodies, while those in the center can claim knowledge as unmarked by embodiment, the work of "pure" rational minds. This map also demarcates a knowledge politics wherein knowledge claims made by those in the center are shaped by invisible and implicit norms that make them seem neutral and "objective," although those claims are in fact deeply entwined with the social and political perpetuation of those norms.

The way into disrupting this mapping and the episteme of rational mind-man versus Other-body is to reclaim those marginalized bodies as sites of knowledge production and to center the positions of those at the periphery as loci through which to see and know otherwise, and therefore better. In this sense, standpoint theorists answer my introductory question regarding who gets to be *only* a body by positing that very embodying as a means to produce knowledge challenging that of rational man.

An example of thinking of embodiment as knowledge practice in standpoint theories is the differential mapping of claims to objectivity and the locations where bodies are marked and unmarked. For example, take the symptomology of heart attacks, typically characterized as a tightness in the chest and pain down the left arm. However, these are the typical heart attack symptoms of a cisgender man. Cisgender women may lack such symptoms and present, instead, with wholly disparate indicators such as stomachaches and shortness of breath. Failure to acknowledge these latter symptoms leads to an alarming number of deaths and misdiagnoses. Further, data regarding noncisgender people's heart attack experiences is scant, as are data on the effects of race, poverty, and indigeneity in preventing access to treatment and causing misdiagnoses. Simply put, the science behind heart attacks, not to mention the setting of ideal building temperatures, the design of seat belts, and the modeling of the clitoris, is tacitly based on data about cisgender, usually white, usually able, often neurotypical male bodies: that is, the data underlying these "facts" feature specific bodies as both norm and ideal subject, but claiming them as facts generates understandings that remove this specificity, for they are seen as pertaining equally to all bodies, effectively making invisible the specific bodies that ground them.[40]

One might also look to the history of photographic film, optimized for white skin colors well into the 1980s, when furniture and chocolate makers' protests led to the development of film stock better able to represent ranges of brown tones.[41] For philosophers such as Sandra Harding and Patricia Hill Collins, such examples underscore how *all* claims to knowledge, along with the material workings of technology and technosciences, have "fingerprints" on them: they are shaped by the social positions of the knowers making claims (not to mention their funders and audiences).[42] That is, all knowledge claims and "facts" are rooted in bodies, and the disavowal and rendering invisible of those bodies is part of the larger legacy of the denial of bodies in favor of the mind of rational man. The universality of these "facts" and practices is disrupted when it becomes clear that only certain bodies are involved in their production. Feminist standpoint theorists argue that those positioned outside or on the margins of the mappings of political and epistemic power and identity are better able to identify these fingerprints, biases, and invisibilized normative bodies, because they do not benefit from the power dynamics that shape such claims. Their very marginalization and supposed demotion to being merely or simply bodies makes them more capable of registering and therefore challenging the knowledges and power dynamics ongoing in the center, or on top.

Inherent in this critique is a challenge to objectivity, for no knowledge comes "unmarked": *all* knowledges have fingerprints on them. Standpoint theories disallow what Donna Haraway terms the "god trick," knowledge claims that emerge from a seemingly all-seeing nowhere. Standpoint theorists are careful to identify how specific experiences of embodiment, knowledges rooted in fleshliness, need to be valued in order to counter the ascendancy of seemingly objective but in actuality deeply biased and normative claims to wisdom—claims whose fingerprints have been wiped, as it were.[43] An ethical response to the problem of the tacit norms involved in claims to knowledge is to start by being reflexive, by noting where one's own knowledge claims are coming *from*, by actively claiming the bodily positioning of one's own knowledge production, and by interrogating how that embodiment has been shaped through both Othering and the lack thereof.

A wonderful example of the sensual and what Haraway might term "situated" knowing prized by standpoint theorists emerges in the work of Audre Lorde, who writes: "The white fathers told us, I think therefore I am; and the black mothers in each of us—the poet—whispers in our dreams, I feel therefore I can be free."[44] For Lorde, feeling is a way into understanding, one that works apart from the rigid confines of Cartesianism. And, for Lorde, poetry provides a means of expression for this knowing, for "poetry is the way we help give name to the nameless so it can be thought."[45] Working within the confines of a language rooted in the episteme of rational man, Lorde finds in poetry a means to make thinkable what has been denied in the effacement of bodies and bodily knowings. This knowing is both ontological and liberatory, a means of escaping not just the parameters of rationality as conjoined with that unmarked knower man, but the ways of being allocated to his Others.

Key to Lorde's work is her self-identification as "black, lesbian, warrior, mother, poet," claims that demarcate both her embodiment and her placement on the fringes of knowledges in a mapping that centers a seemingly unmarked "rational man."[46] These ways of knowing emerge from loci that are not available for claiming by just anyone. For example, the celebrity Kanye West's April 2006 assertion, in the wake of the mass devastation and deaths caused by the structural violences of racism and poverty in the wake of Hurricane Katrina's impact on New Orleans, that President George W. Bush "doesn't care about Black people" is a far cry from his January 2019 tweets supporting President Trump and his "Make America Great Again" slogan.[47] The marginalization that allowed West to identify the racism in the federal response to Katrina does not seem to shape his embrace of a slogan that glorifies the United States' history of enslavement and genocide. Indeed, it is important not to assume immediacy or transparency in particularly positioned experiences or embodiments and related moves to knowledge claims. The location that any one of us might self-ascribe does not necessarily enable us to understand the experiences of another positioned almost identically. As a white, middle-class transmasculine queer person with U.S. citizenship, for example, I am not automatically attuned to the knowledges and experiences of another white, middle-class transmasculine queer person with U.S. citizenship. Coming to a standpoint, to speak from a position in a way that does not erase disparities or, as in West's case, reinforce a continuing history of violence, requires work; one must labor not to simply speak for Others even when one can claim a position of Other.

Related to the question of acquiring standpoints, the bodily knowledge Lorde conveys is neither repeatable nor translatable, for there is no way to encapsulate the knowings she describes in any alternative format. Put another way, the knowings Lorde puts forward cannot be transmuted into what the philosopher Bruno Latour might term an "immutable mobile"—a codification of knowledge gleaned, such as a map, that might travel to other sites without changing shape or content, and which can then be combined with other similarly extracted and discrete pieces of knowledge, such as records of shipping routes, which together can be used for the development of strategies of conquest or war.[48] Given these factors, the question of how someone not positioned in such a way might relate to such knowings and even attempt to know in a similar manner becomes paramount. Here I turn to the work of María Puig de la Bellacasa, whose conceptualization of "thinking-with care" seeds my approach in this book.

Thinking-with Materiality

Puig's thinking-with care, a mode of thinking that takes up the togetherness of the prepositional -*with* through an explicit engagement of care, expands on the work of standpoint theorists. Beginning with an understanding rooted in materiality, Puig argues that "thinking matters of care in more than human worlds" requires an understanding "where knowledge is not just 'knowledge' but practices and sociomaterial configurations." In this conceptualization, knowledge indexes not just abstractions, ideas that reference systems of logic—"I think, therefore I am," for example, yields a mind/body abstraction but also the doings, social mappings, and related material shapings through which abstractions emerge and pertain. For example, "I think, therefore I am" emerged and persists today as a mind/body division through the materiality of an ableism that routinely regards people with bodily impairments as incapable of making decisions and so unthinking that communicating with them requires baby talk. Puig joins this understanding of knowledge with an affective, or emotional, mapping, arguing that "standpoints come to be through a transformation of habits of perception, thinking, and doing that happen through attachment to particular concerns, interests, and commitments"—that is, through care.[49] She notes that "care itself is relational" while also affirming that "beings do not pre-exist their relatings."[50] What follows from this understanding is the work of thinking-with care. The choice of preposition reads as an extension, a positioning nearby, a sense of solidarity with, rather than thinking, writing, or speaking *as*, *from*, or the even more distant *about*. Thinking-with care takes up the responsibility of the reflexive knower—a knower who has worked to identify their own positionings in terms of body, power, and oppression—who, in engaging with and thinking through standpoint theories, expands on the meaning of knowledge itself to encompass the many doings and materialities that shape and are shaped by such knowers, and claims the very emotional attachments that impel such practices, thinkings, and doings as key to their work. Further, because beings emerge through relatings, or what Karen Barad terms "intra-actions," and because care is relational, thinking-with care engenders knowledges as practices, doings, and ways of understanding that emerge not through a static mapping of self, body, and identity, but through a dynamic relationality that emerges and shapes not only self and other but knowledge itself.[51]

Puig's attention to knowledges as emerging through materiality—she points to "practices and sociomaterial configurations," engaging literal "things" as part of knowledges—connects to a prominent area of thought in feminist science and technology studies: new materialisms. Thinkers in this area, such as Jane Bennett, take as a starting point that "things," that is, nonhuman and nonanimal objects, are actors, disrupting the subject/object divide that follows from the mind/body dichotomy. Bennett's *Vibrant Matter* asserts the "vibrancy of matter and the lively power of material formations" in which "things" act as "quasi agents or forces with trajectories, propensities, or tendencies of their own."[52] For example, consider plastics containing bisphenol-A (BPA). Research into their health effects is ongoing, but it is generally recommended that people avoid ingestion. This advice is reflected in the now-common "BPA-free" label on many plastic products. "Things" such as BPA demonstrate how objects are "lively," exhibiting a range of actions and, affecting humans, nonhuman animals, and other objects of their own accord.

The verb *to affect* reflects a particular scholarly formation entwined with new materialisms, which is the theorization of *affect*, a noun I use often with reference to bodily movement and shared or transmitted emotions and feelings. The philosopher Brian Massumi gives a more formal definition: "an ability to affect and be affected . . . a prepersonal intensity corresponding to the passage from one experiential state of the body to another and implying an augmentation or diminution in that body's capacity to act."[53] *Affect* engages bodily motion as part of emotions, emotions that surface as bodily movements, and movements that, in turn, are conveyed to others through feelings and touch. My dog Annie's hypervigilance becomes my own. A bodily travel of feeling—both of us become tense—disrupts the many divisions between us, including that mediated by the leash. In claiming the ability of matter to *affect*, new materialists thus track a sense of movement that blurs not only the subject/object divide, but the boundaries of bodies themselves. The beings that emerge through the relatings that Puig and Barad highlight are but one result of the imbrication of theories of affect and new materialisms.

However, the work of new materialist and related theories of affect often loses the thread that is central to standpoint theories. In a world where bodies are unbounded and "prepersonal intensities" do the shaping, the sources of power and oppression are elusive. The writings of Mel Chen, a theorist in queer, trans, and critical ethnic studies, can help elucidate how new materialist–style thinking retains these commitments. Chen's focus on *animacy* intervenes in and retheorizes "current anxieties around the production of humanness in contemporary times."[54] Focusing not on liveliness but on calibrations of "life/death," Chen's purpose "is not to reinvest certain materialities *with* life, but to remap live and dead zones away from those very terms, leveraging animacy toward a consideration of affect in its queered and raced formations." While new materialists tend to inject hope into readings where matter becomes animate, for Chen, the fact that the seemingly neutral bodily descriptor of "'being moved' becomes twisted into the image of the overanimated racialized subject," a subject who is often policed to the point of exclusion from the social, underscores how animacy can, in reality, mark a proximity to social death rather than life. Further, for Chen, "animacy tugs the categories of race and sexuality out of their own homes."[55] To return to the example of photographic film, Chen might read early norms of celluloid film production not only as animating the life-giving qualities of cinema but as engaging and producing racialization in ways that go beyond the representation of the bodies in the image. Chen might identify anxieties about BPAs, the harmful effects of which include mimicry of the hormone estrogen, as animating concerns about a rise in human gender nonnormativity that, given the white norms undergirding Western conceptions of gender, are also deeply racialized.

Central to Chen's thinking in *Animacies* is the role of animality in these mappings of life and death. They take up "animality as a condensation of racialized animacy" and as a locus for queerness understood as "improper intimacy" in reading cultural texts.[56] Chen shows that practices that seemingly reinforce hierarchical designations, such as the tacitly normative "center" elucidated by standpoint theorists, in fact betray anxieties and divergences. For example, Chen analyzes a "Rough on Rats" poison advertisement from the late 1800s—the era of the infamous Chinese Exclusion Act in the U.S.—that depicts a Chinese man eating rats. The advertisement claims to clear out "rats, mice, bed bugs, flies, roaches" because "they must go." The advertisement not only implicitly casts the Chinese *as* rats but also engages contemporary discourses of hygiene, wherein "the homosociality of bachelor households, the 'improper intimacies' of opium dens, and the shared parenting of Chinatown working women . . . participated together in white domestic discourses of racialized hygiene and public health."[57] For Chen, then, the ad evokes not only racialization by animalization but also the movements of feelings—the affect—of a queer and racialized anxiety that animates such ads in connection to but also well apart from the bodies of literal humans and nonhuman animals.

Standpoint theories, Puig's "thinking-with care," and Chen's analytic of animacy represent key interventions that respond to the ways in which "rational man" and his Others continue to dominate our episteme. This conceptual web has been formative to my own approach to questions such as how one might claim subjectivity and agency for dogs while they are denied to many humans. However, taking up these theories together is problematic, for their logics and approaches do not mesh easily. The mapping of standpoints leans on somewhat immutable ideas of bodies, embodiment, and identity: the very choice of the term *standpoint* (rather than *walk-* or *movement-point*) underscores the metaphorical stasis of the approach! Further, the bodies evoked by Puig have a temporality to them, emerging through relationships and affective connections: their boundedness arises after the encounter of a relationship, another difference from standpoint-style approaches. And Chen's tracking of anxieties reveals an approach distinct from Puig's, seeing race and sexuality as tied to power in ways that might be masked by claims to care—after all, the term *eugenics* comes from the Greek *eu*, meaning "good" or "well-born."[58]

Yet these approaches share key themes, for affect, seen as bodily, shifting understandings of bodily boundaries, and webbings that situate humans and nonhuman animals in terms of power and oppression can and do surface together in the production of knowledges in the dog worlds I examine in this book. Through a turn to the knowledge politics of these worlds, I draw from and connect thinking-with, affect, materiality, and questions of gender, sexuality, and race in putting forward my own epistemic disruption of "rational man."

Knowledge, Language, Affect, Vision

Virtually all knowledge claims in animal shelters and the overlapping work of "rescue" conjoin vision, feeling, movement, and claims to speech through bodies and body language. The knowledge politics of dog shelter and rescue worlds are concerned not just with bodies and embodiment but with the registering of those bodies and their movements, the rendering of those bodies into a language, and the exercise of human bodies as expressing language. Vision is the primary sensory mode through which humans "read" bodies, feelings, and movements, but hapticity, or touch, assumes great importance when working with dogs, for body contacts become movements that are also feelings, and both humans and dogs express and acquire knowledge through haptics. In this section I trace the emergence of meaning through a complex congeries of haptic, sensual moves, sometimes affective and sometimes not, in order to translate and register how bodies engage and enact knowledge.

This entwining of vision, reading, feeling, contact, touch, bodies, and language often engenders contestations about expertise. My descriptions illustrate not only the prominence of affect and bodily movement in knowledge claims, but also disparities in understandings and in the ways the claims themselves acquire meaning. Many of these descriptions are autoethnographic, for this element of my anthropological work involves my own changing understandings, through my immersion in these worlds, of what it means to know. Through this exploration, I examine what it means to attempt to be *sensible* to the many ways of making meaning in these human-dog worlds.

Seeing in this context means understanding (or attempting to under- stand) dogs' bodily movements and stillness as feelings. Contestations frequently involve what humans see in dogs' bodily movements or lack of movement, and how humans translate that seeing—or perhaps more accurately, how that seeing becomes a mode of registering movement and stasis as expressions of feeling. For many of my interlocutors, especially those with formal training from trainers and behaviorists, looking at a dog means tracking its stance, its hackles, the corners of its mouth, bodily looseness or stiffness, pupil dilation, "whale eye" (eyes widening to show the whites), sniffs, lip licks, yawns, where the dog looks and doesn't look, and other cues.

The poster *Doggie Language* by the artist and dog thinker Lili Chin translates body movements into desires and feelings, with an emphasis on how to read dogs' attempts at conflict avoidance in their bodily movements. This type of looking as affective reading is key to many of my interlocutors' building of understandings and knowledges. It functions as the means

DOGGIE LANGUAGE

starring Boogie the Boston Terrier

By Lili Chin www.doggiedrawings.net

ALERT

SUSPICIOUS

ANXIOUS

THREATENED

ANGRY

"PEACE!"
look away/head turn

STRESSED
yawn

STRESSED
nose lick

"PEACE!"
sniff ground

"RESPECT!"
turn & walk away

"NEED SPACE"
whale eye

STALKING

STRESSED
scratching

STRESS RELEASE
shake off

RELAXED
soft ears, blinky eyes

"RESPECT!"
offer his back

FRIENDLY & POLITE
curved body

FRIENDLY

"PRETTY PLEASE"
round puppy face

"I'M YOUR LOVEBUG"
belly-rub pose

"HELLO I LOVE YOU!"
greeting stretch

"I'M FRIENDLY!"
play bow

"READY!"
prey bow

"YOU WILL FEED ME"

CURIOUS
head tilt

HAPPY
(or hot)

OVERJOYED
wiggly

"MMMM...."

**"I LOVE YOU,
DON'T STOP"**

Lili Chin, *Doggie Language*. Reprinted with permission from Lili Chin, doggiedrawings.net.

to figure out a dog's needs, desires, thoughts, and intentions—which are, of course, often inextricable. This is seeing as affective knowing.

This knowing frequently involves the seer's own affective response. In theorizing affect rather than emotion, Massumi and others emphasize the shared rather than individuated nature of bodily feelings and movements. The knowings involved in my fieldwork illustrate this sense of affect. I had a series of interactions with a shelter dog I will call Herman, whom I found troubling. Going into his kennel just to interact with him and get him used to the presence of humans, I discovered he knew the cues "shake" (to proffer a paw to be clasped by my hand) and "sit." However, as soon as I looked away from him, he growled, even though the rest of my body hadn't moved. I shared my reactions with Donna, a Latinx woman in her early thirties with a long history of pit bull–related activism. Lacking words, I said: "And I was just like—the hairs on my arms, I was just like, 'Dude, I . . . '" Donna responded, "Yeah, no, your intuition tells you things that you don't." I replied, "Yeah, and my body was like—" and demonstrated by stiffening my shoulders and torso.[59] My own affective response shaped my knowledge. Even as my "reading" of the dog, using knowledge gained from seminars on dog behavior, included noticing whether his commissures (mouth corners) were forward, and whether his body was stiff and leaning forward—indicators of a dog's intention to transmute fear into aggression—in truth, it was the hairs on my arms that made me decide not to stay in that kennel that day. I later learned that the shelter had euthanized the dog roughly a month after this interaction for biting a human.

The bodily and affective knowing I describe extends to movements toward engagement as well as away from it. Here the affect incorporates both vision and the registering of movement as touch—what the queer theorist Eve Kosofky Sedgwick might characterize as "touchy-feely."[60] My field notes describe my first encounter in a shelter kennel with a dog I'll call Piglet, a fawn-colored pit bull type:

> I slowly let myself in, and, avoiding eye contact, slowly sit down next to her and toss some treats on the ground. She eyes them but doesn't move. Very slowly, I extend my hand under her chin, and she, just as slowly, sniffs it. She doesn't growl, and I don't see "whale eye." I gently

stroke her chest, and she turns to me, surprised, but I think pleasantly so. She rests her head on my hand and I continue to stroke. Then she gets up, noses at the treats on the ground, and settles again next to me, her body a warm lean against the length of my thigh.[61]

Our interaction here hinges on an initially tentative and then solicited bodily contact. Being touched gives Piglet pleasure, and her affect yields important information for me and the shelter regarding her behavior toward people she does not know. This movement is joined with visual information—Piglet does not exhibit whale eye, a clear indication of fear—but, again, it is a bodily understanding that leads me to move toward her in this encounter. This bodily knowledge affects me as well— many psychology-related studies attest to the pleasure of petting a dog.[62] Indeed, the ways that contemporary usage of the verb *to pet* often conjoins with those designated as *pets* (dogs, cats, and similar critters)—one pets one's pet—underscores how bodily, affective contact is centered in such cross-species relatings.[63]

The concatenation (or . . . con*dog*enation!) of language, knowledge, affect, and vision I write with here is subject to contestation. This became increasingly apparent as I spent more time at shelters, "rescues," seminars, and the like, and heard variations on what Cynthia, a white straight upper-class woman in her late forties, noted to me: "The 'rescue' groups are filled with people, in many cases, like me. Middle-aged women." For Cynthia, this dynamic informs claims to knowledge, or lack thereof. She argues that these women (who are also predominantly white) "are out to help love animals, [but] don't have the vaguest idea of what they're doing."[64] This description reflects how the affective storying of "love" and the covering over of other knowledges described in chapter 1 evolves into an all-encompassing reference to action, bodily and otherwise. Knowing and doing, or knowledge and praxis, are thoroughly interwoven in the contestations of these worlds.

Assertions like Cynthia's almost invariably involve another person's failure to "see" correctly. Consider this excerpt from my field notes, which describes my experience walking a brown and white pit bull–type dog, Bubba, who was mildly leash-reactive: he would stiffen and sometimes bark at other dogs when we passed within about twelve feet of them.

As we're walking, I spy an elderly white man . . . with another of the shelter dogs on leash. I've never walked the dog, but it's clear that his dog is quite interested in meeting Bubba. Wary of interactions that might start either dog down the path toward leash-reactivity, I position my body between Bubba and that of the other dog, and we cross to the far side of the street (there's rarely much traffic on this road). I find myself getting irritated, for the man is doing absolutely nothing to stop the dog from initiating a staring contest with Bubba. These are the kinds of interactions that lead the dogs to develop bad habits, and I can see from across the way that . . . he's an advanced volunteer. Why the hell is he letting this happen? I hurry Bubba along and we practice "sit" and "down" a bit farther away to get him to focus back on me and away from this other dog.[65]

The behavior I am trying to prevent is visible to me and, of course, to the dogs themselves, but it is not perceived by this other human, whom I'll call Alan. My carefully attuned watching—many a dog owner uses the phrase "eagle eye" when speaking of their dog(s)—in conjunction with my perception of Alan's lack of seeing points to disparities in not only our knowledges but also our actions, in the form of bodily movements, as part of those knowledges, for I first block Bubba's line of sight and then move him and attempt a different kind of engagement with him.

When I shared this interaction with Yolanda, a straight Latinx shelter worker in her twenties, she sighed knowingly to me: "There's some common sense that's not there." When I asked her to expand on this—was this just Alan, or more folks?—she said it applied to both, and gave me another story. Two advanced volunteers—that is, folks whom the shelter deemed qualified to work with its more difficult dogs—had Pretzel, a new arrival to the shelter, out in the lobby on a busy day. They paused to try to adjust the fit of her harness. Here Yolanda shifted modes in her telling and gestured toward me, reaching over my head. Visibly tensing herself, Yolanda recounted that Pretzel "backed up, started licking her lips, going like this—" Yolanda ducked her head back and looked away from me. At this point, Yolanda and another shelter staff member yelled, "Stop!" Yolanda continued: "In my head, [I] already saw the bite happening." Frustrated, Yolanda told the volunteers: "This dog is telling you in three different ways, she doesn't want you touching her right now!" to which one responded, "Oh, okay! I'm just gonna fix the harness!" Yolanda's voice quickened and gained urgency as she noted that the volunteer "went in *again*," still trying to adjust the dog's harness. The second volunteer, who was holding Pretzel, "was kind of oblivious, also, to what was happening." Frustrated, Yolanda and the other staff member told the volunteers: "Stop. Just stop. Walk away. Back away from the dog." Yolanda turned to me, representing the dog's point of view: "How many warning signs was she gonna have to give before something happened in the front lobby?"[66]

In Yolanda's story, the volunteers' failure to see marked a potentially fatal misreading, given that shelter dogs who bite humans are usually euthanized. This failure to see, coupled with Yolanda's characterization of Alan as lacking "common sense," points to a failure to *know*, and specifically a failure to know what is expected of most folks in this setting, the "common" logic of shelter worlds. And while I doubt this was Yolanda's intent, her reference to *common sense* encapsulates what might be claimed as "good" knowing: *sense* as *sensibility*, as attending to senses and sensory experiences, both human and dog, in building better knowledge.

Perhaps unsurprisingly, a failure to "see" and therefore to know or sense is often invoked in contestations about whose knowledge is more accurate. Nathan, the shelter worker whose thinking informs much of my first chapter, told me about a husky that had come through his shelter whom he read as "*really* creepy. . . . The reason he was creepy is that sometimes he would do, like, a freeze, and then a bow that was play. And then other times he would freeze and then, like, get worse. I mean, really threatening." Nathan's ultimate reading of the dog combines a visual reading of the dog's bodily signs with the word *creepy*— quite a touchy-feely word, especially given its roots in "having a creeping of the flesh": "Nope. This dog is scary. This dog is not okay, this dog should not leave our shelter."[67]

This reading was not shared by another volunteer, who posted a video of the dog claiming that the shelter staff didn't "know how to read a husky's typical freeze-play behavior." Nathan responded: "And I was like, 'You know what, I actually *do* know the difference between freeze-play, and freeze-not-play, and my concern with this dog is that he does both.' And . . . he's like, 'Well, I don't see it.'"[68]

The dog was adopted out to a home in Arizona, "bit four times, and was then euthanized." The volunteer in question contacted Nathan to apologize and tell him he was right, but for Nathan it wasn't about being right: "Like, I'd rather have, honestly—if the dog was gonna leave our building, I would have rather been wrong."[69] Nathan's tale illustrates how much is at stake for both dogs and humans in not seeing and not feeling or sensing.

Although the end goal for Nathan—and likely the volunteer—is not simply to win an argument, Nathan's story highlights the question of expertise: a person claiming breed-specific expert knowledge challenges a person with expertise in dog behavior more generally. Both forms of knowledge rest on the ability to read dogs' bodies accurately. Nathan further commented: "But it's, again, the like, if they can't see it, they don't believe it. And it did take a good eye to read this dog because of the fact that he did both of those behaviors" (freeze-play and freeze-not-play).[70] The invocation of belief here reveals how seeing not only ties into knowledge but also provides the grounds for accepting an understanding and not disavowing or overwriting it.

The type of overt contestations Nathan and Yolanda describe are widespread in dog shelter and rescue worlds. For example, take the "dog autistic" comment I noted at the beginning of this chapter. Felicity, a white, upper-middle-class queer woman in her forties, was out with me one day working with Beth, a cow-colored, sixty-five-pound pit bull type, when we passed another volunteer, David, a white middle-class man in his early thirties. I told Felicity I had heard that David had encouraged Beth to chase a squirrel while on leash. Given Beth's habit of not paying attention to her handlers, encouraging this behavior spelled trouble and would make her less adoptable (although it was undoubtedly fun from Beth's perspective). In response, Felicity snorted: "He thinks he's the dog whisperer, but he's really the dog autistic."[71]

Felicity's comment expresses a specific form of denying others' knowledge, for autism is understood to demarcate a lack of ability, a lack of knowledge—that is, a lack of emotional knowledge. It also expresses an opinion common among my interlocutors, which is that the people who claim to be experts are the ones to watch out for.[72] My fieldwork involved an encounter with Brewster, a smaller, black and white pit bull type with a history of reacting to dogs and humans while on leash and in certain spaces (such as kennels and houses with windows where other dogs were visible). When we returned to the shelter from a walk, there was a small dog on the steps of the shelter involved in an adoption interaction. This was a time-consuming process, and waiting for the other dog to move was not an option. Walking Brewster was a volunteer who was white and appeared to be in her early forties, and who had Brewster on a taut leash with a prong collar (a punitive device that pinches when a dog strains at a leash or when a human pulls at the leash). She was accompanied by another white woman in her late twenties whom I knew to be a shelter volunteer.

As they walked up the steps, I hastily stood up to block Brewster's view of the other dog, as I could see from Brewster's bodily stiffness and the whites visible around her eyes that she was struggling with fear and frustration from being close to another dog while on leash. It seemed as if she had moved "over threshold": that is, she was not calm enough to engage with her handler. However, the second woman held up her hand to me and said, "Don't worry, she's a trainer, she knows what she's doing." I snorted in response and said, perhaps a bit too loudly for an anthropologist, "Uh, no, she doesn't."[73]

I "saw" Brewster's situation quite differently from the second woman. What I saw was a dog being subjected to a punitive training technique. Given that most barking and lunging on leash emerges from fear and the inability to escape the situation, the experience would lead Brewster to associate fear with pain, exacerbating the behavior rather than remedying it. Further, I saw a dog whom I had learned to read as being "out of her body"—that is, a dog so overcome by fear that asking her to consciously attempt a different behavior, to learn and enact a new response to that fear, was impossible.[74] My dismissal of the trainer's supposed expertise was thus rooted in a counter–knowledge claim: I read the trainer's actions as showing inattention to the emotions of the dog. It is human understandings of dogs' bodies as affective—as movement and emotion that one reads, feels, senses, and responds to—that matters most in these situations. Here the trainer seemed to disregard Brewster's affect—was *insensible* to it—and instead attempted to dictate a wholly different bodily and therefore emotional experience for her in a way that likely only made her behavior and experience worse.

My attempt here to trace the interplay of knowledge, vision, affect, language, touch, and movement reveals what Haraway would describe as a particular form of *response-ability*. The affective sensing and response of the human knower also matters, be it through particular training practices or in countering other humans' reading practices.[75] The affective state of the claimant to knowledge is part and parcel of the knowing. The sensibility at work in these spaces is perhaps most tellingly revealed by Nathan when he comments on the emotional experience of working in an animal shelter: "I think one of the things that's really hard . . . is that we do have the training to read the unhappiness in the animals that we're working with."[76]

Conscientious efforts to claim knowledge of dogs emerge through a specific form of thinking-with that works as a bodily, affective relay of responses, a response-ability that works through the sensory. These efforts reveal a knowledge politics that emerges through bodily relatings, one that in fact emerges as a way of navigating relatings. These efforts demonstrate a knowledge politics that functions as what I term a *sensibility*. In these ways of knowing, bodies are paramount. These practices entail the claiming of bodies as a means of knowing, really a claiming of bodies *as* knowing, wherein sense is central to common knowings. This is another form of Lorde's claiming of bodies as knowing, but with an additional mapping, expanding on standpoint theorists' and Chen's work by disrupting the conceptualization of animal as Other—and, I hope, Other as animal—in claiming nonhuman bodies as knowing, and shared human and nonhuman bodily movements and related experiential knowledges as knowings. That is, *sensibility* counters what Chen terms "anxieties around the production of humanness . . . particularly with regard to humanity's partners in definitional crime." Notions of animality (the first "partner" Chen lists), as conjoined to or working through race, nation, sexuality, and gender, lose their hold in the context of knowledges involving the bodily movements of animals and their affectional effects on and interrelatings with humans.

From this sensibility emerge the kinds of knowledges as sociomaterial practices and doings that are key to Puig's thinking and the affective work she claims. *Sensibility*, as the work of being open to and connected with a dog's bodily experience while staying alert to one's own, is certainly a form of thinking-with. Yet the affects involved here go beyond care. As Cynthia's disparaging remark about middle-aged (white) women indicates, there are certainly ties between particular bodily locations and this welter of human-animal knowledges, although this naming of position is a bit more static than Chen's. That said, the sensibility I describe reveals a knowledge politics that gives texture and variance to the conception of animal as Other. The fact that this sensibility reflects a thinking-with between and among humans and nonhuman animals disrupts the simplicity of the invocation of the animal that is central to the emergence of race, gender, and sexuality in the rise of rational man. In the following section, I trace out more formally philosophical reclaimings of nonhuman animal bodies in an effort to build my sensibility into a more clearly articulated knowledge politics.

Umwelt, Naturecultures, and More

While the philosophical works I cite tend to rest on an abstract conceptualization of animality, that is, the animal as Other to rational man, the living animals that emerge in my ethnographic excerpts stand (or, more aptly, move, posture, play, rest, growl, and snuggle) in stark contrast to this abstraction. As Chen notes, the animal "has served for the human as such a rich comparative repository . . . because it is kept significatorily empty." That is, because the animal (with emphasis on *the*) operates so thoroughly as an abstraction, it lacks referents in the real world.[77] Haraway, among others, takes issue with this philosophizing, arguing that approaches to the animal index a "misplaced concreteness," that is, they mistake the abstract for the literal and the concrete.[78] Here I examine several approaches that valorize the thinkings and doings of living nonhuman animals in order to articulate a knowledge politics rooted in sensibility.

Haraway argues across a large body of work for the importance of what she terms *naturecultures*.[79] This concept challenges the (mostly scientific) practice of reading human norms into renderings of animal sociality. A standout example is the shifting understanding of wolves in twentieth- and twenty-first-century sciences. In studies published between roughly the 1930s and 1960s by scientific luminaries including L. David Mech and Rudolf Schenkel, wolves were written about as hierarchical social beings, with alpha wolves positioned at the top and (depending on the author) beta and omega wolves below. This hierarchy aligned with a human world in which stories of by-nature dominance and subjection circulated widely through practices such as eugenics and narratives of patriarchy and racism. However, in the 1980s, Mech retracted his original publications, arguing that they were flawed because they focused on captive wolves: the social organization of noncaptive wolves was based in a compassionate heterosexual family unit.[80]

Mech's retraction has done little to challenge the wholesale embrace of dominance theories by today's dog owners in the talk of "pack leaders" and the like. His turn to family also reflects a different political moment, in which the family as a site emerges as the primary locus through which to not only imagine a future but also protect the innocent, as evidenced in Focus on the Family and related campaigns.[81] Here scientific claims are identifiable as projections of human-specific concerns and cultures onto nonhumans: as Haraway might phrase it, Nature is a story that culture tells itself.[82] Haraway's elision of *nature* and *culture* underscores that there is no way to ever render nature without producing it through the lens of culture, that is, without the fingerprints of subjectivity.

However, Haraway's thinking with naturecultures extends beyond a critique of, say, a hetero cisman's arguing for his need for multiple sexual partners by pointing to a vulgarization of genetic science of the "sowing wild oats" variety: she uses the term to point to the ways that entities in nature engage in their own productions of cultures.[83] Examples include the matriarchal organizations evident in orca pods, whose social systems reveal complex patterns of sharing knowledge involving migration, food, and predatory threats.[84] Another example is a baboon troop that subsisted mostly on food filched from a particular dump: when a number of the more senior males of the troop died off because they were poisoned through this food (to which the males had ample access because of their higher social status), males in subsequent generations were witnessed as engaging in more cooperative social behaviors, indexing a shift in the troop culture away from the achievement of high status through competition and aggression.[85] These examples speak to the ways that entities perceived as "natural" build and practice their own cultures.

In tandem with naturecultures, I want to add a concept put forward by the biologist Jakob von Uexküll in the early twentieth century: *Umwelt* (which translates roughly to "environment world"), consisting of signifiers (or, alternatively, "carriers of significance") that shape the meaning and lives of the nonhuman animals in them.[86] Key to Uexküll's thinking is the assertion that human and animal worlds are not quite shared; as Giorgio Agamben comments, "Where classical science saw a single world that comprised within it all living species hierarchically ordered from the most elementary forms up to the higher organisms, Uexküll instead [supposed] an infinite variety of perceptual worlds that, though they are uncommunicating and reciprocally exclusive, are all equally perfect and linked together as if in a gigantic musical score, at the center of which lie familiar, and, at the same time, remote little beings called *Echinius esculentus, Ameoeba terricola*, [etc.], [or the] sea urchin, amoeba," etc.[87] Uexküll positions knowers not in a web of power and relationships but in discrete worlds that only seem to occupy the same spaces; further, these knowers, who acquire knowledge through their interpretation of various signifiers, are not just humans but also sea urchins, dogs, and others—that is, nonhuman animals.

Most striking in Uexküll's writing are descriptive segments that reveal what one might term the worldviews of his nonhuman knowers. For example (and this is perhaps my favorite), there is the tick:

> This eyeless animal is directed to this watchtower by a general photosensitivity of her skin. The approaching prey is revealed to the blind and deaf highwaywoman by her sense of smell. The odor of butyric acid that emanates from the skin glands of all mammals acts on the tick as a signal to leave her watchtower and hurl herself downwards. If, in so doing, she lands on something warm—a fine sense of temperature betrays this to her—she has reached her prey, the warm-blooded creature. It only remains for her to find a hairless spot. There she burrows deep into the skin of her prey, and slowly pumps herself full of warm blood.[88]

Agamben is quick to note the tick's desires: while "one might reasonably expect that the tick loves the taste of blood, or that she at least possesses a sense to perceive its flavor," in fact ticks eagerly absorb any liquid "corresponding to the blood temperature of mammals."[89] The fact that the tick wants a specific temperature of liquid, not blood per se, demarcates how her desire and its meaning, for her, are about getting a "just right" temperature rather than vampirism. Here, the tick's *Umwelt* consists of a narrow range of signifiers, namely odor, temperature, and skin surface, whose translation by scientists into the metrics of chemical formula, degrees centigrade, and skin typology already render them as holding vastly different meanings than those experienced by the tick. This sense of the tick as living in a sensory world that is also a world apart from, say, my own humancentric world quite clearly decenters the human and, arguably, the Anthropocene, in articulating alternate renderings of what it means to know and understand.

Haraway and Uexküll augment my understanding of sensibility, for *naturecultures* validates the perspective that dogs engage in a culture, or many cultures, of their own, while *Umwelt* elaborates the working of sensory ways of making meaning—odors, movements, "body language," bodily sensings.

To these theorizations I add one more from a philosopher of science, Vinciane Despret. In her studies of ethologists (those who study nonhuman animal behavior), Despret argues for a cross-species practice of knowing that she identifies as *embodied empathy*.[90] This begins with "the process by which one delegates to one's body a question, or a problem, that matters and that involves other beings' bodies."[91] This question posing is evident in the work of the wolf researcher Farley Mowat, who experimented with a diet consisting entirely of mice in order to emulate that of the wolves he researched. His purpose was to demonstrate, through his body, that wolves stayed in place and decimated mouse rather than caribou populations during the caribou's summer migrations.

This kind of bodily thinking is further evident in the work of the primatologist Shirley Strum, who in her fieldwork with baboons in Kenya went against the then-accepted approach of staying in the Land Rover and observing from afar, instead approaching and entering the troop. One of her interactions involved refusing a baboon's request for help with a "no" that she signaled by moving away and turning her back to him. Despret argues that Strum builds on the sense of bodily query evident in Mowat's approach: in entering the baboon troop, she makes her "body available for the response of another being."[92] This sense of embodied empathy as a careful cross-species choreography of question and response analogizes bodily form and function and, in doing so, shapes a kind of knowledge. By entering the baboon troop, Strum becomes vulnerable in a literal and epistemological sense in a way that changes her perceptions of both baboon life and herself.

The sensibility I outline as emerging through the welter of seeing, knowing, affect, and bodies in shelter worlds draws from and builds on the challenges to rational man invoked by standpoint theorists through the claiming of bodies as knowing. This sensibility also engages the circulation of affect in the work of both Puig and Chen, for affect as bodily movement, feeling, and sensation that moves and even emerges through relatings is fundamental to the sensory work of seeing and movement in dog worlds. Further, dogs engage in cultures of their own, for bodily postures are understood to "speak," and sensory signifiers, to use Uexküll's terminology, are paramount in these body languages.

In addition, moments of what I have called *insensibility*—as with the self-proclaimed dog expert who fails to identify Brewster's state of hyperarousal—index failures to become "available" in the sense delineated by Despret. That is, when knowledge claims fail, part of what tends to be missing is the bodily questioning Despret elucidates. *Sensibility* thus joins together key facets of the varied approaches to knowledges posed as challenges to rational man and his episteme. However, my sensibility also falters when it comes to the mappings of power and oppression critical to standpoint theories, not to mention the work of race, gender, sexuality, and nation central to Chen's writings and my own approach of interspecies intersectionality.

The Sensibility of Feminist Fuzzy Sciences

The points of friction between human and dog approaches to worlds and shared spaces are many: for example, the labor of washing a dog following an ecstatic session of rolling in the fragrant remains of a dead creature reveals just one of many disparities in human and dog ideas (and ideals) about bodies and cleanliness. In this section I examine such points of friction: specifically, I look to loci where sensibility emerges in the form of advice, helpful tips, and similar efforts to share knowledges. These examples demonstrate not just the peopling of these worlds by the mostly middle-aged white women referenced by Cynthia, but the work of tacit norms connected to larger projects of gender, race, colonialism, and nation.

The interventions I examine include the work of dog trainers and behaviorists as well as popular media such as memes and Lili Chin's superb work. I term these labors *fuzzy sciences* because they involve an array of practitioners, some trained in scientific disciplines like psychology (sciences in a more formal sense), some who have taken seminars and the like, and some who have simply learned from dog trainers or even friends who may or may not have taken formalized classes (sciences in a lowercase, informal sense that are disseminated in and through a range of loci and actors, many with no formal credentials). *Fuzzy* not only captures these informal modes of learning and building knowledge but also (delightfully) reflects the fuzziness of dogs themselves.

In the contemporary realm of the fuzzy sciences of dog training and behaviorism, a battle rages between advocates of positive reinforcement (R+)—say, giving a dog a treat for presenting a "sit"—and those who use aversive methods and punishment, the latter typified by the television celebrity Cesar Millan, who has been known to kick dogs when they exhibit behaviors such as guarding a food dish. Because these latter approaches are invested primarily in human dominance over dogs— Millan emphatically insists that owners must gain their dogs' "respect"— they evince a decided anthropocentrism that many, myself included, find deeply unethical.[93] Further, aversive work relies on responding to unwanted behaviors with punishment, which can take a variety of forms: for example, using a collar that delivers an electric shock when a dog does not come when called. As such approaches effectively rely on inflicting pain and discomfort, they are also remarkably insensible to dog emotions and experiences.[94] For these reasons, I have selected the following examples from writers and thinkers who are, to the best of my knowledge, committed to avoiding aversive methods and embracing R+ approaches, although the anonymity of the internet hinders a precise accounting in that regard.[95]

One point of friction between humans and dogs concerns bodily contact. A key intervention centers on the practice of humans hugging their dogs—what the trainer and ethologist Patricia McConnell describes as a typical primate behavior.[96] Numerous posts on Facebook, Instagram, and other social media sites feature paired pictures of dogs responding differently to hugs: one dog is clasped by a human (almost always a child), body tense, whites of the eyes visible, licking lips, and looking away, while another dog leans into a human, body relaxed, eyes often closed. Many of these posts include arrows pointing to these differences, attempting to make legible what might otherwise go unseen by the casual viewer.[97] Less frequent are analogous posts featuring dogs wincing from head pats, another typical human behavior that these images illustrate as distasteful to dogs.

Notable in these interventions is their decentering of the human. Indeed, McConnell's enumeration goes so far as to detail the pervasiveness of embraces in the work of the primatologist Jane Goodall: hugs as a form of ventral-to-ventral contact are a typical primate behavior that humans, as primates, are exceedingly prone to exhibiting. Conversely, McConnell points out that you would be hard pressed to find an instance of one dog hugging another dog in the affectionate manner common to humans, as such "embraces" are associated mainly with mounting behaviors. Advice on human bodily contact with dogs promulgates an attention to interspecies intimacies as requiring alertness to the body language of both parties, dogs' bodies in particular. And this attention reveals a curiosity, a desire to learn from dogs, requiring human sensitivity to reading bodily movements (or lack of movement!) as emotions, as affective. In these interventions I identify the sensibility necessary to begin to think-with dogs, for they require an openness to how dogs experience touch, the *Umwelt* in which hands register as threatening rather than caressing.

Additional aspects of the sensory also emerge in such interventions, and here it is worth noting that I am invested in taking up *sensory* as far exceeding the typical five senses many humans are taught about through early schooling. For example, the issue of temporality and how humans and dogs register—sense—the passage of time surfaces with regard to dogs' rummaging in the trash or chewing on shoes—behaviors that typically happen when a dog is unsupervised and whose effects are discovered later. Frustration, anxiety, and even boredom can negatively shape dogs' sense of time: what may be counted as just a matter of minutes to humans can seem like a frantic, endless stretch to dogs, relieved only by chewing and sniffing things that may be understood by both human and dog as off-limits in calmer moments. In their discoveries of these infractions, humans frequently respond with anger, yelling at the culprit and even asserting, "Oh, she *knows* why I'm mad!" These assertions are rooted in expressions of woe and related appeasement gestures presented by the dog, such as lying flat on the floor and licking hands. However, dogs' knowledge in these situations differs considerably from that of humans.

Aside from the obvious fact that human trash is dogs' treasure, dogs' sense of time here is quite different from that of humans. In addition to disparities in experiences of time's duration, there are also disjunctions that can be read as more cognitive than sensory, for much research in this area asserts that dogs have no idea why humans get mad about trash break-ins unless they are caught in the act; dogs remember quite differently than humans.[98] The apparent remorse humans witness when scolding their dogs emerges from dogs' response to human anger in the present, not memories of past wrongdoing.

Blog posts urging people not to yell at their dogs (McConnell also notes that making lots of loud noises is representative of typical primate approaches to conflict) highlight the futility of after-the-fact chastisement.[99] Suggested alternatives include managing the problematic behaviors through crating while the human is absent, securing trash and shoes where dogs can't get at them, and practicing cues such as "leave it" through R+ training. All of these approaches are rooted in a sensibility that assumes disparities between dog and human time and memory.[100] The dog *Umwelt* (not unlike that of the tick, for whom time lapses of up to seventeen years between feedings are sustainable) incorporates immediacy of memory and a wildly different temporality.

Geographies and sensoria augment these disparate human and dog temporalities. For example, dogs will often respond to a "sit" cue in the home but not the dog park. For dogs the context of the solicitation of a particular behavior matters in a deep way that is often not apparent to humans.[101] And to these disparities one might add the primacy of senses, for dogs are far more likely to pay attention to human body language than to voices. It is actually much easier for a human to teach a dog a new trick using just body language than with just voice cues.[102] Thinking-with dogs requires a sensibility attuned to these distinctions rather than the denial of them.[103] And this sensibility leans, in turn, on attention to naturecultures, for it requires that humans take seriously what the trainer Jean Donaldsen terms the "culture clash" between human and dog understandings of each other's worlds.[104]

Additional geographies come into play with regard to dog needs and exercise. For example, a blog post titled "I'm a Professional Dog Trainer and I Don't Walk My Dogs" by Stacy Greer flies in the face of common wisdom. While Greer acknowledges that exercise is important for dogs' health, she argues that the paramount concern is mental stimulation, which daily walks often fail to provide. Greer laments that it "has been drilled into dog owners' heads that physical exercise will fix all the things!" when, in fact, the equation "An exercised dog is a tired dog, and a tired dog is a good dog" does not address the many behavioral issues Greer identifies in her clients, whom she describes as "stressed dogs, dogs riddled with anxiety, dogs with lack of boundaries and training, and dogs not set up to have their brains enriched in the way that they should."[105] Greer lists numerous alternative activities, including training, play, relaxation exercises, and even camping, that can provide dogs with the mental stimulation and rest they need to perform well and even thrive in the decidedly humancentric geographies of our shared spaces.

Another blogger, Martha Knowles, underscores the value of mental enrichment in a piece titled "The Importance of Allowing Your Dog to Sniff." She laments that "too often I have seen guardians impatiently yanking their dogs away if the dog stops to sniff even for a moment. I have observed dogs that are walked obediently to heel and not permitted to stray to sniff." Noting that "the mental stimulation from sniffing and exploring can be just as tiring as physical exercise," Knowles goes on to posit that sniffing can signal a dog's emotional state:

> If my dog responds to an environment in a manner in which he is comfortable to investigate it—in an in-depth manner with calm sniffing—this indicates that the walk is going well and the environment is suitable for him. If my dog is pulling, moving erratically and choosing not to engage with the environment by sniffing, this is a telltale sign that he is not coping for some reason. So sniffing calmly and engaging with the environment can give clues as to the internal state of your dog.[106]

Here Knowles renders sniffing as not only an important form of mental activity but also a bodily movement and behavior that indicates a dog's emotional state.[107] Indeed, in training sessions with my dog Annie, I encourage her to sniff, roll on the grass like a bug on its back, shake herself, and basically have the leisure to take breaks on her own timeline in order to enable her to stay calm enough to work. These approaches reflect the sensibility this chapter foregrounds, for attending to dogs' actual desires and needs rather than humancentric imaginings of them emerges out of an attention to the differences between their sensory worlds, their *Umwelten*, and those of their human caretakers. Here again is a move to learn-from where and how others' desires map differently from what humans want or perceive.

These examples evince the sensibility I highlight, responding to the vexed interminglings of affect, reading, touch, and knowledge. Their perspectival reorientation works as a form of relating attentive to disparities in feeling, thinking, understanding, and sensing combined—a sensibility that, in turn, responds to Puig's call for thinking-with. While multiple affects operate in these approaches to relating, key among them is care, for sensibility works as a corrective in expressing care for dogs in a way that is both legible to them and responsive to their desires. And in some respects, this caring sensibility counters the white feminine innocence and entwined saviorism that results in the "it's a rescue" over-codings Donna derides in the previous chapter and the love that Cynthia points to as getting in the way of knowing what one is doing with dogs. A caring sensibility pushes those who take it up to work to understand dogs in all their materiality and fleshliness.

However, this sensibility and the thinking-with I propose falter when subjected to the analytic of interspecies intersectionality, not to mention the analytic of animacy put forward by Chen. The same is true of other theorizations I invoke. For example, Uexküll was no exception among his contemporaries in positing as Other humans whose experiences struck him as far removed from his own experience of the world; describing how he asked "a young, very intelligent and agile Negro . . . from the heart of Africa" to climb a ladder, Uexküll details how the man protested, exclaiming "How am I to do that, I see nothing but rods and holes?"[108] In a chapter dealing entirely with hens and dogs until this point, this example positions Africanness at a similar sensory remove from the human (of which Uexküll is the representative) as the nonhuman animals.

The analytic of interspecies intersectionality also troubles Despret's use of *empathy*, a term with a complex history in American studies. According to Merriam-Webster, empathy means "the action of understanding, being aware of, being sensitive to, and vicariously experiencing the feelings, thoughts, and experience of another." Yet the invocation of *vicarious* in this definition indexes an attempt to feel *as* an other. The literature scholar Saidiya Hartman problematizes this sense of empathy in the context of white abolitionists' accounts of slavery, arguing that empathy functions as a "projection of oneself into another in order to better understand the other" in a manner that "fails to expand the space of the other but merely places the self in its stead."[109] This empathy obliterates the other and makes a space where the white "witness comes to stand in, as proxy, for the victim."[110] In this regard, both empathy and *Umwelt* in many ways conjure precisely the rational man this chapter opposes.

While my use of *sensibility* in drawing from Puig's thinking-with disrupts the logic of the proxy with which Hartman takes issue, the disparities I evoke lean on a fairly broad and homogeneous understanding of humans—for example, as a species of primates with a propensity for embraces. Further, as in Despret's writings, my sources go unmarked in this latter discussion. While I can definitively state that McConnell belongs to the grouping of white, middle-class, middle-aged women that tend to populate shelter and dog training worlds, my other sources do not include references to their researchers' and writers' race, gender, class, and citizenship status, although I would guess that most of them fit the same profile. Because of these factors, I want to trouble my own use of *sensibility* and expand on it in ways that better address the concerns of this book.

The interventions in dog behavior that I describe in this section emerge through common points of friction. And yet, to whom exactly are these points common? Who are the humans who face these problems with dogs? For example, trash break-ins and the like certainly pose more difficulties for those U.S. households comprised of white settler colonists with 2.5 children than for houseless dog guardians living in tents beneath urban street underpasses. In discussions of the dangers of hugging dogs, the paramount concern is often the safety of children, a concern that often does not hold, or not to the same degree, for those in queer kin arrangements consisting entirely of adults who do not require careful supervision in their interspecies intimacies. The criticism of a walk as insufficiently enriching for dogs, or as failing to allow dogs the mental stimulation of sniffing, may apply to economically stable households whose members have the leisure to take dogs for walks, but it likely doesn't hold for those whose economic survival depends on working multiple jobs, with little or no time for dog-related activities. Thus the interventions I present here as *sensible* presume a specific kind of dog guardian. Such guardians are part of a pet culture examined by Heidi Nast in her critique of the production of dogs, in particular, as objects of affection necessitated by the alienation resulting from modern forms of capitalism, a production through which emerges a racial politics that valorizes the lives and needs of "pets" over those of marginalized humans.[111]

Put simply, ways of knowing that encompass interventions such as "crate your dog when you leave the house," which I delineate as engaging the *sensibility* I aim for in this chapter, take as their starting point a particular kind of human—humans for whom home ownership and 2.5 children are the norm—rather than all humans. Much like the worlds of sheltering and rescue, the worlds that are both built through and presumed in these practices of interspecies relatings emerge in the context of settler-colonial mappings of house, home, and family, in conjunction with white-normative visions of family homes consistent with the much-lauded American standard of living. And although I embrace these approaches and the sensibility they reveal, they fail to address the needs of humans and dogs who live on the margins of these mappings and worldings. That is, even as these practices put forward a sensibility that challenges rational man, they simultaneously reinforce a world order in which only some human-dog relationships matter, an order striated by race, class, sexuality, colonialism, and nation. This differential mattering returns me to the questions with which I opened this chapter, particularly how to build knowledges-with dogs that respond to an episteme with rational man at its center.

Conclusion

A critical means of extending the work of sensibility emerges through a conversation I had with Nathan about specific individuals involved in rescue with whom he had had numerous disagreements. Nathan described an encounter in which well-meaning shelter volunteers traumatized an already borderline dog by placing it in a travel crate, wheeling it to an area where the dog was encouraged to exit the crate for a video, and then essentially using a catchpole to force the dog back into the crate and returning the dog to its kennel. Nathan was livid and appalled. In his view, the dog in question had only recently begun to regard humans in a positive light, and the fright of this episode set the dog back a great deal in the tentative process of building trust.

Nathan was quick to aver that the shelter volunteers most likely to engage in these and similar endeavors, which index an insensibility to the affective experience of the dogs in question, were also those most likely to sport "All Lives Matter" T-shirts and similar paraphernalia. That is, those volunteers who were most notably lacking the sensibility delineated in this chapter were also the most likely to engage in racist political messagings. He observed that "most of the people that I'm really seeing that language from are the people that I already have strong disagreements about, about what to do in sheltering." When I asked him what he did if such language was used by or among people he worked more closely with or found himself in alliance with, he noted: "It doesn't happen as much, and I think that that's mostly because of the group of people that I work with, who tend to have some of the same awareness."[112]

In his reference to *awareness*, Nathan expresses both a sensitivity in keeping with the bodily *sensibility* of thinking-with dogs and an acknowledgment of the structures of racism, and arguably classism, colonialism, misogyny, heteronormativy, and transphobia in which shelter worlds and practices are placed. This latter acknowledgment, which Nathan terms an *awareness*, takes up the affective, sensory curiosity of my *sensibility* and transmutes it into a curiosity about and alertness to the mapping of bodies and identities that emerges in my discussion of feminist standpoint theories; *awareness* connects the more localized thinking-with that emerges in my use of *sensibility* with the larger systems and structures, the intersections, interspecies and otherwise, that shape bodies and position them as such.

Further, Nathan's observation that individuals insensible to dogs' needs are also unaware of racism underscores a failure to identify the workings of racialization as it travels in and through the bodies of dogs and their geographies. Shirts with the slogan "Straight Outta the Shelter," referencing the N.W.A. album and biopic *Straight Outta Compton*, were also common attire amongst these individuals.[113] I can only guess that the wearers had not seen the movie; at any rate, the substitutive like-race thinking in such labeling certainly went unnoticed, according to Nathan. In this regard, a lack of awareness signals a failure to notice racialization in these shelter spaces, while its awareness can be characterized as being attuned to these movements and the affects that travel with them. Awareness thus carries with it something of the analytic of Chen's *animacy*. And in this understanding of awareness conjoined with sensibility I find the potential for large-scale disruption within the episteme of rational man.

Earlier in this book I point to not just the possibility but the necessity of thinking-with the concerns of marginalized humans and nonhuman animals together in order to counter the zero-sum thinking wherein care for animals is seen as somehow taking away from or taking priority over care for marginalized humans, especially people of color. Sensibility, coupled with the awareness Nathan puts forward, offers one means to accomplish this work. The bodily sensibility of thinking-with, and the reworking of this bodiliness into an alertness to larger systems and structures that shape and mark bodies, provides a means to intervene in these structures and the episteme in which they manifest, thus prompting thinking in constellations, not isolation.

When the levees broke in New Orleans in August 2005 following Hurricane Katrina, chaos ensued. Those most severely affected by the flooding were the most marginalized of New Orleans. Thousands were unable to flee because of lack of transportation, not to mention a paucity of resources available to help those with mobility needs and related disabilities. And the areas most heavily affected and damaged by the storm and its aftermath were areas primarily populated by people of color, many of them poor—and their animals. The efforts undertaken to rescue and rehome those animals is the focus of Geralyn Pezanoski's film *Mine*.[114]

Starkly clear throughout Pezanoski's film is the fact that even as the rescue industry provided vital assistance to the animals affected by Katrina, social stigma and the legal system worked together in a manner that deeply harmed humans who were already victims of structural violences. Shelters and rescues become legal owners of animals when those animals are determined to be abandoned or loose, strays; many readers are no doubt familiar with the holding period (typically three to seven days) applying to dogs who are taken into the shelter before they become available for adoption. Following Katrina, this meant that humans who were forced to leave their animals behind—for instance to board Coast Guard boats and helicopters rescuing them from rooftops—were legally deemed to have abandoned their animals and relinquished their rights as owners.

Concomitant with this legal framing is the popular perception highlighted by Nicole of the *Redemption Dogs* blog: "No one ever thinks to give dogs who look abused or neglected a second opinion—no matter where they came from, whoever owned them was a bad person."[115] Such assumptions pervade the interviews in Pezanoski's documentary and are evident in the obstacles faced by original owners and their allies in trying to locate their dogs and secure their return. Many of these efforts failed.

One story in particular stands out: that of Jessie Pullins, an African American man trying desperately to reunite with his dog, J.J. (short for Jessie Junior). Mr. Pullins, formerly houseless and now living in the ruins of his home, and whose family members have left the state in search of work, eventually locates J.J. in the hands of an out-of-state rescue. However, here he is stonewalled. While *Mine* stages multiple heart-wrenching scenes in which new owners, often extremely reluctantly, return dogs to their original owners, Mr. Pullins's calls go unreturned, and he is faced with the fact that he has no legal means of recovering his dog. At the close of the film, Mr. Pullins remains alone, the flood-marked walls of his home delineating the empty space formerly occupied by his family and his dog.

Mine exhibits the joining of sensibility and awareness, for it demonstrates at once a careful and deep attention to the needs of animals for shelter and companionship—a thinking-with dogs in a bodily sense—and a stark alertness to the ways that structural inequities encourage and make possible certain relationships—those of newly rehomed dogs in often-lush circumstances—while denying others. The film visually connects these structural inequities with the flood-devasted structures emptied by pervasive race- and class-related injustices. The film also links dogs' health with structural privileges and injustices. Interviews with rescuers highlight widespread problems such as heartworm and, anathema to such organizations, unspayed and unneutered dogs, while interviews with New Orleans residents and former residents underscore how racism, poverty, ableism, and misogyny undergird the life circumstances of these dogs and their humans.

The film solicits emotional responses on numerous levels. The opening footage of initial rescue efforts features gaunt-eyed dogs and cats. The film then proceeds to tearful and urgent interviews with both original owners and new owners of "Katrina dogs." The *New York Times* reviewer Manohla Dargis writes in response to the film: "Go ahead and get a tissue to wipe your tears. I did."[116] And while I will not delve into debates about cinema, ideology, and affect, what appeals to me about *Mine* is precisely how it elicits a response on the part of the viewer to the plight of both the animals and their humans in the face of a structurally unjust rescue industry. The film engages in work both to think-with animals, in a rather stark sense—care is provisioned through access to food, water, and shelter—and to share an awareness of the structural inequities that shape the lives of marginalized animals and humans.

The structural injustices *Mine* highlights are everywhere, not merely in post-Katrina New Orleans. They include the eviction of humans from rapidly gentrifying areas and the shame and stigma they encounter at the doors of animal shelters when they try to relinquish their pets. Such cases dramatically illustrate a need to think-with both nonhuman animals and the larger social structures in which they and their humans are placed. Such work is crucial to building not only better understandings but also different worlds in which currently marginalized humans and animals can thrive.

Mine and many other undertakings disrupt the sedimentation of structural violences in an increasingly harsh animal rescue and shelter world as well as the episteme of which that worlding is a manifestation. This disruption entails the decentering of not just "the human" of the Englightenment but also the human who serves as the tacit norm for knowledge-related interventions in dog behavior and training. While sensibility counters the deep anthropocentrism inherent in rational man, awareness prioritizes the structural violences, movements, and emergences of racialization, colonialism, gender, sexuality, species, nation, and breed. And in this shifting and decentering I find hope for a different kind politics of rescue, for a different conception of giving shelter, for a different way of engaging dogs, and, above all, for the imagining of a different kind of world.

3

Becoming in Kind

Race, Class, Gender, and Nation in Cultures of Dog Rescue and Dogfighting

In September 2002 I adopted a pit bull–type dog I named Haley. "Rescued" from euthanasia at the hands of animal control, Haley made the rounds of several foster homes before our meeting on a sunny San Francisco street. She accompanied me through the many life experiences of a twentysomething graduate student: marching with me in protests and pride parades, moving with me to Santa Cruz and then back to the Bay Area, and walking by my side through numerous public spaces.

This last element of our relationship merits some discussion, because during our time together, I transitioned from presenting as feminine to masculine. While the social is always part of the personal in trans*, transgender, and transsexual experiences, Haley's presence deeply shaped my world. When my appearance was at its most liminal, when I felt vulnerable as a visibly transgender person, she ensured my safety. Concurrently, my whiteness, queer identity, and middle-class status encouraged other humans to read Haley as less threatening in my presence. Each of us shaped who the other was. This enmeshment of our identities exemplifies what I term *becoming in kind*.

Becoming in kind builds on my thinking regarding interspecies intersectionality by signaling the deep imbrications of not just identity but also being in many relationships between humans and nonhuman animals. Haley helped make my gender expression possible, for my gender was shaped by the space between us, just as her experiences of species and breed were shaped by my race, class, and sexuality. The *kind* of *becoming in kind* indexes the role of identity categories in relationships between humans and nonhuman animals. *Becoming* indicates the fluid nature of these relationships, a sense of negotiating togetherness as a process, described by Rosi Braidotti as "an affect that flows, . . . a composition, a location that needs to be constructed together with, that is to say in the encounter with, others."[1]

Becoming in kind speaks to the joint building of a sense of togetherness, a *we*, and the kind of beings we become. In that respect it focuses not on epistemology, the key concern of my previous chapter, but, instead on ontology. It is inflected by Donna Haraway's *becoming with*: it is a "dance of relating" in which "all the dancers are redone through the patterns they enact," a process of human and nonhuman animal encountering in which each becomes "jointly available" and through which each is changed.[2]

Haraway's *becoming with* is deliberately set against Gilles Deleuze and Félix Guattari's *becoming animal*. Their formulation elucidates connections that challenge patrilinear genealogies, connections with others produced not by resemblance or filiation but by alliance.[3] These becomings are ways of being that bring into doubt individual subjectivities through relatedness without descent, kinship despite kind. However, Haraway is critical of the way Deleuze and Guattari write against "individuated animals, family pets," as participants in modes of Oedipalized subjectivity that the authors abhor, which she sees as a commitment to the sublime altogether disconnected from the ordinary fleshly relationships between humans and nonhuman animals.[4] And while my own sense of becoming is also invested in unexpected connectivities, I find that Deleuze and Guattari's *becoming animal* misses the ways that ontologies and identities are often mixed, for it fails to address how a statement about one's being, such as "I am transgender," can be a statement about one's categorical kind that is caught up in and shaped by one's encounters with nonhuman animals—that is, identifiable through the analytic of interspecies intersectionality. My becoming in kind is indebted to Deleuze and Guattari as well as to Haraway, but by pairing *becoming* with *kind* I aim to connect the ontological stakes of jointly crafted ways of being and unexpected connectivities with the identity categories of larger social worlds.

Becoming in kind builds on interspecies intersectionality in thinking through the more overtly ontological relationships among categories such as species, breed, race, class, and gender. *Kind* is both category and divider, a taxonomy that shapes and is shaped by these connections. Deleuze, Guattari, and Haraway linger in this sense of *kind*, for it is rooted in difference rather than analogy. *Becoming in kind* deliberately contrasts with the parallels introduced by animal advocates between, for example, species and race.[5] My sense of *kind* also contrasts with the notion of difference inherent in the term *speciesism*, introduced by the philosopher Richard Ryder and adopted by the philosopher Peter Singer, which relies on analogies with racism and sexism as explanatory mechanisms—that is, the like-race thinking I trouble in the introduction.[6] Becoming in kind offers an alternative way to understand the connections between species distinctions and human-specific categories: instead of drawing parallels or analogies, becoming in kind describes the more ontological dimensions of the relatings and intersections I read through the lens of interspecies intersectionality. These intersections reveal how relationships between humans and nonhuman animals provide the conditions of possibility for specific experiences of race, gender, class, sexuality, species, and breed. Because of this focus, becoming in kind has the potential to change how we understand the ontological relationships among the categories that define humans and nonhuman animals. This understanding has important implications not only for animal studies but also for scholarship invested in critical race, feminist, and queer theories.

The specific relationships I explore this chapter are those among pit bull–type dogs, dog rescuers, and dogfighters. Debates about so-called dangerous dogs and dogs perceived to be in danger provide apt cases for thinking through the intersections of race, species, gender, breed, and nation because they reflect social conflicts about identities. What constitutes danger, and in which bodies should it be localized? What kinds of measures should be taken to address the problems related to dangerous dogs or dogs in danger, and at whom should they be aimed? These and related questions come up all too frequently in debates about pit bull–type dogs and the people connected to them, and it is here that becomings in kind are easiest to identify.

The Pit Bull

Any casual Internet search about dangerous dogs today would lead one to believe that the top contender, what one might term America's most wanted dog, is the pit bull, a descriptor with what the essayist and cultural commentator Malcolm Gladwell names a "category problem."[7] This is because there is technically no such thing as a pit bull. Because contemporary dog breeds are regulated and determined by kennel clubs, not biologists, this category problem is partly due to the shifting history of breed politics: the American Kennel Club (AKC), in an effort to distance its registries from dogs with reputations as fighters, began to recognize the American Staffordshire Terrier (AmStaf) in the 1930s, while the United Kennel Club (UKC) continued to register the American Pit Bull Terrier (APBT) throughout the twentieth century. In addition, the American Dog Breeders' Association (ADBA) also has a registry for APBTs.

Even when *pit bull* is understood to be a broad reference to all of the breeds listed above, the question of phenotype, or physical characteristics, complicates matters. An Internet-based test developed by the pit bull advocate Marcy Setter illustrates the difficulties of identification: "Find-a-Bull" features a grid of sixteen dogs ranging in weight from thirty to eighty pounds, all registered members of bully breeds—dogs descended from those used in the sport of bull baiting in nineteenth-century England, usually with breed names including some variation of *bull* in conjunction with *terrier*, who are all fairly squat, muscular, and short-haired.[8] Only one of the dogs is an APBT. Setter's point, that very few people can accurately identify any of the pit bull–type breeds just by looking, is compounded by the fact that many dogs identified as pit bulls or pit bull–type dogs are not registered with the AKC, UKC, or ADBA at all. In conflicts over dog bites, there is very rarely a means of attesting a dog's parentage, papers, or conformation to a breed's ideal phenotype. In this sense, dogs labeled as pit bulls experience breed as a formulation in the eye of the beholder, a variation of "I know it when I see it." A recent study contrasting perceptions of breed by workers at dog adoption agencies and animal shelters with DNA samples showed only 36 percent agreement between the label of *pit bull* or *pit bull–type* and genomic markers specific to the APBT or AmStaf breeds.[9] Thus, while dog breeds are regulated by kennel clubs, popular understandings of the ways breed inheres in physical characteristics, varying understandings of the specifics of those characteristics, and the fuzziness of the term *pit bull* itself make for a tricky situation. The term *pit bull–type* I use throughout this book casts a broader net but does not, in fact, solve these category problems.

Of course, a more precise taxonomy would not address the problem of the dangerous dog as a moral category. The practice of labeling particular breeds of dogs as dangerous requires some context. Harold Herzog points out that problems with dogs such as pit bulls and Rottweilers often reflect an increase in numbers rooted in boom-and-bust cycles of breed popularity.[10] Shifting understandings of breed also affect matters: the researcher Karen Delise observes that the most dangerous dog of the nineteenth century was the bloodhound, a dog designated not by its appearance but by its purpose of tracking people escaping from slavery, detailed at length in the African American and African studies scholar Bénédicte Boisseron's wonderful monograph *Afro-Dog*.[11] The concept of breed as expressing phenotype rather than purpose emerged in the twentieth century.[12]

Unfortunately, these category problems are often perpetuated in law, as evidenced in the passage of breed-specific legislation. BSL, which ranges from banning particular dog breeds and mandating their euthanasia to requiring muzzles and enclosure inside fencing of a specified height, is problematic in both its logic and its consequences.[13] Bans have resulted in the forcible seizure of dogs that are then killed by animal shelters. Following a 1989 breed ban in Denver, Colorado, even elderly dogs with no history of conflicts were subject to seizure and euthanasia. Mandatory fencing and related restrictions can be prohibitively expensive, making it next to impossible for people with lower incomes to keep their dogs.[14] Notably, BSL has also been documented to be ineffective: the National Canine Research Council points out that "citizens of Denver continued to suffer a higher rate of hospitalization from dog-bite related injuries after the breed ban than the citizens of breed-neutral Colorado counties."[15]

The language of BSL reflects the complexities of breed designations. The laws of different municipalities target "pit bulls," "pit bull terrier dogs," "American Pit Bull Terriers," "Bull Terriers," and "pit bull–type dogs." The addition of *type* is telling, as are common addenda to lists of specific breeds that read "or any dog displaying the majority of physical traits of any one or more of the above breeds."[16] However, these laws are fairly uniform in ascribing dangerous traits to dogs because of their breed. For example, Des Moines, Iowa, defines *vicious dog* to include "the American Staffordshire Bull Terrier and the Pit Bull Terrier."[17] Thus these laws locate viciousness in the bodies of specific kinds of dogs that are nevertheless characterized by fairly fuzzy criteria. In practice, these criteria include a loose conglomeration of physical characteristics such as "exaggerated jaw muscles, heavy necks and shoulders, and large physical mass," pointing to what one might term pit bull profiling.[18] In this legal sense, BSL produces pit bulls and pit bull–type dogs as criminalized beings. As the American studies scholar Colin Dayan notes, legal rituals make and unmake particular humans and nonhuman animals, and the legal rituals surrounding dangerous dogs participate in producing the very kinds of beings they regulate as criminalized by designating them as criminal by nature.[19]

Dangerous Dogs and Race

Pit-bull identities are crafted not only through the frequently contested processes outlined above but also by connections with specific categorizations of humans. The most prominent among these is race. Pit bull advocates routinely employ race-related language to garner sympathy for their cause. Intent on transporting dogs out of Denver after the passage of the breed ban, owners and allies developed a "pit bull underground railroad," evoking emancipation from a race-based system of slavery.[20] In a similar vein, some advocates refer to BSL as "breed-discriminatory legislation" and to the practice of differentiating pit bulls from other dogs as "canine racism."[21] Op-ed pieces criticizing anti–pit bull activists often introduce parallels between breed stigma and race: "I'm white, but if an African American or Hispanic person were to murder my entire family I wouldn't go to my local paper and call for the demonization of all African American and Hispanic people."[22] This logic persists in one adopter's analogy: "I think it's awful what people say about 'pit bulls' or dogs that look like 'pit bulls.' It's like racism, except against dogs."[23]

While much of the like-race thinking endemic to pit bull advocacy tends to appropriate rather than speak from the experiences of subjugated peoples, others with direct experience of human race-based profiling also make such connections. The film *Fruitvale Station* depicts the death of an unarmed African American man, Oscar Grant, at the hands of police in 2009. It includes a scene in which Grant, played by Michael B. Jordan, pulls a pit bull–type dog from the street where it has been fatally injured by a car and holds it as it dies. In an interview, Jordan said: "Black males, we are America's pit bull. We're labeled vicious, inhumane, and left to die in the street."[24] This tangle of connective language reveals the many ways that debates involving pit bulls touch on, join, and participate in perceptions of race and practices of racialization.

Less analogical thinking also emerges in the media, where both implicit and explicit connections among pit bulls, race, and criminalization are common. Writers decrying the presence of pit bulls in urban areas characterize the dogs' owners as "thugs," "gangstas," and "white trash."[25] Stories about dogfighting center on and vilify prominent African American public figures, such as the NFL quarterback Michael Vick and the rapper DMX. These stories frequently imply that rap and hip-hop cultures are central to contemporary social problems in which pit bulls are linked to violence.[26] The language used to describe the dogs also frequently resonates with that of nineteenth-century sciences of race. The criminologist Cesare Lombroso's characterizations of criminals as being excessively large of face, overly muscled, and possessing enormous jaws, and Samuel George Morton's depiction of so-called lower races as being encumbered by protruding jaws, are echoed in the contemporary characterizations of pit bulls.[27]

Breed histories reflect the connections with human racial categories, for while APBTs and AmStafs were primarily owned and bred by white men in the rural southern United States for much of the nineteenth and twentieth centuries, in the 1980s there was an influx of urban men of color into breeding circles.[28] In pointing out these connections I am not positing that literal pit bulls "have" race, a move that ignores disparities in histories of violence and species; the violences of, say, the transatlantic slave trade are not a history that these dogs can or should claim, and no actual pit bull walking through a drugstore is tailed as a potential shoplifter. However, racialization features prominently in the production of the pit bull category, exemplifying the work of becoming in kind. Pit bull figurations connect to and draw from practices of human racialization, and their animality at the categorical level of breed is most definitely a locus for what Mel Chen terms "racialized animacy."[29] This is especially evident in a prominent legal case involving pit bulls, dogfighting, and a famous African American man.

Bad Newz Kennels

The 2007 conviction of Michael Vick on dogfighting charges drew national attention. A talented African American quarterback—a position long reserved in the NFL for white men—Vick was an important public figure because of his race long before his conviction. When the federal government indicted him, stories began to surface of his cruelty to the dogs he owned, alleging his involvement in strangling, shooting, hanging, and electrocuting dogs that would not fight. A media storm followed, with protests staged against Vick across the country, some of which harked back to practices of lynching.[30] Images of Vick in his football uniform, choking a dog, were spray-painted onto concrete walls, and pictures on social media showed him shackled to a snarling dog as if he were enslaved.[31] The case was hotly debated along racial lines among dogfighters, many of whom saw in it the denigration of the sport by street fights known to be staged in urban areas by men of color.[32] The case shaped public perceptions of who Vick is and was.

The cultural geographers Glen Elder, Jennifer Wolch, and Jody Emel have argued that when practices involving animals deemed problematic, such as dogfighting, "occur in racialized and marginalized places, such as ghetto areas, the prospects of racialization on the basis of animal practices rise higher."[33] They point out that "animal bodies have become one site of political struggle over the construction of cultural difference and help to maintain white American supremacy."[34] Vick's trial by both the judiciary and the court of public opinion transformed him into a convicted criminal in serious debt with a major image problem. This transformation changed how people read Vick's African American masculinity. It was not just his conviction—or his exile from the elite fraternity of the NFL for the duration of his eighteen-month prison sentence—that transformed public perceptions but also the relationships with animals on which his conviction was based.

Jim Gorant's 2010 best-seller, *The Lost Dogs: Michael Vick's Dogs and Their Tale of Rescue and Redemption*, reflects the role of race in these changing perceptions of Vick. Gorant, a *Sports Illustrated* writer, describes Vick by highlighting features such as "a strong jaw that made him look as if he had an underbite," and asserts that Vick's appearance, "while handsome, could be fairly described as almost canine."[35] This description codes Vick as animal-like, Othering him in a manner deeply reminiscent of the earlier projects of human racialization through animal likeness detailed in chapter 2.[36]

Media coverage of the dogs taken from Vick's Bad Newz Kennels also affected public perceptions. Gorant's book, which contains italicized passages narrated from the viewpoint of one of the dead dogs, was part of an advocacy movement on behalf of the dogs. Initially understood as "some of the most viciously trained dogs in the country" by Wayne Pacelle, then head of the Humane Society of the United States, the dogs were subsequently dubbed "Vicktims."[37] As a result, the danger initially seen as inhering in breed came to be localized instead in the person of Vick, an African American man. The dogs' transformation from fighters to victims played a central role in altering public perceptions of Vick. His relationship with his dogs was and is a becoming in kind.

The American studies scholar Megan Glick explores the "frameworks of logic" involved in these transformations. She notes that following Vick's trial, his dogs were initially described as awaiting "execution," terminology generally employed only for humans. Glick argues that the humanization of the dogs through this language reflects a connection between racialization and speciation in the context of what Achille Mbembe terms a "necropolitics."[38] Necropolitics rests on rendering "inhuman" peoples whose lives or, more aptly, bodies, are made disposable by the state, as is the case with eugenics: nonhuman animals are likewise associated with "death worlds," even as they influence who or what is classified as human. This tendency is evident in President Donald Trump's 2018 remarks regarding Latinx migrants to the U.S.: "These aren't people. These are animals."[39]

The valorization of Vick's dogs demonstrates how contemporary patterns of racialization in the U.S. facilitate necropolitical understandings. For Glick, the dogs' shifting status, and their eventual positioning in a narrative of redemption twinned with Vick's own, demonstrates how their humanization worked as "a means to an end," that end being Vick's imprisonment and excision from society. Given the extraordinarily high rates of imprisonment of Black and brown men in the U.S., Glick reads the Vick case as a reflection of "the banality of criminality, . . . the banality of monstrosity, that shape popular imaginings of black masculinity."[40] Ascription of humanity to the dogs thus feeds into a politics wherein Black and brown masculinities are firmly emplaced in Mbembe's "death worlds."

The political scientist Claire Jean Kim also examines Vick's case, arguing that race "in the sense of a taxonomy of bodies and a set of enduring, structured meanings about those bodies," constituted "the very cultural frame through which the story came to be read." She posits that part of the case's explosiveness emerged from the fact that "its central players were, in the American cultural imaginary, the most animal of humans (the Black man) and the most human of animals (the dog)." Kim, like Glick, points to language that humanizes the dogs and animalizes Vick: the dead dogs found on Vick's property were described as "having been executed," and "critics called for Vick to be caged, neutered, or placed in a fighting pit." Kim argues that animal advocates put forward an "optic of cruelty" inextricably entwined with race, while Vick's defenders advanced an "optic of racism" that ultimately denied "the other set of moral claims" involved in the case, namely extreme and intentional cruelty to nonhuman animals.[41]

For Kim, both approaches involve a disavowal: even as animal advocates proclaimed, "This is not a race issue," and denied the salience of skin color with remarks like "I don't care if Michael Vick was black, white, green, or purple," Kim drily notes that "no one in [the U.S.] has ever been enslaved, auctioned off, or lynched for being green, purple, or orange." Further, Kim identifies the tendency among Vick's defenders to "affirm both that Blacks are human and therefore more important than animals, and that animals do not merit much moral consideration." Kim argues for a politics of "avowal" wherein animal advocates' condemnation of dogfighting might engage "the context of anti-Black racism" and through which "race advocates . . . would resist the reflexive moves of asserting human superiority and reducing animal advocacy to anti-Black racism."[42] In the following section, I explore in depth how the Vick case facilitated the production of a particular formation of innocence conjoined to whiteness, intrinsically shaped by the dynamics Kim articulates.

Whiteness to the "Rescue"

Typically, federal, state, and local governments euthanize all dogs present at a dogfighting bust, including those that work as government informants (as participants in fighting rings staged to set up busts).[43] Workers at animal shelters commonly call such dogs "kennel trash," for as they wait for their inevitable death, they take up shelter space that could be used by adoptable dogs.[44] In Vick's case, however, the federal government permitted the dogs to be evaluated, rehabilitated, and, if possible, placed with families. This policy shift changed the connections between the category of pit bull and race. Narratives about the dogs uniformly emphasize tropes common to both neoconservative and neoliberal projects of citizenship, recuperating them into a tacit whiteness.

An internet video titled *See Them Now*, posted by BADRAP, a pit bull advocacy group involved in the Vick case, features photos of several of the rescue dogs accompanied by a voice-over from Donna Reynolds, the group's cofounder. Emphasizing that the dogs' job is to "show America that pit bulls aren't monsters," Reynolds tells us that they "remind us that everyone wants and needs to be treated as an individual." Hector, a dog covered with bite scars, has "wonderful play manners." Ernie is a "big dork" who "wants to be friends with everybody" and happily lives in a home with a child. And Uba, who now lives with a dog and a cat, knows that "the cat is his boss, and he's happy to take on a cat as part of his family."[45] In his book, Gorant uses similar language, pointing to the dogs' "dorkiness" and "pure unfiltered love."[46] The dogs are almost uniformly described as happy, unique individuals who are excellent and loving family members and have good manners.

This language is also central to contemporary constructions of U.S. citizenship. Writing at the beginning of President Bill Clinton's administration, the American studies scholar Lauren Berlant noted how "the intimate public sphere of the U.S. present tense renders citizenship as a condition of social membership produced by personal acts and values, especially acts originating in or directed towards the family sphere."[47] This agenda has persisted in contemporary U.S. politics, not just in the neoconservative Focus on the Family campaign, but also in the push for gay marriage, which deployed rhetoric and images tying queer identities into the norms of American kinship practices. The stories of the Vick dogs reveal how nonhuman animals participate in these practices of good citizenship and national sociality. Many of the Vick dogs not only met their rescuers' goal of finding "forever" homes and families but also became aspiring citizens in another sense: one of the rescuers' main goals for all the dogs was that they pass the American Kennel Club's Canine Good Citizen Test.[48] Where and how canine citizenship intersects with the acts of citizenship of family-oriented dog rescuers, and how both parties relate to "tacit whiteness," merits further attention.

For Berlant, two figures are central to the discourses of reactionary conservative politics: the American fetus and the American child. She calls them "supericons," reading them as "the last living American[s] not yet bruised by history . . . not yet caught up in the confusing identity exchanges made possible by mass consumption and ethnic, racial, and sexual mixing." She notes that the lack of knowledge, agency, and accountability common to the fetus and the child give them ethical claims on the adult political agents who write laws and administer resources.[49] As imaginary figures who exist outside the real material social world of the U.S., the American Fetus and Child emerge as in need of protection from and seemingly unmarked by social divisions. But this is only a seeming unmarking, for in the contemporary U.S. the supposed absence of race, when closely examined, reveals the active construction of whiteness. For example, when the author of a novel fails to remark on characters' racial identifiers such as skin, hair, kinship practices, or even language, it communicates not a lack of race but rather the presumed norm of whiteness (not to mention able-bodiedness, heterosexuality, etc.).[50] Berlant's innocent supericons, not yet citizens, not only require that others advocate on their behalf, but also, in their seeming lack of overt racial identifiers, do so through what can be understood as a tacit whiteness.

The rescued and rehabilitated Vick dogs, cleansed of the taint of dogfighting, represented as innocent victims, and transformed into iconic family members, participate in the national public sphere in ways remarkably similar to Berlant's supericons. Indeed, the very shift in federal policy that enabled their salvation—the saviorist language of "a second chance" runs rampant in their stories—is a case of adult political agents' acknowledging the dogs' ethical claim on both the law and the resources at its disposal. Of course, unlike the fetus and the child, these dogs will never become real U.S. citizens. Rather, through participating in training practices directed by their human handlers, and specifically training oriented toward passing the Canine Good Citizen Test, many of the dogs became, instead, good cultural citizens. Publicity on behalf of other rescued pit bull–type dogs deploys similar tropes.

Rescue groups that work with pit bulls routinely describe them as fun-loving, exuberantly happy, sweet, affectionate dogs that crave human attention.[51] Pictures of dogs engaged in cross-species love with humans and other animals and acting as productive members of society abound in this type of media. For example, stories about dogs like Ruby, a pit bull–type dog who now works with elderly folks in a nursing home, are common.[52] Leo, another Vick dog, earned the nickname "Dr. Leo" from hospital staff because of "the healing joy he brought to cancer patients" in his work as a therapy dog.[53] Affective labor in the most literal sense, these dogs' work affirms their place in American families and homes.

The changes undergone by the dogs taken from Vick's kennels relied on changes in their relationship to the categories of race and nation. No longer partnered with "thugs," the dogs were very publicly removed from their position as victims of abuse and recoded as "unique individuals" with stories to tell and love to give. They came to participate in families and social settings in ways that connected their very ways of being to a tacit, normative whiteness. They became pit bulls committed to the greater social good, pit bulls with stakes in home life, pit bulls whose loving families needed to advocate for them in order to distance them from their "bad rap." In living, training, and becoming with the humans committed to their rescue, these dogs underwent (and continue to undergo) alterations in their experience of kind.

Becoming in Kind through Rescue

The experiences of dog rescuers involved in the Vick case and others like it are also forms of becoming in kind. Gorant describes the labor and emotional toll of Nicole Rattay, a volunteer who worked with the Vick dogs during their shelter confinement. Noting that "Rattay was quickly growing attached to the dogs and this caused her distress, . . . [and that] they made her cry . . . every night," Gorant sympathizes with Rattay's admiration for "how resilient and loving" the dogs were.[54] One can join this narrative with that of the pit bull advocate and writer Ken Foster, who finds that each time he rescues a dog, he experiences ambivalence, "wondering if I'm doing it for them or whether in rescuing them, I'm actually doing something for myself."[55] Another dog rescuer, Terry Bain, notes that dog rescue can transform your heart, giving it "an even greater capacity to love."[56] The sense of a self transformed and made more whole by the act of rescue is common. The prominence of the term *rescue* in these personal accounts reveals an identity rooted in salvation and sometimes inflected by religion: one Vick dog adopter, upon meeting her charge, is moved to help "this beautiful soul."

This salvation also relies on geography, for it entails moving these dogs out of the woods or the streets, out of animal shelters, and into homes.[57] While the spaces into which these dogs are moved are inflected by whiteness, as Berlant makes clear, they are also shaped by class.[58] In many U.S. municipalities it can be difficult to rent a home where any dogs are permitted, much less pit bull–type dogs. The looseness of this category is no impediment to home insurers' denying coverage or charging higher rates. Thus the homes made more whole by a rescued dog are homes made possible by the financial resources of the middle class, including intergenerational wealth—wealth that connects directly to racism, given the histories of redlining, blockbusting, and racist bank-lending practices in the U.S.[59] The identities of the animal rescuers whose hearts and homes are made whole reveal becomings in kind shaped by class as well as race.

Affective Politics

A story from outside the U.S. underscores the effects of breed-specific legislation. Through this narrative I examine the work of affect in conjunction with like-race logic in pit bull advocacy politics and my larger argument regarding becomings in kind.

In April 2010, a dog named Lennox was seized from a family in Belfast, Northern Ireland. After measurements performed with a "worn dress-maker's tape," Lennox was sentenced to death for being a "pit bull." Pit bulls were and are outlawed in Northern Ireland, but their legal definition is quite murky. The use of the tape enacted an arguably extralegal maneuver to bolster a determination rooted in the approach of "I know it when I see it" rather than a predetermined metric. Lennox's family and numerous advocates vigorously contested this label through DNA analysis and other methods, sparking a legal battle followed around the world.[60] According to one report, the "battle for Lennox became an international campaign" that "went 'viral' on social media websites and attracted tens of thousands of well-wishers."[61] Even celebrity dog trainers leapt into the fray: *Animal Planet*'s Victoria Stilwell offered to rehome Lennox with a family in the United States. However, the Belfast authorities were not persuaded, and in July 2012, the city council issued a statement: "The dog Lennox, an illegal pit-bull terrier type, has been humanely put to sleep."[62]

Lennox's case directly reflects many of the dynamics I outline throughout this book. When an image of Lennox surfaced, it was accompanied by commentary about the concrete "prison" in which he was being held.[63] Advocates spoke of his two-year stay with the council dog wardens as "solitary confinement," referred to the weeks before his death as his time on "death row," and pointed to the problems of "racially profiling dogs such as Lennox."[64] For U.S. observers, given the legacy of the racist prison-industrial complex in the U.S. and its disproportionate population with persons of color, it is impossible to read these prison references apart from racial formations. The direct ascription of racism in these examples suggests that like-race thinking ran strong in this case, with Lennox perceived as Black. However, in pleas from Lennox's advocates such as "This could be YOUR family, please help fight this injustice," the emphatic positioning of Lennox within the innocence of the family sphere, as outlined by Berlant, joins with an additional dynamic.[65] In prepending *your* to *family*, Lennox's many advocates not only circulated Lennox's story through connections with race and family but did so in a manner that solicited the participation and feeling of readers and observers: the "you" of "your family."

In the public displays of mourning that followed Lennox's death, moves to propagate connections to Lennox through appeals to feeling transmuted the like-race thinking through which his case was understood into troubling practices of identification. This is because immediately after the announcement of Lennox's euthanasia, many photos of humans and dogs appeared on the internet with the caption "I am Lennox."[66] This campaign occurred not long after protests in response to the February 2012 murder of Trayvon Martin, a young, unarmed African American teen shot and killed by George Zimmerman, a self-identified neighborhood watchman, who was acquitted of murder charges on the basis of Florida's "stand your ground" law. Those protests included an internet meme in which people posted photographs of themselves in black hooded sweatshirts—the garment Martin was wearing when murdered—captioned "I am Trayvon Martin." While the Martin meme highlighted the racial profiling at work in Martin's death, it also acted as a form of public mourning, a way to express sadness, anger, and rage about Martin's death and the social order that, in exonerating his killer, condoned it. In deliberately evoking this meme, the "I am Lennox" campaign sought to bring the like-race understandings of pit bull profiling into an affective politics. "I am Lennox" encouraged people to take up not just the reasoning that pit bulls experience stigma in a way that works "like" racialization, but also the emotions evoked by the public mourning of a racially profiled young man.

In "I am Lennox" clicktivism, what appears to reflect an ontological premise that transcends human-animal boundaries reflects instead a substitutive claiming that erases important and human-specific elements of marginalization. This is not a becoming in kind, but an appropriation of kind. Just as the many white commentators who posted selfies in hoodies after Martin's death are clearly not Martin, the dogs depicted in the "I am Lennox" memes are very much *not* Lennox. In the equation of Lennox's and their experiences with the implicitly state-sanctioned, race-based killing of Martin, mostly white denizens of the internet claim to feel-as, to suffer injustices that are palpably demonstrated as *not* theirs through the simple fact that the images are of them, not of actual victims of injustice. Rather than becomings in kind, these activisms and the images that circulate in and through them are *erasures* of kind, appropriating the reality of racist injustice and centering whiteness as victim. This erasure is made possible through a movement of affect, a claim to share in feelings that are thereby emptied of their actual race-based conditions of emergence.

Becoming Perpetrator and Victim

Contemporary discussions of race and racialization in the U.S. frequently invoke what the scholar Robin DiAngelo has described as *white fragility*: white people's difficulty, anger, and frustration in discussing or addressing the role of race, particularly as it bears on their own actions. For example, when a white person is told that, say, their ability to own a home emerges from white privilege tied to intergenerational wealth, schooling, bank lending practices, employment practices, and so on, and the person subsequently expresses fear, panic, or anger that impedes further discussions, that behavior fits into the framework of white fragility.[67] Claims of "reverse racism" further exemplify this dynamic, underscoring a sense of individual victimization on the basis of whiteness that disregards the systemic oppressions of actual racism. And while white fragility is certainly prominent in much of today's politics, and strongly evident in court cases related to affirmative action, some of its most brutal circulation inheres in its conjunction with gender and sexuality, in particular as rendered through the history and present of what Angela Davis terms "the Myth of the Black Rapist."[68]

For Davis, "the fraudulent rape charge stands out as one of the most formidable artifices invented by racism," such that "the myth of the Black rapist has been methodically conjured up whenever recurrent waves of violence and terror against the Black community have required convincing justifications." The notion of sexual aggressiveness as innate to Black masculinities dates to the beginning of enslavement (especially as tied to animality, as detailed in chapter 2), but Davis, citing Frederick Douglass, argues that its political weaponization was most virulent in the aftermath of the U.S. Civil War. With the erosion of the pretext for mass lynchings (themselves vehicles for the sexual assault of Black women) on the basis of countering Black aspirations toward political supremacy, "the cry of rape emerged as the major justification for lynching."[69] Today, cisgender Black men are far more likely to be prosecuted and imprisoned for sexual assault than their white counterparts. The perception of specifically Black masculine sexual violence directed toward white women persists.[70]

This mythology connects to one of the more telling dog stories involving pit bull types in recent years, that of "Dog Park Diane." This moniker resembles those conferred on numerous other white people recorded in the act of harassing or calling the police on Black people engaging in ordinary activities like shopping, going swimming, or holding a barbecue in a public park. Videos of such incidents are posted and widely viewed on the internet, with the vast majority of commentators excoriating the racism of the white folks involved. In February 2019, a white woman at a dog park in Attleboro, Massachusetts, accused the dog of Franklin Baxley, an African American lawyer, of "assaulting" her dog by humping it. Baxley filmed the incident, including the arrival of the police officer, who chided him for leaving his vehicle running and for gesturing with his hand in front of his chest—which, according to the officer, could be interpreted as assault.[71]

From the video it appears that all three dogs involved in this incident are pit bull types, although this is of course a tenuous identification. Baxley, an employment attorney, points out to "Diane" that she is using the language of assault, along with the fact that numerous other dogs at the park had exhibited the same humping behavior, and yet none of their owners had had the police called on them. The case quickly took on a life of its own through the online circulation of Baxley's videos, and the incident was added to a growing public list of spurious, racially motivated complaints to the police by white people. However, given that the discourse of assault in circulation here works entirely through the bodies of dogs, it offers another example of the work of becoming in kind.

In Diane's use of the language of assault on behalf of her dog lies a claim to victimhood that emerges entirely through the mythos Davis describes. When a dog belonging to a Black man is perceived as assaulting a dog belonging to a white woman, the first dog represents the threat of Black masculinity to Diane's white femininity. Perceptions of Baxley's Black masculinity are tied to and co-constituted by what is read as overly animalistic (though in fact common) behavior on the part of his dog. Both dog and man are interpreted as threatening, a charge compounded by Diane's insistence that Baxley's tone is overly loud and the police officer's reference to hand gestures as suggestive of assault. Doing Black masculinity in public is rendered threatening through its association with a seemingly out-of-line behavior by a dog. In this lies an uncomfortable becoming in kind.

Moreover, Diane's claim to injury echoes the false characterizations by white men and women of Black men that Davis highlights in her writing. Among dogs, humping is a rude behavior, but not one that tends to result in the immediate expulsion from other canine company. Further, as the animal psychologist Marc Bekoff notes, "Mounting and humping by dogs are among those behavior patterns about which humans make lots of assumptions but we really don't know much about them." In spite of talk of dominance and the resemblance of humping to mating behaviors, says Bekoff, humping is not only "a normal part of a dog's behavioral repertoire" but also a behavior that, in of itself, is not particularly gendered, for "both males and females hump."[72] Thus for Diane to claim that Baxley's dog is assaulting hers is to turn a normal behavior into a gendered and racialized threat. Given that the videos Baxley shares all feature fairly normal and cooperative dog play, Diane's accusation entails investing her dog with her own whiteness and femininity. Her actions and language bespeak an uncomfortable becoming in kind that reflects much larger discourses of race and rape rather than any issue rooted in dog behavior.

While the very moniker "Dog Park Diane" reflects the widespread hostility expressed on social media toward Diane following the incident, only Baxley was identified: Diane, as of this writing in spring 2020, remains anonymous. This suggests an avoidance of accountability on the part of the woman involved. However, I find hope here nonetheless, for that same widespread circulation has almost certainly influenced others who might have been inclined to act similarly: no one wants to be the "flavor of the day" on Twitter. While Diane herself may or may not have taken up the necessary work to disrupt future iterations of this becoming in kind, the publicity generated by the incident almost certainly pushed others, specifically white dog owners who are similarly positioned, to question their assumptions and, hopefully, to act, think, and engage differently. In this manner the dissemination of Baxley and Diane's story on social media, unlike the case of Lennox, likely facilitated the disruption rather than reification of similar becomings in kind through the relatively simple move of identifying and making public, making recognizable, the dynamics of race and gender at stake in such interactions.

Becoming Dog Men

Both Diane's and Baxley's experiences of becoming in kind contrast with the writings of white Southern dog men.[73] Dogfighters, or dog men, are seen as the diabolical enemy by dog rescuers, humane organizations, law enforcement, and most animal lovers. While contemporary dogfighting involves dog men from both urban and rural locales, often divided along racial lines, throughout much of the late nineteenth and twentieth centuries, most American dog men were white men located in the Southern states. Importantly, these men communicated through underground breed magazines and semisecret publications in obscure presses; dogfighting was outlawed in all U.S. states by 1976, although law enforcement attention varied widely until fairly recently.[74] Because it is difficult to gain access to web-based contemporary discussions, I focus here on writings from underground publications dating from the 1970s through the 1990s.[75] These writings reveal an alternative process of becoming in kind, one with stakes in a different kind of whiteness, but one, like that of the rescuers, cemented by kinship and love.

The unique traits of the individual pit bull, so prominent in stories about the Vick dogs and pro–pit bull media, are also central to the narratives of dog men and game dog (fighting dog) fanciers. Ed Faron and Chris Faron, the authors of *The Complete Gamedog*, describe their mistake in setting up a fighting match for Pinky, one of their fighting dogs, as a failure to recognize her individuality and her youth: "Instead of looking at each dog as an individual, a lot of the time we would tend to assume that if a dog acted hot and was at least 18 months old it was 'ready'[to fight]."[76] They exhort their readers to tailor their conditioning and setting up of test matches to the individual dog. They include elaborate accounts of individual dogs' matches and descriptions of prized dogs' personalities.

Genealogies, both human and canine, are essential to these tales. Like rescued dogs, fighting dogs participate in human families. Writing of the death of Mean Jolene in a match against Sadie, the Farons assert that she died doing what she loved and add: "We bid farewell to you, Jolene, and feel privileged to have been able to call you one of our family."[77] They mention another white Southern dog man, Thomas Garner, who proudly displays an eleven-by-fourteen-inch picture of his stud dog Ch Pedro beside his children's pictures on his office wall.[78] And while game dogs' names are often prefaced by the kennel in which they were bred—Wildside's Mean Jolene, for example—it is also common for them to include the name of their breeder, as in the Boudreaux line of dogs. Descriptions of fights often conflate human and nonhuman identities, as in the description of Roadblock's kennel's grand champion: "Joey beat three top dogmen with good dogs for his championship, and then went on to beat two champions and a grand champion for his next three matches."[79] (It is impossible to tell here whether "Joey" refers to the dog man or the individual dog.) Because dog men retain breeders' names to track dogs' genealogies, and because dogs are often given to or fostered by other dog men, the dogs cement a kinship network among dogfighters and dog men. (Generally speaking, *dog men* refers to the men who breed dogs but do not fight them, men who both breed dogs and fight them, and men who purchase or receive dogs but do not breed them. Dogfighters are all dog men, but not all dog men are dogfighters.)

Dog men's relationships with their dogs also explicitly incorporate an affect often tied to family: love. Bobby Hall, an old-time dog man, describes a moment when a woman asks the famed dog man Earl Tudor, "'Just what kind of S.O.B. does it take to fight dogs?' Per Hall, Earl replied, 'Lady, it takes a man who loves dogs very much.'" This love comes through in Hall's writing about handling, the job of the person in the fighting pit with the dog. Tudor tells Hall: "I have watched you and you have picked up and handled each dog as if you were in the pit with them." Hall replies, "It makes me feel closer to them." He describes Tudor's response: "Peering gently over the top of his glasses, he cleared his throat so the emotion feeling would permit him to reply in a low church tone and with tenderness he said 'Bobby, it makes them feel closer to you, too.'"

The exchange between Hall and Tudor reveals how dog men navigate masculinity through the bodies of their dogs. Indeed, after offering this church-toned encouragement, Tudor congratulates Hall on a recent win, and Hall notes, "Well, after he told me this it was all I needed, a little pat on the back from the master."[80] Tales traded among dog men tend to be filled with paeans to the older dog men who introduced the younger ones to the game. While some tributes are brief—"I owe everything I know to Ron"—others, like Hall's, are more intimate. Established dog men not only bring newcomers to underground fights but also let them buy into their dog bloodlines. Introductions take the form of an apprenticeship: "If you're lucky, someone who is already established in the game will take you under his wing and teach you everything he knows."[81] These ties between older and younger dog men reveal a sociality in which masculinity is fundamentally shaped by connections with other men through the bodies of pit bulls. Not only is this masculinity very homosocial, as Hall and Tudor's exchange reveals, but it is also white.

Ed Faron's description in *The Complete Gamedog* of being arrested on suspicion of dogfighting while living in North Carolina highlights his understanding of race: "I found myself in a cell block where I was the only white person, which I guess was just another way they were trying to mess with my head." His sense of not belonging in this jail space increases the following morning, when he is overwhelmed and irritated by the "Motown music" played by his fellow prisoners, almost all of whom are men of color. He also notes that he had met many of them previously, through seizing their belongings while working as a repo man.[82] Faron's placement in this space signifies a change in his experience of white masculinity, for his association with dogfighting means that his whiteness and socioeconomic status no longer buffer him from presumptions of criminality: his body is placed in the same space as the bodies of men from whom he had previously taken possessions. Faron's arrest reveals how he and other dog men become in kind with their fighting dogs, for their experiences of the intersections of whiteness, class, and masculinity are fundamentally shaped by their relationships with pit bulls.

Some Kind of Love

All the relationships I examine in this chapter involve love. Even Michael Vick has gone on record to affirm that he loves dogs.[83] But what kind of love is this, when it is neither innocent nor liberatory? And how is this love part of becoming in kind? What of the loves involved that are more aptly described as appropriations of or substitutions in kind? *Becoming in kind* speaks to the overlaps in identity and ontology experienced by humans and nonhuman animals and to the changes individuals undergo as the result of an encounter. As the stories of dogfighters reveal, their experiences are not becomings in kind that necessarily build better shared worlds. In exploring how becoming in kind is caught up in specific affects, like love, I am in conversation with not only Haraway but also Vinciane Despret.

Despret thinks through *attunement* as a way of articulating the changes to both humans and nonhuman animals enabled by practices of relating. Describing an experiment in which students were given ostensibly smart and dumb groups of rats to raise in order to see whether the students' expectations of the rats would influence the rats' performances of maze navigation (which they did), Despret finds that the rats and the students became "attuned."[84] She argues that the students conveyed their trust and expectations to the rats through caressing, manipulating, handling, and encouraging them. According to Despret, "these beliefs brought into existence new identities for the students and for the rats" through the touches exchanged between them.[85]

Love and touch are key to the interspecies ontologies Haraway and Despret describe. Referring to the trust that makes the students and rats available to each other, Despret quotes the philosopher Isabelle Stengers, who notes that "trust is one of the many names for love, and you can never be indifferent to the trust you inspire."[86] Despret reads trust as a practice of love that facilitates the ontological shifts prompted by attunement. Haraway's characterization of love is less wholesome. She describes her relationship with her dog as follows: "Significantly other to each other, in specific difference, we signify in the flesh a nasty developmental infection called love."[87] Both kinds of love shape experiences from which humans and nonhuman animals emerge changed. Love is part of becoming.

The loves that shape the becomings in kind I read among pit bulls, pit bull rescuers, dog park goers, and dog men are similar to those outlined by Haraway and Despret. Hall describes his use of massage as part of his "duty and obligation to give 100% total dedication to this gladiator going into battle," a form of love conveyed through touch.[88] And dog men's stories not only allude to the ways the men are driven by "the love of this great dog" but also mention it in accounts like that of Mean Jolene, who the Farons claim died "doing what she loved best," a claim that is of course impossible to verify.[89] Love is omnipresent in dog rescuers' stories that tell of the ways rescue expands one's heart and highlight how rescued dogs act out of love as canine good citizens. Love is apparent in Dog Park Diane's identification with her dog, as well as in Baxley's defense of his dog's right to simply be a dog in public. The appropriative claims made by mostly white pit-bull owners to Lennox's identity evince a love that seeks to shoulder a race-based injustice but instead overwrites it. Love is also central to rescuers' advocating a better kind of death. Arguing against the outsourcing of the work of rescue to poorly funded animal sanctuaries in cases where dogs become too unsafe to keep in homes, the pit bull activist Jessica Dolce advocates to owners another form of love: "Putting them to sleep, in your arms, can be the greatest act of love you can give to your pet."[90] These are undoubtedly funny kinds of love.

Dogfighters' loves are laced with power dynamics. Like Despret's rats, the dogs are often eager to move into the identities their handlers desire. Unlike the rats, these dogs are directed into violence. While many dogs love to fight—an attitude called "dead game" by proud handlers—many others, also bred by dog men, would be happy never to fight. "Gameness" itself is a complicated term, but it can be generally taken to index a dog's desire to pursue an activity beyond the point when most other dogs would give up or walk away, and in the context of dogfights it is often taken to mean that a dog would fight to the death if not stopped: hence the prepending of *dead* to *game* here. Dog men like Hall express a love that makes me uneasy, not only because the maiming and killing of dogfighting is terrible to witness but also because this love, even when the dogs also "love" to participate in fighting, is a means of extracting profit from the bodies of dogs. The love of Hall and others is a love shaped by power, money, and blood, not a love invested in the well-being of dogs.

The loves under discussion here are inextricably tied to contemporary political discussions about race, gender, and nation. Perceptions of love are often the basis for discussions about whether a relationship with an animal is good or ethical. The love that animal rescuers speak about is drawn from the language of a larger political discourse that tends to see love as a panacea for social ills, one where love is introduced as an answer to cries of injustice—the love proclaimed in the Beatles song "All You Need Is Love." However, as Hall and others reveal, love is never easy, nor is it innocent. Indeed, uneasy and noninnocent loves are central to the becomings that emerge from human and nonhuman animal encounters. As Haraway notes, love is "often disturbing, given to betrayal, occasionally aggressive, and regularly not reciprocated in the ways the lovers desire."[91] The woman who asks Tudor, "Just what kind of S.O.B. does it take to fight dogs?" sees a lack of love, not to mention care, in dogfighting, even as he steadfastly avers its presence as formative to his labors. The presence or absence of love, or its perceived presence or absence, does not directly address the ethics or politics of becoming in kind, for love of one kind or another is everywhere in these stories. Becoming in kind offers a way to better understand and even challenge these uneasy and different loves.

Conclusion: Loving Differences

Let me revisit the story of Haley and me as a story in which a dog, a middle-class white transperson, safety, and love become together. Like pit bulls, transgender identities bring with them a number of category problems. Legibility is an issue, but there is also the question of whether one even wants to be read as, say, a white male. When I first began transitioning, thoughts of running into the likes of Newt Gingrich in the bathroom made me very nervous. I did not want to share a category with such a man. Becoming in kind was a way for me to think through the ways that who I was—no longer a woman, but not quite a man, and not really interested in being a man—were facilitated by my relationship with a pit bull. Becoming in kind was a way for me, as a feminist and white transperson, to understand how the categories that shape many humans' existences and against which many folks chafe—such as race, class, gender, nation, and transgender—are caught up in relationships with nonhuman animals. Becoming in kind also made me uneasy about my love with Haley, for it pushed me to consider how narratives of animal rescue and salvation are caught up in these category problems. It also pushed me to think critically about how to disrupt the connections among these enmeshed human and nonhuman identities.

However, becoming in kind did not necessarily help Haley in the way that it helped me, for problems of categories and kinds are problems that dogs in Haley's position cannot themselves contest. She could not express ambivalence about her legibility as a pit bull, nor could she "look back" or return my gaze in a way that might assert a different understanding of the connections among categories and kinds I outline here, the latter being a human-specific form of making meaning.[92] This chapter thus falls into a long line of animal representations in which advocacy is mixed with seeming anthropocentrism.[93] This problem leads me to consider the formulation of a more hopeful and hopefully less anthropocentric politics that stems from becoming in kind, a formation inflected by what one might term "becoming in kindness."

The political stakes of my elucidations are twofold: recognition and disruption. In proposing *becoming in kind*, I extend my use of interspecies intersectionality in an effort to understand how the overlapping categories of difference that divide human worlds are part and parcel of necessarily intermingled human and nonhuman worldings where ways of being and doing commingle with and are shaped by the power dynamics.[94] In particular, the recognition of different ways of being participates in conversations among scholars in animal studies, in feminist, critical race, labor, environmental, and Indigenous studies, who are concerned with how we might inherit the violences that have shaped our more-than-human worlds. This recognition can help us interrupt and disrupt the ties among these identity categories for the better.

When I advocate disruption, I am invested in taking up the uneasy loves I read with, the affects that move within and into the ontological work identifiable in becomings in kind, and finding ways to interrupt their attachments to the norms of rescue, race, gender, and nation.[95] A disruption following from becoming in kind might mean understanding how some forms of uneasy loves, like that of the person whose pit bull–type dog is skinny and has heartworms, shape and are shaped by classism and racism, and how help, if offered, should address these factors rather than propose salvation by separation. A disruption might also mean exploring the potential for restorative justice rather than lengthy prison sentences when dealing with people who have been involved in dogfighting, challenging ties between notions of justice and a growing and deeply racist prison-industrial complex.

Disruption might also mean facilitating loves outside homes and apart from narratives of normative kinship. Downtown Dog Rescue, a Los Angeles–based organization, was founded by Lori Weise and Richard Tuttlemondo in 1996. Concerned with the ballooning stray dog population in LA's "skid row," they wanted to help by facilitating the spaying and neutering of the dogs. They quickly learned that many of the seeming strays—most of them pit bull types—had owners.[96] Rather than attempt to part people from their dogs, they tried to connect them with not just spay-and-neuter resources but also more general veterinary care. Tuttlemondo notes that a key lesson from this process was to "accept the dog owner as he or she is now, no judging their lifestyle choices."[97] This sense of a person who lives outside—Tuttlemondo is careful to note that folks prefer the descriptor *living outside* to *homeless*—as a dog owner who should not be judged reveals a form of understanding well versed in funny kinds of love. Tuttlemondo points out that "people love animals regardless if they live inside or outside."[98]

Downtown Dog Rescue pays impound fees and medical bills, provides an address owners can use when obtaining dog licenses, and offers transportation to a vet, leashes and collars, dog food and training, and letters of recommendation for housing applications. These practices respond to how the lives of these dogs and owners, their ways of living and being, are shaped by intersections of racism, classism, sexism, speciesism, and, given the predominance of pit bull types, what I will call "breedism."[99] Moreover, these practices do not attempt to assimilate owners or dogs into normative or wholesome patterns of, say, home building and kinship, but rather encourage their continual disruption.

The work of Downtown Dog Rescue is attuned to becoming in kind; it is work whose politics is about understanding uneasy loves and facilitating their disruption of contemporary American conceptions of home, family, and family dog. This work is savvy to the use of dogs as victims to racialize and denigrate humans, and it is invested in helping pit bull–type dogs thrive without having to bring them into families and affirm their connections to an implicit and normative whiteness. Downtown Dog Rescues also understands that dogs love and are happy with folks who live outside: it recognizes that what is good for dogs, according to dogs themselves, is not necessarily a fenced backyard and pit bull–inclusive insurance. This is a work that pits kindness against kind. No community outreach efforts are ever innocent, but the work of Downtown Dog Rescue strikes me as uneasy and uncomfortable in a good way. It is this kind of work that I hope thinking with becoming in kind can encourage—work that I think makes for a better and jointly shared world, for it takes up the troubles identifiable through interspecies intersectionality and finds ways to encourage different ways of becoming in kind.

4

Queer Imaginings and Affiliative Possibilities

As we get near the grassy area, we see another dog, and all of my rewarding for responding to my cluck that I've been doing with Beth . . . falls apart—Beth only has eyes for the other dog. Cora brightens and says maybe we could try . . . arcing around the other dog with a treat in hand to lure Beth along. . . . I try this and it utterly fails—Beth is only intent on looking at/staring at this other dog. . . . Beth drags us to the grass, her favorite favorite thing, and proceeds to roll over and wriggle around in the greenness. We end up all sitting—or in Beth's case, lying down—on the grass . . . , and we play with Beth, doing "nose touch," "look," "sit," and "down." At one point, I pull Beth onto my lap and kiss her nose. This is really lovely and I think both of us enjoy it. It's also important because Cora and I have noticed that Beth has a strong tendency to ignore people, focusing entirely on other dogs and the environment around her. Getting her to show some form of affiliative behavior is a step up for sure.

While we're on the ground, a dog walks by, just as I have my arms around Beth. I squeeze her neck and hold a treat in front of her, telling her "look" and pointing at my eyes. She does this, and Cora is impressed, noting that Beth will do this in this context, in spite of being completely tuned out when we're out walking.

—AUTHOR FIELD NOTE, SPRING 2013

The above note documents my work with Cora, a white, middle-aged, upper-class straight woman, in taking Beth, a cow-colored pit bull–type dog we guesstimated to be about three years old, on a walk outside the shelter. We had first gone to an enclosed play area where we had worked on playing fetch. Throughout our interaction I had been working my hardest to get Beth to pay attention to me, making clucking noises and rewarding her with freeze-dried liver bits whenever she turned her head. Our goals with Beth were simultaneously complex, in that they were aimed at shaping Beth's behaviors through cues, such as a proffered palm eliciting a "nose touch," and relatively simple, in that we were trying to get Beth to engage, to attend to us, to relate, or, in dog-world speak, to evince "affiliative behavior."

In this chapter I attempt to extend my thinking-with dogs and humans through a paired sensibility and awareness that interrupts saviorist storyings and the types of becomings in kind detailed in the previous chapter. To do so I engage several senses of *affiliative* and *affiliation*. The first is the sense Cora and I were aiming for with Beth, a responsiveness and positive interest in interacting. This is significant for dogs in shelters because it is strongly tied to a dog's perceived adoptability—adopters tend to want dogs who like humans, even just a couple of them, rather than those who are seemingly disinterested. This sense of *affiliative* has everything to do with the bodily engagements, thinking-with, and movements of the sensibility I explore in chapter 2; it entails connecting and relating primarily through bodies and sensoria.

The second sense of *affiliation* I work through and draw from is that of affiliation as a belonging, but not necessarily a claiming: one can be affiliated with multiple political parties, for example, without having to claim just one of them. Less directly focused on bodies and behaviors, this second sense of *affiliation* operates between or among different practices, doings, or ways of understanding, without being associated with, say, the family. Further, while this usage of *affiliation* works as a neutral descriptor, my investment here is in queer affiliations, in Mel Chen's sense of *queer* as "social and cultural formations of 'improper affiliation.'"[1]

This chapter builds on the work of multiple queer theorists. In her early contributions to queer studies, Eve Kosofsky Sedgwick notes how "'queer' seems to hinge much more radically and explicitly on a person's undertaking particular, performative acts of experimental self-perception and filiation." Here *filiation* emerges as part of the practice of doing and claiming or, more ontologically understood, being queer.[2] The queer theorist Gayatri Gopinath describes "a queer diaspora" as acknowledging "the spaces of impossibility within the nation and their translation within the diaspora into new logics of affiliation."³ While I depart radically from the context in which Gopinath writes—hers is an interrogation of queer of color diasporic meaning-making in film and literature—I draw from her sense of *affiliation* in conjunction with *queer* as a means to identify new logics that might emerge where, in alternative renderings, there were spaces of impossibility.

In joining a very doggish sense of affiliation with specifically queer invocations of affiliations, I consider affiliations as *sensible* connectivities, with the potential to move away from what I term, following Chen, "proper" relatings, and toward *awareness* of the structures—violences, epistemes, norms—that undergird human-dog worlds. More specifically, identifying queer affiliations acts as my method in this chapter, disrupting saviorist storyings and the normative logics of becomings in kind, and, through attention to queer affiliations' very doggish sensibility and potential movement toward a more structural awareness, I aim to interrupt the "rational man" of an anthropocentric episteme. The queer affiliations endemic to human-dog worlds reveal alternative ways of understanding, the "logics" introduced by Gopinath, that hold promise for different patterns of relating, different ways of thinking, and different modes of building human-dog worlds.

Affiliation itself counters a move endemic to both queer studies and human-animal studies, which is the claiming of kinship and family as innately hopeful or promising. For example, some scholars point to the need for an embrace of a proliferative sense of kinship as a way to decenter the human and embrace a more-than-human connectivity—Donna Haraway names this with the phrase "make kin, not babies"—while gay and lesbian activists' slogan "Love makes a family" is widespread in the wake of the campaign for gay marriage.⁴ However, because conceptions of kinship and family emerge from particular histories of both settler colonialism and structures of racialization in the U.S., I find the terms themselves troubled and troubling in a way that makes me hesitate to use them. Indian boarding schools sought to erase Indigenous family formations and force children into a colonialist ideal of nuclear family formations. This same ideal is evident in white-normative policings of heterosexuality whereby denying the status of *family* to African Americans has yielded poverty, precarity, and state-sanctioned sterilization.

Kinship emerged from early anthropological approaches that were part and parcel of ongoing projects of colonization.[5]

Because of these histories and their present-day workings, my investment in identifying queer affiliations in human-dog—and dog-dog— relatings emerges from a desire to identify connectivities without reproducing or reifying the normative logics of the family home, the family, or kinship. I also continue the troubling of love with which I closed the previous chapter, for while the connectivities I examine are certainly imbued with and shaped by affect as a bodily movement and feeling, in the very haptic sense of the term, to call that affect *love* would miss the many ways that other feelings shape the relatings in question, as with Cora's and my concern and even worry for Beth. Finally, with queer affiliations I continue to trouble the problematic *like* or *as* logics often invoked in animal advocacy, whereby animal lives are ascribed value through rhetoric specific to race-related injustices, such as rabbit rescuers' claims to running a "Bunderground Railroad." These moves erase the actual humans whose experiences of violence and injustice they evoke.[6] With queer affiliations I hope, instead, to introduce alternative imaginings of how to think humans and nonhuman animals together in these worlds.

Queer affiliations can take many and varied forms. Above I describe a moment when Beth consents to rest in my lap and snuggle against me, even giving me her attention in the form of a "look" when another dog walks by. Keeping in mind that Beth is in no way "my" dog, or Cora's, what occurs in this moment is a form of intimacy, but one that falls well outside structures of family and kinship. We certainly connect physically— we touch, and I proffer a kiss. And we connect visually, for Beth gives me a "look" to the exclusion of focusing elsewhere. Our eyes meet, and we hold that gaze for several seconds. We are intimate and connected, and yet Beth will never become part of my kinship formation or participate in my domestic life. Ours is a public and temporary intimacy that, even though it involves kissing, certainly does not entail either home or family. It is, in key ways, an improper relating.

The geography of this moment also bears mentioning. The park in which we were sitting had been something of a gay cruising zone, primarily for working-class men, a practice that heavy policing had quelled. It was and remains a specific kind of public space where intimacies were and are deliberately constrained. Given the social and legal norms through which nonheterosexual contacts are heavily policed in public spaces—queer theorists Lauren Berlant and Michael Warner analyze this issue in discussing how heteronormativity was central to New York Mayor Rudy Giuliani's efforts to "clean the city up" by legislating the closure of gay sex shops, which was concomitantly an effort to close down a public culture of queer sex positivity—and the fact that such intimacies are increasingly relegated to private space— *Lawrence* v. *Texas* legalized sodomy, but only in the privacy of the home!—one could argue that Beth's and my cross-species connectivity, as a nonheterosexual intimacy undertaken in the public space of a park, was some kind of queer.[7] This type of connectivity— sensible intimacy outside the bounds of "proper" actions and locations— is one of many queer affiliations I explore in this chapter.

In what follows, I examine human-dog and dog-dog intimacies in popular culture as a means of both examining and troubling connections among queerness, family, and kinship. I take up the role of racisms in both hetero- and homonormative formations in order to delineate the kind of queer theorizations I am invested in both avoiding and engaging. I then turn away from the politics and practices of visual recognition and into the sensory through fieldwork encounters. I explore the affective, queer affiliations engendered through positive-reinforcement (R+) approaches to dog training and interaction. More negative affiliations at work in temporalities and geographies then lead me to the question of refusals of relating.

A Certain Kind of Queer

The term *queer* holds many different meanings, and only some of them align with my argument. I want to give something of my own intellectual genealogy in this regard, both personal and cultural. When I began this project, I focused on my own practices of human-dog relating, first with Haley and then with Annie (Haley passed in 2014). To me, both Haley and Annie, like many queer and trans* folks I knew, seemed to be cut off from their families and placed, instead, in makeshift networks that involved, if not the overt choice one might find with "chosen families," at the least, necessity; I read ours as queer relatings. In witnessing the disgust and dismay with which some scholars reacted to Donna Haraway's description of kissing her dog, Cayenne, in her *Companion Species Manifesto*, I saw in these makeshift kinships a disruption of the staid politics of the Anthropocene, wherein only human-human intimacies merit recognition and acceptance.[8] And—rather hopefully and naively—I thought that many practices of human-dog familiarity, or of becoming-familiar and becoming-family, held at their core a kind of queer deviance: they countered a larger culture where an adage delightfully phrased by a former student, "straight until proven gay," seemed to hold.[9] In a world where virtually every film and TV show involves heterosexual romance, where visibly gendered deviance is frequently met with violence—that is, in an overwhelmingly heteronormative world—I found hope in these relatings.

A wealth of examples from popular culture support this reading of human-dog connections as potentially queer. In a prominent publicity move in February 2019, staff at the Kennebac Valley Humane Society in Maine staged a wedding between two elderly, bonded pit bull–type dogs, dubbed "Jack" and "Diane" by staff, whose original owner(s) they had been unable to locate. The "bride" wore a white collar and a gauze veil that resembled a cape, while the "groom" was decked out in a black and pink necktie over his blue martingale collar. The happy couple were encouraged to pose for photos by staff dangling treats in front of their noses, their leashes visible in the background even as the humans holding them were hidden.[10] Meant to ensure that the two dogs would be adopted together, the dogs' marriage makes sense as such in the context of an era that postdates a lengthy gay-marriage campaign and its legitimation by the U.S. Supreme Court: the bond of "marriage," more than any other kind of marker, cemented and made visible a form of connection—the dogs' mutual bond—that might otherwise go unnoticed. And at a time when stories about animals are perceived as offering respite from a depressing political reality, the dogs' story circulated far and wide. The story's celebration of the institution of marriage via dogs seemingly demonstrated a joyous extension and even transposition of human-specific practices of making kinship and family legible. This move could be read as queering marriage itself, especially in light of common conservative reactions that condemn gay marriage on the basis that it will lead to marrying nonhuman animals.[11] Jack and Diane could be read as standing together at the top of a slippery slope!

The politics undergirding the Kennebac Shelter's decision are also evident in a 2014 Subaru commercial titled "In the Dog House." In it, a car containing a dog "family"—consisting of a longer-coated golden retriever (the "father" and driver), a yellow Labrador (the "mother" and front-seat passenger), and two golden Labrador–type puppies in the backseat—drives up to a stop sign. While the car is stopped, a female poodle (the lack of belly fur reveals no penile sheath) saunters across the crosswalk, and the "father" watches her movements to the accompaniment of the song "Je t'aime." The "mother" emits a low growl from the passenger seat, and the "father" seemingly reluctantly turns "his" eyes back to the road as the vehicle moves through the intersection. The intertitles "Dog Tested" and "Dog Approved" appear on the screen, which then fades to white with the word "LOVE" in bold black type. This in turn vanishes in a swoop, to be replaced by the Subaru logo.[12]

This ending to the commercial shifts its meaning rather markedly. The "Barkley" family are certainly represented as heterosexual through both their setup in the car—the "dad" as driver and therefore lead decision-maker, the "mom" as the more passive passenger, and the "kids" in the back—and the ogling of the poodle represents a simulta-neous violation and affirmation of the norms of monogamous straight marriage. But the invocation of love "unstraightens" this family. Subaru has a long history of coded advertising that targets gay and lesbian con-sumers, and it was one of the first major companies to offer benefits such as healthcare to same-sex partners. The "LOVE" text conjoins the dogs of the commercial with the larger political movement for gay mar-riage, the central slogan for which was "Love is love."[13]

Connections of family and intimacy with queerness are also evident in rescue and pit bull advocacy. For example, articles linking gay rights to dog rescue feature pictures of "these amazing pets and the parents who saved them." One adopter notes that he is grateful for the chance to help these animals have "a chance of being who they were born to be," echoing the language of the "authentic" and "true" self that circulates widely in LGBT advocacy.[14] Many rescue and advocacy organizations bring dogs to gay pride parades: BADRAP has marched in the San Francisco Gay Pride Parade since 2002. The straight couple that founded the organization march in honor of a gay friend with AIDS who was evicted from his build-ing because his service dog was a pit bull type.[15]

These examples seemingly evince a queerness common to dog-dog and human-dog intimacies, with gay marriage in particular standing out as a practice that has wriggled its way into an enthusiastic embrace. However, they also fit well within contemporary and deeply normative notions of family and domesticity, the very terms I trouble at the outset of this chapter. I am reminded of a post on the satirical website The Onion featuring a fictitious interview with a golden retriever, titled "Dog Doesn't Consider Itself Part of Family"; such a denial of kinship or intimacy illuminates the norm it satirizes.[16] Further, the kinds of intimacies and family formations involved in these labors are subtended by the ways that sexuality—queer or no—is shaped by and works as a "vehicle of articulation," to reference Sarah Lamble and Gail Mason's writings, of racial and colonial formations.[17] The connections valorized in these representations and practices are deeply involved in larger structural projects and attendant violences, particularly white supremacy.

While the close of the Subaru commercial seemingly embraces nonnormative families, the choice of dog breeds featured—golden retriever- and golden Labrador–type dogs and the anonymous poodle—points to a racial subtext. The humans most prominently associated with these breeds of dog are white. Poodles are additionally read as highly feminized. Thus, the love the commercial embraces, putting doggie-style heterosexuality in the service of sloganized gayness, rests on a norm of whiteness. Indeed, this commercial would signify quite differently if it had instead featured black Labradors, or brindled American Pit Bull Terriers, or Jack Russell Terriers (which is not to say that such breeds would not raise their own problematic connections).

It is tempting to argue that queerness emerges with any action that signals, "Take that, heteronormativity!" While heteronormativity certainly entails the policing of visibly gay and lesbian acts, such as LGBT-positive literature being proffered in schools, it is also fundamentally a racial and colonial project.[18] As the political theorist Cathy Cohen describes in her essay "Punks, Bulldaggers, and Welfare Queens," heteronormativity deems deviant not just overtly lesbian, gay, and queer kin formations and their attendant sexualities, but also those of nominally straight people of color—as in Ronald Reagan's denigration of "welfare queens"—whose heterosexuality is highly regulated by the state in light of its perceived deviance from nuclear family–style, tacitly white- and settler-normative kinship.[19] Nonconsensual sterilizations—colloquially known as "Mississippi appendectomies"—were widely practiced in the southern United States into the late 1970s. These sterilizations were motivated by the perception that the sexuality of Black and brown women was "wild" and "uninhibited" and warranted regulation.[20] This attempted genocide demonstrates how heteronormativity deems deviant not just gay and lesbian acts, but also the sexualities and sexual activities of people of color.

I also want to question the embrace of marriage invoked in Jack and Diane's example. Marriage emerges from the recognition of particular kinds of families and kinship units to the exclusion of others. These connections are evident in critiques that highlight problems with not only heteronormativity but also homonormativity.[21] For example, in a collective interview, the scholars Marlon Bailey, Priya Kandaswamy, and Mattie Udora Richardson answer the question "Is gay marriage racist?" with a resounding "Yes!" Richardson points to the way marriage "has been used against African American people," in particular, as "an impossible standard of two-parent nuclear household that pathologizes the extended families that are integral to both . . . African ancestral and African American cultural lives." Even when marriages are recognized, they have done little to protect "Black families from destructive state interventions like incarceration and the seizure of children."[22] Analogously to Cohen's thinking on heteronormativity, Richardson finds that marriage not only fails to provide protection from a racist state and social order but is also frequently weaponized against African American communities in order to deem other kinship formations deviant. Further, as Kandaswamy notes, "In the U.S., race is the strongest predictor of whether or not the state chooses to recognize your parental ties," for "Black families are the most likely of any racial group to be disrupted by Child Protection authorities." Marriage, she observes, "doesn't protect straight Black families from having their children taken away."[23]

Building on these insights, one can also look to the material violences faced by many LGBTQ* people. Houselessness resulting from family rejection is a huge problem—roughly 40 percent of houseless youth identify as LGBTQ* (a statistic that predates the 2020 COVID-19 pandemic)—and it remains legal to discriminate against LGBTQ* people in housing, employment, and, increasingly, health care. Gay marriage has done virtually nothing to change this situation.[24] The extension of marriage to lesbian, gay, and bisexual humans serves to uphold normative family formations—white, socioeconomically secure, monogamous, normatively gendered—while ignoring the needs of the more marginalized members of the LGB community.

Critiques of gay marriage and homonormativity are nothing new: the ascension of marriage-based politics simply reflects a long-standing trend in U.S.-based gay and lesbian activisms of ignoring and even reinforcing injustices arising from race, settler colonialism, and class. The work of the Asian American Studies scholar David Eng furthers my critique of the more homonormative flavors of queer. Eng explores how the "increasingly normative vision of acceptable queer identity and lifestyle" of LGBTQ* advocacy has facilitated an increasing concentration of whiteness and property in the family as an affective unit in the U.S.[25]

For Eng, the "racialization of intimacy" emerges through a division between public and private inaugurated by capitalism. Specifically, capitalism produces a family unit firmly seated in a private sphere, divorced from the public space of political life and waged labor, as the primary and therefore proper locus for the emotional life of individual subjects. Given that the transatlantic slave trade and various projects of colonization were critical to the emergence of capitalism—the transition from feudalism depended on an extractive global economy of death and violence that inaugurated race as we now know it—Eng's writing leans on what the critical race and ethnic studies scholar Cedric Robinson terms "racial capitalism."[26] For Eng, the family unit produced by racial capitalism demarcates a white-normative space, especially in law.

Eng's central example is *Lawrence v. Texas*, the 2003 U.S. Supreme court case that legalized sodomy (in the private sphere of the home). Eng notes that the case began not with a concern about sodomy per se but with a call to the police about a "n—— going crazy with a gun" in a backyard. The case emerged from what Eng terms "intimacy as a racialized property right": an intimacy in which whiteness shapes the geographies of family and home, and undergirds and legitimizes intimate contact on the grounds that it occurs on private property.[27] Put another way, the case would not have proceeded if it hadn't been for the perception that an African American man was trespassing—the marking of a nonwhite body as out of place by the racialization of the suburban family home. Thus to see the case solely as a landmark decision in favor of gay rights is to occlude the way that race, and the norms of whiteness and class, played a role in its inception. For Eng, such occlusions are writ large in contemporary gay and lesbian politics and their concomitant homonormative craftings of home and family.

To build on Eng's thinking, one might also consider the "like race" thinking so prominent in gay and lesbian advocacy. Many in the queer community viewed *Obergefell v. Hodges*, the 2015 U.S. Supreme Court case that legalized gay marriage, as "our *Loving*," referencing the landmark 1967 *Loving v. Virginia* case that legalized interracial marriage. However, as Eng and the queer studies scholar Siobhan Somerville note, the *Loving* decision was handed down within months of a decision directly bearing on gay rights. In the 1967 case *Boutilier v. INS* (Immigration and Naturalization Services), the court not only rejected the petition of the openly gay Canadian Clive Boutilier for U.S. citizenship but also ordered his deportation on the grounds of his being an "alien homosexual" and therefore by definition a "psychopathic personality."[28] Claims to *Obergefell* as parallel to *Loving* thus ignore the fact that the same court that arbitrated *Loving* had shored up specifically heterosexual claims to legitimacy and citizenship not long before. In addition, invocations of *Loving* as a parallel ignore the racial realities Richardson and Kandaswamy detail. In spite of *Loving*, equality under the state has never been realized for communities of color in the U.S., as the Black Lives Matter movement makes clear. Moreover, as wonderfully detailed in Kami Chisholm's 2016 film *Pride Denied*, the *Obergefell* decision grounded the "right" to marriage in the desire of the extremely wealthy to avoid taxation: the plaintiffs in *Obergefell* sued primarily on the basis that an individual inheriting property after the death of a loved one to whom they were not allowed to be married incurred higher taxes than a widowed spouse.[29] Put plainly, the decision helped shore up intergenerational wealth in the hands of an almost entirely white citizenry whose ancestors were never subject to redlining, land seizure, genocide, or related practices.

Many seemingly queer connectivities enact a politics that elides injustices related to race, settler colonialism, and class. Marrying a pair of dogs in a manner that echoes the politics of a larger movement for gay marriage reinforces rather than questions the ways marriage itself works to reinforce norms of whiteness, class, and gender. For many, gay pride parades symbolize not a joyful claiming of public space as queer, and therefore safe for the many whose deviance from social norms positions them this way, but rather a "pinkwashing," a corporate takeover with the goal of profit, often at the expense of the most marginalized members of the LGBTQ* community. For example, when the very corporate entities whose real-estate purchases and predatory business practices have been central to the gentrification that has driven many residents out of historically gay, lesbian, trans*, Latinx, and Black neighborhoods in the San Francisco Bay Area are brought in as supposedly staunch supporters of the LGBTQ community via sponsorship of pride celebrations, many constituents have cried foul, arguing that this sponsorship ignores and covers over—"washes"—the ways those same corporations actively harm marginalized communities.[30] In addition, the deployment of pride as an occasion for municipal and corporate profiteering elides the history of LGBTQ* social movements: the first pride event was a riot, not a corporate-sponsored, police-led explosion of glitter.[31] Given these concerns, the incorporation of pit bull advocates and various rescue dogs into pride festivities signals not some kind of queerly liberatory claiming of cross-species deviant kinships in a larger tradition of antistate protest, nor a kind of queerly deviant reclaiming of public space, but rather their assimilation into homonormative discourses wherein LGBT family formations participate in rather than interrupt structural violences, particularly those enjoined by the state.

Finally, these ostensibly queer extensions of kinship and intimacy erase the sensibility I highlight in this book. Positioning dogs *as* humans, that is, marking dogs' participation in human kinship formations through practices specific to human-style, state-based recognitions of family, obscures how dogs themselves experience relating. The Subaru ad characterizes dogs' experiences of relating in terms of human kin relations, such as *mother* and *brother*, and elides the fact that such language means literally nothing to dogs. Depicting dogs as participating in human patterns of relationship entails an erasure and overcoding rather than an articulation of their own ways of relating.

Moreover, the kin-oriented claim made by gay adopters, of facilitating dogs' becoming who "they were born to be," collates canine experiences into a particular narrative endemic to LGBTQ activism today. Such language draws from assertions of an individual and seemingly natural truth of nonheterosexuality that merely needs to "come out" and find spaces of affirmation in order for an individual to exercise what is viewed as freedom. However, these assertions are specifically Western and Anglo-normative. The "freedom" of "coming out" is almost exclusive to those who are gender-normative and white, for gender norms are themselves white-normative: think of the politics of "good hair" as tied to femininity, with dreadlocks or locs thus always already gender-deviant. Further, much like representing a dog as a child, pulling a dog into such an understanding of ostensibly queer "truth" erases and overcodes what it might mean to a dog herself to be, well, anything.

The sense of *queer* that I engage, then, is not one of pride parades or corporate-sponsored sales of rainbow-themed merchandise. Nor is it the kind of queer evoked in the campaigns for gay marriage and related homonormative politics. It is a sense of queer evinced by one of my favorite buttons, "Not gay as in happy, but queer as in fuck you"—that is, queer as a political stance oriented toward changing a staid and hetero- and homonormative world. But it is also a sense of queer that understands hetero- and homonormativity as white supremacist projects. This is a sense of queer that engages with queer of color theorizing, a field with a genealogy in many ways distinct from early interventions in the field of queer studies. The theorist Roderick Ferguson positions queer of color theories as emerging more directly from the material attentions to difference that are endemic to scholarship about and by women of color and, in fact, counter to the largely white-normative understandings pervasive in early queer studies discourses. Queer of color theorizing engages the production of sexuality and gender as racial and colonial projects.[32] And while I am a white transperson, I hope that my own queer interventions in this writing honor and contribute to larger conversations in both queer studies and queer of color scholarship.

About-Face

Most of the examples I have given in this chapter involve looking, being looked at, and categorizing looks. The critiques I leverage, such as that of the problematic whiteness of the family imaginings in the Subaru commercial, involve a practice of reading that begins with looking. However, much of today's lesbian, gay, and, increasingly, trans activism also leans on a politics of visibility whose approach goes something like this: "If more gay, lesbian, and trans* folks become visible, our social worlds will become more accepting." The thinking here twins visibility with political change, as if one necessarily entails the other. For example, promotional material for the "trans day of visibility" describes the event as a day "dedicated to celebrating the accomplishments and victories of transgender & gender non-conforming people while raising awareness of the work that is still needed to save trans lives."[33] And yet being seen and read—or, "clocked," in the language of the transgender studies scholar Eric Stanley—often has the opposite effect: rather than increasing acceptance, it frequently leads to violence and even death, with trans women of color being the most vulnerable and most frequently targeted.[34] Further, as is evident from the comments section of virtually any online article centered in a trans* person's experience of this kind of violence, media coverage of such incidents frequently generates even more bellicosity. Thus actions centered in a politics of visibility can effectively reinforce rather than challenge the political status quo for marginalized LGBTQ* people. One way to address this problem is to move away from it and go, well, elsewhere. This is, in part, my aim in focusing on sensibility and awareness.

For scholars of animal studies, questions of looking also index what could be described as failed philosophical projects. For example, looking at animals brings to mind not only Jacques Derrida's naked staring at his cat in "The Animal That Therefore I Am," but also the work of Emmanuel Levinas, whose writings on ethics are rooted in an openness to and responsibility for the other in facing the other.[35] Not surprisingly, Levinas had thoughts about dogs as well, noting that although "the phenomenon of the face is not in its purest form in the dog, . . . one cannot entirely refuse the face of an animal."[36] The philosopher David Clark takes Levinas to say that "the animal both has and does not have a face."[37] Many question the implicit humanism of both philosophical interventions: why are human faces privileged for Levinas, and why does Derrida end up talking entirely about himself and not at all about what interests his cat?[38] Further, in many ways the humanism at work here is the same brand detailed in chapter 2, wherein the rational man is constructed through the crafting of his Others as animal. To decenter this sense of the human and engage in a different kind of politics, I now make an about-face into the *sensible*.

A key aspect of the dog *Umwelten* I discuss in chapter 2 lies in approaches to sociality. As I like to remind friends and family who take offense when dogs present them with their rear ends, most dogs live in a "butt culture." When two dogs meet head on, they are quick to turn and sniff the other end. The loose-bodied, curving approach of dogs sniffing each other's behinds is often the first step to their becoming acquainted, and is certainly part of how they come to recognize each other.[39] Butts and smells are central to the ways dogs come to know the worlds and the cultures, canine and human, in which they participate: that is, butts are key to the meaning-making, the semiotics, of dog *Umwelten*.

Additionally, butt cultures underscore the primacy of olfaction in dog *Umwelten*. Scenting involves molecular contact: to smell is to engage a process of sensory recognition initiated by the work of scent receptors on contact with chemicals and molecules inhaled through the nose. Dogs, unlike humans, utilize an auxiliary olfactory organ in the roofs of their mouths: the vomeronasal organ, also known as Jacobson's nose, through which they taste as much as smell, especially pheromones. Dogs engage their vomeronasal organs through both the flehmen response—visible when a dog's jaws opens loosely, the corners of the mouth curl slightly, and she draws in air through her mouth—and the licking of their noses or external objects. Through these actions they take in larger molecules (often pheromones) in what could be described as a mode of tasting.[40] The ability to switch between using this organ and the nose what enables dogs to track scents: by switching, they do not become acclimated to a scent the way humans do (consider your friend whose house smells overwhelmingly of cat litter to you, but not to them). If a dog closely sniffs you and closes the interaction with a short lick of your skin, you have likely been the object of the vomeronasal organ in action![41] I highlight this commingling of scenting and tasting because while I and many of the people I think with have spent a lot of time looking at dogs' faces, we have also done our fair share of kissing those faces, and, crucially, being kissed and therefore being scented and tasted ourselves. Through these processes various signifiers that are, at once, part of us and indexical to who we are—including our pheromones—are brought into contact with dogs by being brought inside them. Most humans already participate in canine meaning-making through scenting that is at once tasting and sensory signification, building understandings in ways that transcend the visual.

In their crafting of meaning, common human-dog interactions frequently go beyond "looking" in that they also involve tactile actions such as petting heads, rubbing bellies, and scratching butts. All of these contacts are part and parcel of the sensibility I identify as a means to better think-with dogs, for while humans lack vomeronasal organs, we certainly participate not only in dogs' use of this organ but a range of intimate contacts rooted in touch, contact, smell, and taste. These intimacies are central to the work of thinking-with dogs. Further, they ground a sensibility rooted not in looking but in a more haptic way of meeting and responding to the world, one that promises not only a way out of politics as usual but also an engagement with a queer potentiality attuned to both bodies and an awareness of structural formations. And while these faceless, unlooking connections may fit within the parameters of normal families and homes—dog butt cultures, belly rubbing, and ear licking, are at work everywhere, including heteronormative homes sporting picket fences and 2.5 children—they also belie this fit, revealing intimacies and relatings that are not quite intimate in the way that Eng critiques, connectivities that are, in fact, promisingly queer affiliations.

In pointing to the faceless intimacies of butt culture and the pervasive haptic and otherwise sensory intimacies of human-dog relatings, I want to highlight and think with the metaphor *stray*. This is the label applied to many dogs as they enter animal shelters and to the journeys they have undergone. Dogs who have moved out of the kinship ties that are named by *family* and *home*, whether or not of their own volition, are frequently described as having gone *astray*. Interspecies contacts without the usual forms of recognition are promisingly queer comings together that have the potential to go "astray" from the normative tropes and politics I outline. *Stray* and *strayings* are apt ways to describe the workings of the queer affiliations I identify. Strayings delineate how, even within a larger normative landscape—the settler colonial mappings of land that subtend the existence of animal shelters, for example—there still exist connectivities, ways of doing and being, ways of relating, that depart from such mappings. In what follows, I explore an array of human-dog and dog-dog relatings that emerge through and expand on the haptics of butt cultures and other sensory intimacies, revealing sensible connectivities that diverge and stray. These strayings promise alternative logics, understandings, and worlds.

Bailey

To begin to demonstrate the promisingly queer affiliations I locate in in human-dog and dog-dog intimacies and their strayings from normative families, homes, and related politics, I turn to another pit bull story. During my fieldwork in an animal shelter, I spent hundreds of hours walking with, playing with, cleaning up after, caring for, and snuggling with pit bull–type dogs. I also interviewed other shelter volunteers as well as shelter staff and members of the general public who entered the shelter. In these encounters I noticed two practices of relating, two modes of affiliation specific to the shelter context, in which faceless recognition and inhuman intimacies run thick. It is difficult to render these forms of affiliating into language—after all, they are rooted in an alternative semiotics of touch and movement. I loosely and clumsily classify them as "intimacy without relatedness" and "relatedness without kinship." Both demarcate promisingly queer affiliations, and both are reflected in the case of Bailey, one of the dogs who came into the shelter as a stray in April 2013.

Bailey is a handsome grey pit bull-type dog whose broad chest, lean hips, and tendency to prance when moving at a trot had me making *Zoolander* male-model jokes soon after I met him. When he underwent his evaluation walk with a fellow volunteer, she noted that he seemed interested in other dogs, but not leash-reactive; he leaned toward them but did not bark or lunge. His manners in general were very good for a shelter dog, and he was quite affectionate; his affiliative tendencies, especially toward humans, were strong. His main vice was tennis balls: when he had one in his mouth, he refused to be parted from it. As this behavior, known as resource guarding, can often be changed through training, a number of us planned to work with him.

In spite of, or possibly because of, his behavioral issues, many of us became attached to Bailey. As a shelter favorite, he went on walks and cuddled with numerous volunteers, practices of relating that were documented on the "walk card" on the front of his kennel and in conversations volunteers shared about him. I took him out a number of times, and each time, we would settle on a bench by a small body of water. He would lean into me and occasionally clamber onto my lap. This was usually followed by a thorough cleaning of one of my ears from his tongue in which his touch and my taste mingled. As his head came to rest on my chest, I would often let out a sigh that he echoed. Just for that moment of relaxation, we moved together. This sense of closeness did not come out of staring into each other's eyes. Nor did it emerge from the recognition of a name, for shelter dogs whose histories are unknown are usually given new names on their arrival. Rather, this was a momentary, provisional closeness, an ephemeral contact rooted in the feeling of moving and resting together.

Notes on Bailey's walk card—"a sweetie," "likes snuggles"—revealed that my experiences with Bailey were similar to those of many volunteers. However, Bailey stayed at the shelter. He did not become part of any one person's home, even as one volunteer affectionately referred to him as "my boyfriend."[42] The touching and caring he experienced, and the responsive attention he gave back, were all forms of an intimacy disjoined from family, much like the experiences I describe with Beth. For half an hour or so every day, he connected with the humans who took him out, leaning on them, moving with them, snuggling and playing with them, after which they put him back in his kennel, then returned to their own homes and, often, their own dogs. In this intimacy without family, in these fleeting, touching relatings unique to shelter contexts, there is a promising mode of connecting, an intimacy without relatedness.

Bailey was fortunate to come to the shelter not long after it began running playgroups, a recent development in many U.S. animal shelters. A typical shelter play session begins with two dogs and can include more, although the Shelter Playgroup Alliance, an innovator in the field, strongly encourages limiting interactions to two dogs.[43] This play is intensely physical, involving play bows—an enthusiastic lowering of the front of the body with an elevated butt and wagging tail to accentuate the gesture—as well as gently mouthing or more toothily grabbing each other's necks or faces or even ankles, humping (although we tried to discourage this behavior), bumping into other dogs' bodies, chest bumping, throwing paws over the other dog's shoulders, and other behaviors. Like much play among other mammals, dog play entails a lot of practice of fighting maneuvers and other social behaviors, but it is punctuated by "check-ins" that establish that the encounter is still play and not something more serious.[44] Dog interactions involve a fair bit of looking: a hard stare was enough to make us decide not to let two dogs meet. But that decision was based not only in the hardness of that stare and unbreaking eye contact, but also in other warning signs, such as a frozen or very still body.

When we first brought Bailey into the playgroups, we introduced him to Peanut, a young grey female pit bull type. We began by taking them out on a tandem walk, during which Bailey put Peanut at ease, or, in one the words of another volunteer (a thirty-something white middle-class woman), "acted like a gentleman."[45] At the end of the walk, we let them play, leashes attached. Over the next several weeks we introduced Bailey to Eliza, with whom he played very well, and to a number of other dogs. There were occasional rude moments of humping, but also play bows and nudgings and mouthings. As Bailey developed relationships with other dogs through their slobbery, exuberant contacts, their encounters revealed a form of connecting that was both temporary and intimate, close but not kin, an affiliation that strays from narratives of family, another form of "intimacy without relatedness."

Bailey's possessiveness about tennis balls had landed him on the list of dogs to be euthanized. Such behaviors are considered unsafe because dogs might interact poorly with children and their toys. He was not an ideal candidate for a family with children, queer or otherwise. The foster team stepped into action. Countless emails were sent out, and he ended up in a temporary foster placement with Shanna, who immediately began working on his behavior by giving him balls and, when he relinquished them, rewarding him with treats and giving the balls right back, so that he began to understand that the loss of a ball is temporary, not forever, and a tasty loss at that. She also took Bailey to training classes and continued to bring him to playgroup. Shanna was only one of Bailey's many advocates: a group of five women planned his walks, feeding, and training through an elaborate communal schedule. This shared labor was especially notable because these volunteers had not socialized much with each other before. Through Bailey, these humans and various practices of care came together.

Bailey's foster situation speaks to the relatedness without kinship at the heart of much animal advocacy. There is intimacy, affection, and undoubtedly love in these relationships; but these are funny kinds of love and different ways of doing intimacy, for the goal in a foster home is to prepare the dog for another home, a "forever home." When people foster dogs, they bring them into relationships with humans and, often, other dogs and even cats, all the while striving to find them other relationships, other families, in other homes (although an increasing number of foster situations are foster-to-adopt, a kind of trial run for the dog in question, and the term *foster fail*, meaning a dog taken in with the intent to foster who is then adopted into that same foster home, is widespread in dog worlds). Providing a foster home may involve forging partnerships with other people to care for a dog throughout the day. These are not your average friendships, for they entail working together to keep a dog alive. These volunteers are not a family. Rather, they are a network cemented through relationships of care. There is kindness here, but not kinship.

Of course, Bailey was also placed in a situation where the norms of whiteness and hetero- and homonormative family values held sway. For example, the shelter volunteer's reference to Bailey's "gentlemanliness" indicates a recuperative reading of his behavior with reference to a classed and racialized descriptor. No longer "astray," he is linguistically incorporated into respectability politics, deemed "suitable for a family home"—a narrative, in all of its tacit whiteness, so central to shelter adoptions. And the gendered longing indexed by the label "boyfriend" underscores this work, for it positions him, albeit playfully, as appropriate for kin-claiming by a mostly white, straight, female, upper-middle-class shelter volunteer network.

These snippets of commentary reflect what Cindy, a shelter volunteer who fits this profile, observed in response to a question about the current landscape of pit bull politics: "I think that there are more people who are accepting of the breed than there used to be." Noting that they are now more common "as pets" than before, she adds that it's now common to "see them on the street with young techies," that "people are like, 'Oh!' You know what I mean? In my mind, those are good people, so they have a pit bull. Maybe it's not such a bad dog. You know what I mean?"[46] Cindy's reference to "techies," an affluent, largely white group whose growth has forced into houselessness hundreds of thousands of working-class, marginalized urban dwellers throughout the U.S., many of them people of color, underscores the connections operating in Bailey's recuperation. Casting Bailey as boyfriend material reflects his movement into white- and middle-class normative spaces.

Yet the touches, contacts, and practices of relating in Bailey's story are promising in that they highlight a sensibility, a way of affiliating through means that certainly include but are not at all limited to vision. Further, these are not anthropocentric practices. There are no words to describe exactly what goes on in these fleeting contacts between dog and human, partly because the anthropocentric work of language and representation simply cannot parse their haptic, olfactory, and auditory aspects. The nuzzles, touches, licks, butt culture, shared sighs, and nudges stray from the visually oriented nature of an anthropocentric politics of representation, revealing joint doings and moments of togetherness that belie a strong division between self and other. In the licking and smelling, the dogs' noses and vomeronasal organs bring the taste of the other within. This is a promising, touching affiliation.

Like Beth's and my intimacy, these contacts are also interestingly queer. Even as Bailey's imagined future hinges on particular notions of family, his present existence involves connectivities, however local, that fall outside the norms of any kind of family at all. And while his "gentlemanliness" bespeaks this imagined domestic future, his many contacts and the intimacies with those around him occur not in a home at all, but rather in an animal shelter, an institution. In these relatings, these sensible connectivities, emerges the kind of queerness described by Chen: "an array of subjectivities, intimacies, beings, and spaces located outside of the heteronormative," which Chen characterizes as "exceptions to the conventional ordering of sex, reproduction, and intimacy."[47]

This is a queerness that reflects the musings of Michel Foucault, who, while decidedly not a contributor to queer of color theorizations, counters family-style narratives in arguing that state recognition of same-sex relationships is "only a first step," and that in fact "we should fight against the impoverishment of the relational fabric" and work to secure "provision for relations of provisional coexistence."[48] It is a queerness reflected in the anthropologist Elizabeth Povinelli's argument for the disentanglement of what she terms "genealogical and intimacy grids," that is, for the disconnecting of intimate acts and practices from mappings of kinship and for, instead, the valorization of, say, fucking that happens without connections to kissing, family, or even partnership.[49]

The "intimacy without relatedness" and "relatedness without kinship" of Bailey's story demarcate an understanding of queer that works without conventional family, without even "chosen families." Further, these provisional, faceless touchings involve a different kind of recognition from that of the family-style politics I critique above, one not rooted in the state and one that cannot easily be seen or made visible, but rather must be felt or smelled or tasted. A different butt culture from that historically associated with the casual cruisings of gay masculinities, these contacts, in their facelessness, are queer nonetheless. The momentary, fleeting contacts centered in touches, tastes, movements, and shared rhythms, in their strayings from the norms of family and home that imbue rescue and shelter work, reveal promisingly queer affiliations.

Queerly Affiliative Bodyings

The joint sighing I describe in my interactions with Bailey, this momentary moving together, is certainly not unique to our encounters: it exemplifies the sensory contacts enjoyed by many of us who live or work with dogs. This jointness frequently transcends the haptic—often when I have been stretching on the floor close to my current dog, Annie, her deep sigh cues my own, even when we are not actually touching. Less stoic than Haley, Annie is an "emotionally available" dog. And this availability stems in part from her attention to my own emotional state. For example, in the months following the death of my father, she seemed to anticipate my spates of crying, along with those of my mother and brother, frequently approaching and leaning against us to solicit interaction and, if we permitted, bestowing liberal face licks. And while these interactions often ended with physical contact—I remember my brother standing in the kitchen wiping his tears on her fur—they began with her attention to us from a distance.

I am interested in the kinds of affective travels and concomitant movements of bodies—*bodyings*—that emerge through human-dog relatings. There is a jointness to these, certainly, with shared sighs and the lick-ish outreach Annie practices, but this affective travel is also evident in the sensory work of the bodyings that emerge through the training practices common to the sensibility on which this book leans. One example is leash reactivity, when a dog barks and lunges at other dogs, humans, bicycles, and so on when leashed to a human. In the world of positive reinforcement (R+)-style training, in which dogs' own emotional states are paramount, such behaviors are understood to emerge not from aggression but from the dogs' fear of being unable to escape from a perceived threat. In R+ approaches, this fear is countered through practices of *desensitization*—encountering the feared object in a muted form while the dog stays "under threshold" (not overwhelmed by fear), and making sure that excellent things happen to the dog during these encounters; and *counterconditioning*—introducing cues for other behaviors that are incompatible with barking and lunging, with rewards for the presentation of cued behaviors while ensuring the dog stays under threshold. Introducing an aversive measure in response to this type of behavior, such as the painful pinch of a prong collar, runs the risk of actually increasing the dog's fear of other dogs seen while on leash, because they are associated with discomfort and even pain.

I have worked extensively with Annie to counter her leash reactivity. We regularly go outside our house and over the varied terrain of sidewalk, street, and grass, and practice her many tricks on leash—Annie is an intermediate-level tricks dog, not to mention a total jock—with bountiful rewards when, instead of anxiously scanning her environment, she attends to me, or really to us. These tricks involve asking her to put her paws on different surfaces so that she will feel them and attend to her bodily feelings rather than the thing she fears. They also involve asking her to climb up stairs, onto wide, low concrete walls, and the like, as she tends to feel more confident when she is higher up. Her rewards vary, sometimes taking the form of small amounts of her dinner, or higher-value cheese and dried fish, and sometimes in the form of increasing the distance between us and the feared object. This latter reward follows from a popular R+ training approach introduced by the trainer and author Grisha Stewart, behavior adjustment therapy (BAT), which works by attempting to rewire a dog's brain by encouraging them to actively choose a method of self-soothing such as looking away, turning away, or sniffing the ground when confronted by a feared object.[50]

In Annie's and my perambulations, I am not entirely in charge—perhaps not in charge at all. Although I hold one end of the leash—which is ten feet long so as to minimize any tautness that might communicate tenseness to Annie—we engage in a choreography of ask and response. I give her a cue, not a command. And my cues generally take the form of hand or body signals, with only occasional voice-overs, because Annie, like most dogs, is oriented more toward reading my body than listening to my speech; this is a deeply bodied practice. And Annie can take a break from our work whenever she deems it appropriate. We have spent ten minutes or more in the middle of a training session with her rolling on her back like a bug in the grass of the nearby park, and I always reward her when she chooses to stop and sniff.

Our engagement through training thus operates through a politics at the center of many contemporary feminist discussions: consent.[51] The dog trainer Suzanne Dubnicka highlights how, in engaging R+ training, her dog "consents every time we work," meaning "she always has the choice to perform the behavior or not."[52] This practice of consent is fairly simple: when an "ask" for a behavior elicits that behavior, the consequence is a reward, while failure to perform a requested behavior simply results in the withholding of that reward. Through this choreography, what might seem a hierarchical practice becomes, instead, a two-way conversation, one enacted entirely through bodyings.

I never introduce these exercises on days I'm exhausted, for I have found that my own emotional availability is critical for Annie's learning. I need the "bandwidth" to keep a clear head, be receptive to and aware of what her body is saying, and attempt to steer her into and, ideally, keep her in a space of calm. I often spend some time engaging in deep breathing and relaxation exercises before we head out in order to ensure that my own body starts off well "below threshold."

The bodyings of affective contact over distance I describe here are not only ethical, especially given the role of consent, but also queerly affiliative. This is perhaps obvious, given that they are rooted in sensible connectivities that emerge fairly directly from the first and most doggish sense in which I define *affiliative*—a desire for contact and movement toward or together. However, I also find these bodyings to be fascinatingly queer because they expand on and work through a form of affective connecting that mitigates what I term, borrowing from Foucault, the paucity of an emotional fabric in our contemporary world orderings. Just as there are far too few terms for and ways of recognizing relationality— think of the expanse of connections between the descriptors *best friend* and *friend*—there are too few ways to describe the traffic and travel of feelings and emotions that make up and deeply shape these connectivities. Moreover, as a result of the racial capitalism critiqued by Eng and others, many feelings and the relationships they shape are deemed unfit for public spaces; and the feelings themselves are collated into and delimited by understandings that claim to merely describe them. For example, friends have jokingly referred to my work with Annie's leash reactivity as a "labor of love," and yet *love* strikes me as a remarkably empty signifier in contrast to the frustration, vivid attention, careful responses, efforts to project calmness, and conscious bodily movements that I experience and engage in while working with her. There is no language to describe the range and travel of emotions, or more aptly, affects—bodily movements that both evince and transmit feelings—in the emotional attunement and traffic of our practices, our thinkings together, especially as she experiences a range of feelings I will never be able to name.

In considering affective movements that emerge through the bodyings of R+ training relationships as queer, I am building on a common critique of marriage, gay or straight: that it privileges one form of relating as primary and central, to the exclusion of others. What of "best friends," or friendships that are neither best nor merely friends? Where do "fuck buddies" and the like fit into this mapping? While this criticism is centered on forms of relating, the affects that work with and through them are also key. Why should intimacy with others be disallowed after the formal recognition of the couple? Why should one be emotionally available only to a spouse and children? The affective intimacies of the bodyings of R+ training encounters, while situated within a fairly comfortable reach of the "home" and "family," also reveal connectivities through feelings that stray from them.

Another way to approach the question of the delimitation of feelings and the need to engage them otherwise emerges in the work of Audre Lorde. Writing about the problems of regarding the erotic as exclusively sexual, she argues that, rather, the erotic is a "creative energy" that is expressed in a range of forms, including "dancing, building a bookcase, writing a poem, examining an idea." Further, for Lorde, the erotic is present in emotional sharing of any kind, forming the joy that acts as "a bridge between the sharers, which can be the basis for understanding much of what is not shared between them, and lessens the threat of their difference."[53] Lorde's writings on this subject are both famous and famously misread. Many have taken her work as a call for sexual empowerment, but it is not (or not only) a call to embrace eros in its sexual sense, but rather to embrace the fullness of an erotic that is "a measure between the beginnings of our sense of self and the chaos of our strongest feelings."[54] For Lorde, the potentiality of these feelings and their transmission promises an alternative world, one that embraces difference rather than regarding it as an impediment. Lorde's understanding of the erotic pushes us not only to valorize those feelings that stretch and connect us, that bring fullness to the self and our relatings, but also to understand them as emerging in both the touch of a lover's body and the feeling of accomplishing a task we enjoy.

In taking up Lorde I am not claiming the erotic as somehow innate to the training practices I detail; rather I follow her thinking as a means to better describe what I find so fascinating and queer about the sensibility of these bodyings. Lorde helps me get at how the affective intimacies of R+ practices are so much more than love and much more interesting than the staid descriptors of *training* or *kinship* suggest. In these bodyings emerge alternative modes of feeling and affective communication that stretch the self and obscure the distinction and the difference between self and other. They give the satisfaction of accomplishing a difficult and important task, and they extend and confound what intimacy even means in the realm of the emotional.

To use my earlier and very clumsy signifiers, these connectivities could be referred to as intimacies without kinship, or perhaps intimacies that exceed kinship. However, I find that I prefer *bodyings* as a descriptor, for these affective intimacies are traceries of feelings that stray from the ideas of family and home in which they are seemingly rooted. And in their mutualistic demands for availability and accountability, in the ways the sensibility of their intimacies moves apart from the anthropocentric norm of human control and canine submission, I find a promisingly queer affiliation.

Finally, R+ approaches also feed into awareness. In firmly avowing an ethic of training that eschews punishment in any form other than deprivation of something the trainee enjoys, R+ approaches embrace a feminist ethics that extends well beyond human-dog worlds. Karen Pryor's inaugural work in the field, *Don't Shoot the Dog*, is replete with examples such as shaping an annoying roommate's behavior through the provision of human-specific rewards—by offering beer when a contentious cleaning task is completed—in place of more aversive methods such as yelling.[55] Proponents argue that R+ methods are "humane": the explicit move away from physical manifestations of violence yields a way of doing, of bodying, fundamentally at odds with a deeply violent political present. The demand for the recognition of and response to an Other's feelings seeds an awareness of the problems engendered by the array of violences constitutive of our current racist, misogynist, homophobic, transphobic, and colonialist social order. This bodily, queerly affiliative prompt to *awareness* gives me hope.

Out of Place and Time

The strayings I have traced thus far have been fairly positive. However, dog shelter and rescue worlds are also replete with connectivities that certainly move in alliance with *queer*—in the sense of deviant from a white supremacist heteronormativity, distinct from the kinships and families of the homonormative—in ways that are not necessarily hopeful at all. Below I address the work of queerly affiliative human-dog and dog-dog strayings that operate somewhat differently from those outlined above, working through the sensory in ways that are both more direct—such as doggish desires for sex—and more elusive—such as the sense of time involved in human and dog lives. These strayings, in approaching and sometimes crossing the norms that bound today's social order, tend to reveal not the potentially hopeful connectivities and concomitant production of the alternative ways of understanding I outline above, but rather the violent logics of said order, evident in stigmatization, harm, and narrowing proximity to, and sometimes literal, death.

Many shelter strays are read as the result of what is termed, with much condescension, "backyard breeding."[56] This terminology refers to the informal practice of breeding dogs, often pit bull-types, as additional sources of income by individuals who take up this work out of their homes, rather than through more formalized spaces such as registered kennels run by state-licensed operators. This terminology also indexes sensible connectivities—the intimacies of dog-dog desires for and engagement in sex—that are widely stigmatized as "out of place."

Generally regarded as a huge contributor to the population of unwanted dogs in urban and semiurban landscapes, backyard breeding certainly defies more formal and more geographically normative practices of biocapitalist production of dogs. However, the pejorative label *backyard breeder* is rooted more in breeders' disparate relationship to capitalism, class, and often race than to their specific practices. Given that all breeding operations monetize dogs, the condemnation of "backyard" operations demarcates a straying from the norms of capitalism—making the private into a space of biocapitalist production—and from the norms of Eng's "racialization of intimacy." And then there is the fact that the materiality of breeding practices belies the stigmatization of "backyards," an exploration of which begins my discussion here.

Condemnations of backyard breeding lean on an implicit comparison with purebred dogs acquired through more formally sanctioned routes. The negative connotations of the moniker *backyard* imply that purebred dogs are, by default, healthier and happier than their backyard-bred counterparts. This is not the case. For example, when bloggers warn that backyard breeders "breed dogs without taking the time to make good genetic matches," they ignore the fact that registered breeders frequently practice "line breeding"—matching sons to mothers, and daughters to fathers—a practice so widespread that those involved in regulating dog breeding argue for the necessity of determining the "coefficient of inbreeding," or CoI, before matching dogs. The very existence of the CoI underscores the suspect nature of supposedly "good" breeding practices. And criticisms of backyard breeders for failing to register dogs "with the appropriate kennel club or breed club" ignore the fact that such demarcations serve a gatekeeping function for an already limited gene pool, through which a propensity to breed from popular sires has led to widespread hereditary disorders. Furthermore, resistance to documentation of such hereditary disorders in purebred circles is formidable.[57] According to Sara, an interlocutor whose work in a range of shelter and rescue contexts gives her a unique background in assessing both purebred fanciers and rescue-oriented advocates, purebred dog breeding today is a "hot mess."[58] Anecdotal evidence suggests that issues with purebreds extend well beyond genetics. Sharon, an interlocutor whose consulting business focuses mainly on dogs who present with dangerous behavioral issues, noted that her business was equally divided between dogs coming from rescues and presumed backyard origins and dogs documented as purebred.[59]

Environment is also critical to the evaluation of breeding practices, and derisiveness toward backyard operations often insinuates that the backyard is inherently a bad environment for puppies. However, one of the central worries for dog breeders today is the potential sterility of their puppy-raising environments, for efforts to make such spaces consumer friendly can end up producing dogs whose worlds are, frankly, impoverished. In contrast, many "backyard" operations can yield good social lives for the dogs in question, for in their very informality they offer exposure to a variety of people, animals, and spaces through which young dogs—specifically those in the critical socialization window between three and five months of age—can learn about their worlds. For example, one of my interlocutors had a neighbor who struggled with drug addiction but whose dogs, because of the high traffic of somewhat erratically behaved humans and their dogs through the house, were almost aspirationally free of behavioral issues. While food insecurity was a significant problem for the neighbor, the dogs were always safe and, in my interlocutor's estimation, happy.[60]

In noting issues with genetics and environments, I am not arguing that backyard-bred dogs are better than purebreds. Backyards are certainly not uniformly rich and safe environments for dogs, and a lack of spay and neuter resources can mean that people become backyard breeders without intending to. What I want to foreground is the fact that there is no easy correlation between *backyard* and *bad dog*. Further, backyard operations demarcate queer affiliations, in terms of sensible connectivities outside the realm of so-called "proper" relatings; the unsanctioned sex they showcase embodies connectivities that defy the staid proprieties of white-normative settler-colonialist domestic spaces wherein the "family home" is definitively separate from the kennel. Moreover, identifying when and how backyard breeders provide good environments for dogs requires an awareness of how designations of class and race stigmatize particular humans and their dogs—that is, the thinking made necessary through the analytic of interspecies intersectionality.

Accusations of "overpopulation" leveled at backyard breeding also merit attention. As the historian Michelle Murphy wonderfully illustrates in *The Economization of Life*, the very term *population*, and especially *overpopulation*, evokes a Malthusian logic through which Indigenous peoples and people of color have long been targeted for extermination.[61] Further, the term *overpopulation* recalls Cohen's argument that heteronormativity polices the sexuality of even straight women of color through measures designed to limit the reproduction of welfare recipients—

think about the well-documented coercion faced by women of color in the U.S. to use long-term and dubiously safe birth-control options such as Norplant and Depo-Provera rather than the pill, or to undergo sterilization.[62] Laments of excess populations of stray dogs and backyard-bred dogs thus can be seen as marking as problematic the production of dogs who have departed from the norms of family and home. These dogs embody a queerly affiliative practice in their unrestrained and "out of place" sexual intimacies.

A common lament I heard during my fieldwork was that large-scale spay-and-neuter campaigns had, in fact, been "too effective" in that they encouraged more "responsible" dog owners to desex their pets while leaving intact (literally) the dogs of more "negligent" people.[63] In these discussions, terms like *negligence* and *irresponsibility* tacitly link reproductive decisions to larger discourses of backyard breeding, which in turn, stigmatize processes of biocapitalist production according to categories of class and race. The humans connected to "overpopulating" dogs emerge as themselves in need of policing, queerly affiliative in their "irresponsible" oversight of out-of-place sexual contacts between dogs.

If questions of "population" point to queer affiliations between ascriptions of the moniker *backyard* to breeding practices and white supremacist heteronormativity, discourses about breed and purity further these connections. For example, while out on a walk with a shelter dog, I ran into Justin, a white, upper-class straight cisgender man in his early thirties. Several years previously, a measure had been proposed in the state legislature mandating that all dogs be spayed or neutered, with a provision exempting those formally recognized as involved in breeding. Justin and I discussed this measure, which failed, and when I mentioned how dog breeds themselves posed problems in terms of general biological common sense, Justin visibly bristled, and burst out: "So you want these people to be able to breed their *mutts*?"[64]

For Justin, the problem of backyard bred dogs lies in their threat to purity, evident in his derisive use of "mutts." A quick foray into blogs on breeding practices reveals that Justin is far from alone in his sentiments; a whole Reddit subforum devoted to the question of whether "reputable mutt breeders" even exist yields the unsurprising general consensus that they do not.[65] To breed mutts, it seems, is already to be "irresponsible." On a related note, most of the guidance I have encountered on "responsible breeding," issued by such august sources as the American Kennel Club, involves a telling slippage in which the expression "breeding dogs" is used interchangeably with "breeding purebred dogs": to be a responsible breeder is to breed purebreds.[66] Then there are the distinctions made between "hybrids" and "mutts," with contentious discussions raging in ascriptions of responsibility to breeders of the former—Labradoodles and the like—but clearly distinguishing them from the latter by virtue of their "mutt-i-grees."[67] Justin's outrage thus echoes a widely shared view in discourses in human-dog worlds that to breed responsibly means to breed purebreds, which entails a politics of bodily purity.

However, Justin's linkage of "mutts" with "these people" reveals how threats of impurity are perceived as coming not just from dogs but also from the humans to whom they are attached. References to "these people" almost universally locate problems as originating among Othered peoples, not "my" or "our" people. In Justin's perception, "these people" tied to and producing "mutts" are people of color. Class is also embedded here, for "mutts" are quite clearly different from the endearing "hybrids" popular among affluent dog owners. This sexual politics of doggish "impurity," emerging from an imaginary peopled by poor people and folks of color, binds humans and dogs together in a queer affiliation through which both are targeted and stigmatized.

While the norms of geographies make threatening the queerly affiliative sexual politics and places of "mutts," "these people," and backyards, temporalities reveal alternative connectivities. Specifically, human-dog worlds are rife with terms like "dog years" as opposed to "human years," for the fact that dogs age differently from humans introduces a sensory mapping out of the regimented time of human lives under racial capitalism. As a transperson who has witnessed innumerable discussions about the expected "second puberty" that follows from the choice to medically transition via hormones, I find a fascinating affiliation between dog temporalities and hormonally reworked trans* temporalities, for both quicken and move astray from human expectations about bodily aging. Further, dogs live in the "now": when a human points to trash on the floor and makes angry noises, dogs understand the need to offer appeasement but do not remember having done something bad in the past in the way the human expects. This temporality of the now resonates with the queer time of people living with "the threat of AIDS" who were "forced to focus on 'the here, the present, the now,'" as the queer and disability studies scholar Alison Kafer reads it, citing the queer theorists Jack Halberstam and Elizabeth Freeman.[68] Both of these examples demonstrate a queer and in many cases trans* affiliation in dogs' sensory worldings, their temporal sensibilities.

While these connectivities border on the promising, in that they upend what queer theorists might call "straight time"—that linear progression of birth, school, marriage, children, and death—the same cannot be said for a third temporal connection, which I will call, very clumsily, death-value time, or a time marked by the valorization of death or proximity to it. The advocacy work that marks dogs' lives as mattering more when they are closer to being euthanized—evident in references to the salvation of dogs on "death row"—demonstrates this temporal sensibility, one remarkably akin to a prominent aspect of contemporary LGBTQ* advocacy: queer lives, particularly those of transwomen of color, emerge as politically important only after they have ended. For example, Trans Day of Remembrance, an event staged yearly on November 20, is meant to commemorate the killing of people claimed as trans*. The observance, during which the names of the dead and the manner of their murder are read off by community members who seek to bear witness—mostly folks in the U.S., Canada, and parts of Western Europe—serves to publicize and make visible not the resilience and beauty of trans lives, but rather the overwhelming violence and sheer numbers of their/our deaths. The dead consist almost entirely of trans women of color.

In the case of dogs valorized in a related manner—chosen for "rescue" because they are on a list of animals to be euthanized, valued because of their proximity to death—this death-value timing often fails, the dogs in question having reached a breaking point in their mental health as a result of their long shelter stay that release from a kennel will not reverse. As I detail in chapter 1, such a supposed reprieve from the shadow of death can quickly become a literal death when a dog exhibits behavioral issues that pose a danger to the dog herself as well as those around her. This sensibility of caring for lives more passionately as they approach their end, and, in truth, far too late, betrays a sobering queer affiliation in the larger worlds of dog sheltering and rescue.

While these temporal and geographical connectivities demarcate strayings in that they depart from norms, they tend to be injurious or fatal rather than courageous or playful. The very nonnormativity of "backyard bred" dogs means that such dogs are seen as a lost cause from the beginning. Reports of backyard-type breeding situations to authorities (animal control or the police, which, in many municipalities, are one and the same) tend to result in punitive measures rather than solutions: for example, the levying of fines and the seizure of dogs instead of referrals to low-cost or free veterinary care or behavioral resources. And when such dogs are seized, they do not always adjust well to shelter life, with sometimes tragic results. One example is Herman, mentioned in chapter 2, who was eventually euthanized for biting a human. Herman was taken into the shelter when a neighbor reported his owners for negligence—evident in his extensive mange, which his owners lacked the resources to cure. His removal from his home and contact with the only humans he trusted, though it was meant to help him, ultimately killed him. I can only imagine the pain of his loss to his humans.

Even if it does not result in euthanization, death-value timing that leads to the placement of dogs with severe behavioral issues in homes frequently leads to further harm for the dogs in question. When new owners are faced with difficult or dangerous behaviors, they often lack the experience and resources (including time!) to engage in the kinds of R+ training practices I describe here. Instead they frequently resort to what might be termed "quick fixes," including those promulgated by television's famed "dog whisperer," Cesar Millan. Sadly, the range of interventions promoted by Millan, including yelling, kicking, applying prong collars, and asserting human dominance or, as he terms it, "pack leadership," are all deeply aversive, and generally exacerbate rather than alleviate problem behaviors: fearful dogs become even more so when they learn to associate pain and discomfort with the humans who care for them.[69]

Then there are policies like the failed spay-and-neuter legislation Justin and I discuss. While rarely taken up at the state or provincial level, such ordinances are widespread at the city and county level. And, in spite of good intentions, such policies effectively demarcate only certain kinds of nonhuman animals and not others ("mutts") as worthy of existing and also inadvertently target more marginalized humans. Those who lack the financial resources to pay for spay-and-neuter services are likely to be fined or even have their dogs seized as a result of such policies.

All of these geographical and temporal strayings reveal queer affiliations that, while certainly identifiable as varying kinds of "fuck yous" to hetero- and homonormative mappings, make them precarious, denigrated, wounded, and even deadly. The logics that such affiliations point to are not hopeful at all, but rather highly normative. Dogs' bodies become vehicles for the stigmatization, policing, and harming of marginalized humans and dogs together and separately, and often to the detriment of both, as in cases like Herman's. These are strayings that yield not promises but rather foreclosures of life, diminishments of life, closer proximity to death, and, at times, literal death. Thus, even as these affiliations map out sensibilities that, in their bucking of norms, join easily into awareness—their very queerness emerges from the ways they can never easily fit into larger social structures—that awareness is oriented toward logics in need of disruption, not embracing.

Refusals in Relatings

While much of this chapter focuses on affiliations as connectivities, refusals of affiliation also merit attention. I begin this exploration by returning to the example of Beth. The opening excerpt from my field notes illustrates that Beth tended toward affiliation primarily toward grass and potentially toward other dogs, and only rarely toward humans. However, details of Beth's story complicate this scant overview.

Much like Bailey, Beth became an enthusiastic participant in shelter playgroups. Because she embraced a rough-and-tumble style of play, she was most frequently paired with similarly exuberant dogs who were tolerant of what might be perceived as borderline or outright rude behaviors. For example, Beth exhibited a strong tendency to take in her mouth the leashes and even collars attached to other dogs, jerking around the dog to whom they were attached. The handlers who supervised the playgroups therefore were careful to either remove these objects or ensure that Beth was partnered only with dogs who were not offended by such gestures. These pairings required knowledge of the dogs' proclivities. After several months in residence at the shelter, with shelter staff attesting to her sociality with other dogs in the playgroups, Beth was adopted out to a family. However, within two months, Beth was returned to the shelter, for while on neighborhood walks with a hired dog walker, she had bitten a small dog and on another occasion a bulldog. She had also made a habit of digging her way out of the backyard. After her return, the shelter kept her for one day, during which select volunteers were allowed to visit with her, and at the end of the next day she was euthanized.[70]

Given my own experiences with Beth, I suspected that an unnamed but likely central reason for her return had to do with her disinterest in humans, for the behavioral problems named by her adopters are issues that many others manage by limiting contact with other dogs and supervising a dog's yard time. Indeed, I have found it necessary to take such measures with Annie. However, despite her behavioral problems, my ties to Annie are strong enough that I simply work around her limitations. She has earned the nickname "Lickety-split" from other members of my family for her tendency toward "drive-by licking," cruising the house with some quick tongue action applied to human knees or hands and then just as quickly wandering away. Knowing Beth fairly well—I spent close to fifty hours walking and working with her during her shelter stay—I doubt she evinced similarly affiliative behaviors to her adoptive family, for she ignored me about 95 percent of the time. My opening field note describes an unusual experience with her.

Beth's disinterest in humans bespeaks a level of disengagement that some of my interlocutors find alarming. This returns us to the question of what counts as a life. For example, speaking about sanctuaries, Veronica, a working-class Latinx woman in her forties, stated: "And the idea of sanctuaries? I'm sorry, I don't think that's a quality of life at all for most dogs, there are plenty of dogs—the dogs that like, look straight through you that are not what we consider social or sociable. . . . Those are the dogs that stay in a kennel in a shelter for two years and are fine. Most dogs shouldn't be fine after being in a shelter for two years."[71] For Veronica, Beth's disinterest in the kinds of human-specific engagement that Veronica and others desire for dogs in their lives outside the shelter suggests a lack of potential for a life of any real quality. Included in this assessment are sanctuaries themselves, which, in Veronica's opinion, do not offer dogs adequate lives at all, given that most sanctuaries keep dogs in isolation from both humans and other dogs. Of course, it is possible that Beth's inclinations were also shaped by the passage of time: she may well have been more affiliative toward humans on her arrival at the shelter and become less so over time.

Beth's story also reveals a refusal of affiliation on the part of the humans who took her in. The day after Beth's euthanasia, I was out on a walk with Haley and encountered Gretchen, an interlocutor who had been involved with multiple rescue organizations in the area. Morose, I shared with her the details of my death-day visit with Beth in her kennel, admitting that it was probably for the better that a biting pit bull–type dog would no longer be out making news. I was surprised when Gretchen reacted to the story with fury toward Beth's adopters: "How could they return her to the shelter? Don't they know how inhumane shelter euthanasias are?" Gretchen believed that the family should have asked their vet to euthanize Beth. "They outsourced her death!"[72] It is important to note that it is unclear whether this was a real option for Beth's adopters. Few veterinarians are willing to euthanize an otherwise healthy animal on the basis of behavior, especially when the behavior can be managed by fairly easy means. But in Gretchen's understanding, the choice to have others euthanize Beth indexed a horrifying refusal of relation on the part of her adopters.

All humans who participate in an open-admission shelter, where euthanasia is generally understood to be part of the work, engage, directly or indirectly, in refusals of relation. Rowena, a white sixtysomething professional dog walker, once told me she thought I was "brave" for volunteering at the shelter and that she couldn't imagine doing it herself. Later she described to me the change that accompanied her own decision to start volunteering: "It's like I grew a callus over my heart."[73] This statement describes a refusal in relating, for even as Rowena contributed to the day-to-day labor of the shelter, she did so while shutting herself off, becoming less emotionally available, rendering herself insensible to the overtly emotional aspects of shelter work.

With respect to failures and refusals of relating, another key facet of human-dog worlds, especially in animal sheltering and rescue, is the species-specific affiliations. Early on in my own shelter work, I noticed that when I took out dogs, other volunteers would hold doors open and be enthusiastic polite, but when I entered the building at other times, dogless, the same people frequently let doors slam in my face. When I shared this observation with my interlocutors, they tended to laughingly agree. As Yolanda put it, "Animal people are in it for the animals, not for the humans."[74] Indeed, early in my fieldwork I worried that my site was so focused on facilitating human-animal relatings that I would observe very little in the way of human-human contact. And, as the slammed doors and general disinterest in polite engagement with other humans reveals, many humans in the animal rescue and shelter worlds consciously choose affiliations with dogs (and cats, goats, chickens, roosters, and rats) over relationships with other humans.

These refusals of relating function as the obverse of intimacy without relatedness, relatedness without kinship, and bodyings. Sensorial in a phenomenological sense—involving movements away, attempts to disconnect, and the denial of touch and similarly faceless intimacies—these refusals delineate another, and in some ways contradictory, queer affiliation. Read through the lenses offered by Mel Chen and Elizabeth Povinelli, turnings away delineate a refusal of propriety and "proper" modes of relating: the choice of, or move toward, an object with which one is not supposed to connect, and the substitution of a different object from that with which one is culturally coded to connect both bespeak ways of relating that resonate with queer interventions.

The queer affiliations I locate in refusals of relating are not entirely positive, as Beth's death underscores. While some are certainly sustainable and demarcate strayings that still work, in a disruptive fashion, within the norms and episteme I describe throughout this book—as with humans who choose dogs over other humans—others seek paths that quite literally do not exist within the confines of contemporary shelter and rescue worlds. A rather bleakly queer connection between Beth's case and discourses of human-based kinship involves the example of the young queer or trans* person who is kicked out of their home because of their inability to conform to normative and expected behaviors. This practice effectively attempts to impose a social death, if not (given the potential psychological and physical harms of such a rejection) also a literal one. Beth's case demonstrates how queer affiliations that work through denials of kinship and intimacy can demarcate strayings for which neither space nor time is allowed, strayings that, for dogs, often end in death. Beth's queerly affiliative strayings wander too far from a normative social fabric and episteme whose geographies, temporalities, bodily politics, and regimes of intimacy disallow the presence of what she has become, a "bad dog."

Queer Understandings and Strayings

At the beginning of this chapter I posited that the connectivities of queer affiliations in human-dog and dog-dog worlds would yield new logics, that is, alternative ways of understanding and even thinking. And yet, just as *love* is an inadequate descriptor for the bodyings of R+ training practices, *logics* only partially delineates my interventions here, for so much of what both excites and dismays me in doggish queer affiliations emerges through the sensory, through ways of feeling and moving. The term *logic* emerges from a lengthy history most easily named through the Enlightenment-era division of mind from body and logic from feeling; there is an air of cold calculation to *logic* that seemingly intimates a denial of feeling.

Here then, while I invoke logics, I also want to convey ways of understanding, because to me *understanding* conveys a coming to knowing that is at once processual—there is a movement to *under* that I find interesting—and interrelational—*under* also implies a positioning in many ways below the other of a knowledge relationship, a positioning that seemingly counters claims to mastery. Of course, *understanding* certainly has moments of overcoding—someone's saying "I understand you" doesn't mean that they actually do—but I find the term encouraging in its motility and relationality nonetheless. And so here I elucidate the new logics and ways of understanding I find interesting, promising, and critical in the many queer affiliations described in this chapter.

The process of identifying intimacy without relatedness, relatedness without kinship, butt cultures, and bodyings entails a move to recognition, an act of marking connectivities that elude the politics of the domestic. This recognition is itself a way of knowing, of coming to understand processes of relating that stray from the norms of family and kinship. However, this form of understanding also valorizes transient and ephemeral connectivities. This valorization suggests that we should take seriously our more transient relationships and not discount them simply because they do not settle into longer-term and, arguably, more easily named and collated practices. The delightful recognition solicited by "butt cultures" asks us to attempt to understand a sensibility that exceeds the limits of primate sensoria, particularly primate noses. Here is an alternate worlding that humans can only begin to appreciate, but whose disparate hapticity and other sensory ways of doing intimacy can certainly extend the understandings of not just human-dog relatings but also human-human contacts: just think if we were to recognize and more deeply engage not just the skin-to-skin contacts that constitute our worldings, but the ways of moving that become intimacies in and of themselves.

The bodyings I delineate through R+ training practices, rooted in an affective sharing and openness to the desires, needs, and body of an Other, clearly disrupt the hierarchy that is the legacy of rational man, wherein "the animal" is always subordinate to the human. These bodyings also transcend the norms of training and ownership, for their goal is not mastery but rather mutual understanding. Such moves to understanding facilitate acceptance. When one attends to fear as a shaper of a frustrating behavior, one is better equipped to—here I paraphrase my interlocutor Sharon—appreciate the dog one has rather than the dog one wanted. However, these bodyings also push against the boundaries of emotions themselves, for their very bodiliness renders inadequate easy descriptors such as *love* and *care*. These bodyings reveal an abundance of ways of thinking, doing, acting, wanting, touching, seeing, and feeling that expand understandings into the realm of affect. And this affective connectivity, as a blurring of self and other through movement and feeling together, in its resonances with Lorde's erotic, reveals a means of building affiliations through rather than in spite of differences, an approach that seeds understanding and awareness. Further, in their commitment to avoid harm, R+ approaches expand understandings of how harm manifests in the first place. When one comes to see that yelling tends not to facilitate learning because of the fear it engenders, one becomes more alert to the work of similar aversive practices in a range of interactions, including human-human relatings. Thus the bodyings of R+ training promote an awareness of violences that pushes its practitioners to think and engage differently well outside the spaces of human-dog relatings.

The fascinating temporalities of dogs' consciousness and their differential aging underscore a particular form of intimacy. While these queer affiliations push for a politics built on the now rather than the future—for example, a politics in which the adults who are now suffering from the ravages of climate change–induced planetary events are the priority, rather than the children who will live on such a planet in the future—

they also reveal a sensory relating that disorders the domestic. For example, the "nowness" of dogs that leads to difficulties in developing shared understandings about the trash tends to yield solutions involving management—that is, preventing access to the trash. Such interventions often take the form of baby gates and carefully closed doors—solutions for a range of problems, including dogs who do not do well with new visitors to their domiciles. In these solutions emerges not just a sensibility attuned to disparate temporalities, but a reunderstanding of space itself, for the proclivities of dogs necessitate different orderings of the domestic. And these reworkings of spatiality in conjunction with temporality reveal small strayings from the ideals of family and home that bring into question how domestic spaces are "supposed to" function, prompting different ways of understanding.

In the less promising queer affiliations among the biopolitics of backyard breeding, mutts, and death-value temporality, awareness assumes primacy over sensibility. Stigmatization reveals points, identifiable through interspecies intersectionality, where disruptions are warranted. "These people" whose "mutts" need to be eliminated experience a form of becoming in kind wherein identity is overdetermined by class and often race. These queer affiliations thus mark connectivities with normative logics that need to be disrupted and separated. In a practical sense this would entail advocacy less focused on "rescue" and more on keeping dogs together with their humans, interrupting the presumption that a backyard-bred dog is a bad dog and the breeder therefore a bad human. This type of advocacy is, by nature, alert to the structural violences that marginalize humans and animals together, and it cultivates awareness by necessity. Somewhat similarly, the death-value timing of "rescue" can be most easily interrupted through a reorientation toward a time of life. In LGBTQ* advocacy such a move might entail engaging and valorizing marginalized members of communities while they are present rather than focusing on their absence—for example, by observing a Trans* Day of Resilience rather than a Trans* Day of Remembrance. In dog worlds, this would mean taking measures to prevent dogs from entering shelters in the first place.

Finally, in considering the refusals of relating I detail through Beth's story, I want to introduce some speculation. My fieldwork site is located in an area where, as in much of California, white folks are fast becoming a minority rather than the majority. It is quite likely that Beth's adoptive family included folks of color. Which leads me to wonder: What if it was not just her disinterest, bites, or escapist tendencies that led to her return to the shelter, but also a desire on the part of her family not to experience the scrutiny exercised by the police (who also act as animal control in the city in which she was adopted) toward dogs, pit bull types in particular, with a known bite history? Given the well-known racism of U.S. law enforcement, what if her family's rejection of Beth also came out of a desire to avoid the likely violent results of such heightened surveillance? I'm sure many readers know of dogs who have bitten not just other dogs but also small children and other animals, but nevertheless remain alive and well, their "badness" shielded by, among other factors, the white, straight, socioeconomic, settler, and/or cis privilege of their owners. What if Beth's family simply did not have the shielding afforded by such privileges?

If this were the case, Beth's family's refusal to relate becomes a choice that in many ways is no choice. "Bad dogs" become "dangerous" dogs in the eyes of the state when they are connected to folks of color, and human-dog connectivities become the catalyst for rather than a refuge from or challenge to violence. When contextualized this way, the "badness" of Beth and dogs like her stems not only from identifiable problem behaviors but also emerges from and reveals a social world whose normative logics overcode and amplify perceptions of those behaviors, transmuting bites into becomings in kind through which both humans and dogs are marked as threatening. This reading of Beth's story underscores how queerly affiliatory refusals to relate can reveal the workings of logics that, in turn, prompt awareness of the need to challenge and disrupt a normative social fabric that sanctions some human-animal relations and not others. Such an awareness could and should involve work towards a social world where ties between public safety services involving animals and systems that perpetuate racist violence are disrupted and even severed; cops should not be involved in animal control and related matters. However, such an awareness also informs the work I point to in chapter 1: the need to prevent cases like Beth's in the first place by making space for such dogs much earlier in their lives and providing resources that enable the original owners of such dogs to thrive with and care for them so that they never enter the space of the shelter to begin with.

Throughout the queerly affiliative connections I trace here, strayings delineate movements apart and away from normative formations and the episteme that shapes them. Strayings underscore alternative ways of understanding, of building knowledges through the inculcation of bodily sensibilities and a connected awareness. And they reveal connectivities that function either within the norms, worlds, and episteme I critique throughout this book or at their limits, demarcating sites for future affiliative interventions. Even as R+ bodyings, spatial and temporal reorderings of the domestic, and stories like Bailey's and Beth's are folded into a social order wherein Eng's "racialization of intimacy" holds strong (for readers who have worried about him, Bailey was successfully adopted) they reveal movements apart from that order, that way of worlding. And while backyard biopolitics, "these people" and their "mutts," and refusals in relating demarcate strayings that move close to or even beyond the norms of this social order, the very awareness of naming them, through the analytic of interspecies intersectionality this book engages, facilitates disruptions to that order. By coupling strayings with queerly affiliative thinking, I identify interruptions and disruptions that might give rise to analyses and practices that work within or at the limits of the social order whose fabric seemingly erases them. Strayings point to ways of thinking and doing already at work within and at the edges of the normative social worlds this book engages. When taken up together with queerly affiliative tendencies, these approaches promise changes to the normative mappings and violences I identify throughout this book through interspecies intersectionality, changes with the potential to reshape our social world into a space where marginalized humans and dogs, together, can thrive.

Conclusion

Imagining Otherwise

It was the 5th of July. New arrivals had been pouring into the shelter all day. A youngish woman, possibly Filipina, came to the front desk roughly five minutes before the shelter closed. Her dog had escaped from the van in which she was living the day before, she tearfully told the animal control officer (ACO) behind the desk. She described the dog—a pit bull type, possibly with some Rottweiler, shy, nervous. I watched carefully—I had seen a dog fitting this description in the quarantine area in the far back of the shelter, where workers had been placing dogs after the shelter ran out of regular kennels earlier in the afternoon. The dog had no collar or microchip, the latter being too expensive and the former an irritant to the dog's tender skin, the woman explained. The ACO stood up and walked the woman back to the dog I had noticed earlier. He was hers! Walking the woman and dog to the on-site veterinary clinic, the ACO inquired about the dog's vaccinations. Learning that some were needed, the ACO scheduled an appointment with the woman to come back for a free microchipping and vaccination update. The woman and dog left together, joined by a leash and soft collar the shelter donated to them, declining the bag of food the ACO held out to them at the door: "We're good," said the woman. I watched as the two snuggled for several minutes in an aging van, which started reluctantly and, eventually, slowly drove off, its sole, semifunctional taillight blinking in fits and starts as the woman navigated the complex intersection outside the shelter.

—AUTHOR'S FIELD NOTES, JULY 5

I begin with this story partly because it reveals the shelter as a space of succor and comfort, one reflective of the verb *to shelter*, where care is extended and hardship mediated, and partly because the circumstances it denotes are fairly typical. July 5 is a terrible day for animal shelters across the U.S. Many nonhuman animals flee their domiciles because of the sheer terror induced by the fireworks set off on July 4. Those who are most affected by this disruption are those who are most precarious, be it through houselessness or through arrangements such as makeshift fencing that safeguards animals on most days, but not when they are driven by fear. But unlike the many other tales and ethnographic jottings that fill this book, this one is made up, because the practices and world it describes do not (yet) exist.

I present a fake field note because I want to highlight the interventions associated with imagining otherwise.[1] I put forward an imagined world, one I aim to make material. This world builds on the analytic of interspecies intersectionality, identifying the connections of marginalization that emerge from a specific human-dog relating and interrupting what might otherwise be a becoming in kind wherein the woman in question is marked as "irresponsible," charged a hefty fine for her perceived lapse in judgment, and likely kept separate from her dog until she finds the means to pay the fine. In such ascriptions of irresponsibility, nonwhiteness in conjunction with pit bull–ness translates into "badness" and even "danger" or "threat."

This field note also imagines a community in which houselessness is not equated with a threat to the domestic, where instead the living practices of those outside the stereotypical family home—that is, those whose practices and doings reveal queer affiliations—are encouraged and facilitated through the provision of medical care and mechanisms such as an address through which to hold a place in a deeply antihouseless world. And this world is subtended by a sense of justice whereby the pain of loss is met with understanding rather than judgment, whereby human and dog needs are seen as entwined and inextricable.

In what follows I detail a host of imaginings, some of which are fairly practical and some of which are not. Many of them follow from the disruptions I argue for through interspecies intersectionality and becoming in kind; many also build on the promises and potentials of queer affiliations to counter the violences of today's world. These imaginings envision a world wherein different understandings yield better and potentially more livable lives. In order to communicate these imaginings in as queer-forward a way as possible—I use *queer-forward* both because this book is not straight and because these interventions circle and twist, evoking the bentness associated with queerness—I have divided them according to the scales of *world*, *shelter/rescue*, and *individual*. I close with thinking that spans all these scales and details one of my larger hopes for this book, an understanding of the multispecies justice necessary to build a new world for humans and nonhuman animals, together.

World

The interventions in this section address changes and practices that pertain to the larger imaginary space where discussions, memes, and ideas about animal shelters, animal rescues, rescue dogs, and pit bull–type dogs emerge. They engage what Michel Foucault might refer to as "discourses"— that is, ways of constituting knowledge, modes of thinking and the meanings that emerge from them, and the circulation of ideas that emerge through language and related practices of representation—common to dog worlds in the U.S., and particularly the worlds of rescue and pit bull politics.[2]

Stop Perceiving Nonhuman Animals as Separate from Human Politics

Interspecies intersectionality identifies how human and nonhuman animals are marginalized together rather than separately. Politics involving nonhuman animals is politics about humans. For example, the common perception of memes about nonhuman animals' "unlikely friendships" needs to be reworked. Such stories should be understood not simply as interesting and fun stories that provide relief from a rather horrible political present but as moves to promote a kind of "Can't we all just get along?" mentality among humans.[3] Much like "color-blindness," this mentality denies disparities and obscures differences, contributing to rather than facilitating antiracist and anticolonialist understandings. To extend this thinking to practice, those invested in animal welfare need to consider just how deeply entwined nonhuman animal needs are with those of humans: that is, to think carefully with Kimberlé Crenshaw's initial invocation of intersectionality and with my own addition of *interspecies*. This approach entails refusing the substitutive logic at work in animal activists' claims that, for example, nonhuman animals are "enslaved" and an introduction of more careful thinking-with both marginalized humans and nonhuman animals. An affinity for nonhuman animals does not exempt activists from considering the workings of racialization, colonialism, misogyny, transphobia, homophobia, and ableism, but rather the opposite: in engaging with nonhuman animals, activists need to pay close attention to the workings of seemingly human-specific processes of marginalization in order to actually build, rather than claim to build, better worlds.

Change the Stories We Tell

A rather discouraging if unsurprising study surfaced in my final phases of writing this book, showing that shelter animals' adoption rates are higher if their photographs seem to convey that they are in need of help.[4] Dogs who appeared more "content" tended to have longer shelter stays than those who ignited a saviorist impulse in the eyes of their beholders. Thus the saviorist storyings I critique in chapter 1 actively shape shelter and rescue practices even on the internet.

The culture and discourses of salvation that feed into perceptions of dogs' needs are subtended by the narrative of no kill. While no kill certainly marked an important intervention when it first surfaced in the mid-1990s, the pendulum has swung too far and in ways that endanger both humans and nonhuman animals in public. The very moralism of no kill needs to be challenged, not just for its white saviorist tendencies but also for its crafting of narratives of innocence that require the production of "badness," be it ascribed to former owners or animal shelters. The moralism of no kill produces, rather than reflects, the persistent ideas in the shelter and particularly rescue worlds that an injustice has been done to an animal and that there is a perpetrator who is not the victim of structural violences such as racism and poverty. The no-kill approach needs to be reworked, interrupted, and replaced with an awareness of the factors that produce shelter dogs and strays in the first place. This storying must change!

In addition, the idea that sanctuaries provide an answer must be exposed for the patent falsehood that it is. Animal sanctuaries are a side effect of the neoliberalization of the shelter and rescue worlds, making private a labor once placed in the public domain. They are not scalable, for they reflect, at most, piecemeal attempts to "save" dogs. Moreover, because sanctuaries themselves are often sites of what is basically (and here I lean on my interlocutor María's thinking), lifelong solitary confinement, what they provide is not what many would regard as anything like a "life." As the American studies scholar Megan Glick might argue, sanctuaries merely place animals in "death worlds," extending their captivity in a manner that completely removes them, for their safety and that of others, from any of the intra-actions that make a life livable. Numerous sanctuaries have been exposed as places of utter decrepitude, with animals living in their own filth, even in cages stacked on top of each other.[5] These are not spaces that give life; rather, they provide a slow death.

Prevent Shelter Dogs from Happening

While much of this book is oriented toward preventing dogs from ending up in shelters, I list here a few examples of measures that can help create a world in which humans, especially those who are marginalized, and their nonhuman animals can thrive together. First, the assumption that nonhuman animals should live only with privileged humans—those who can "afford" them—needs to be done away with. Recognition of the bonds between nonhuman animals and humans and their centrality to making life livable for both needs to come first.[6] Second, efforts to keep humans together with nonhuman animals should be paramount. Such measures include free or low-cost veterinary clinics, shelters that allocate space for both humans and nonhuman animals (including shelters for survivors of domestic violences), free and low-cost training options, active efforts to reunite dogs with owners (rather than waiting for owners to show up at shelters), free and low-cost food options for both humans and nonhuman animals (such as soup kitchens that also provide kibble), free and low-cost advocacy services for those separated from their animals (through natural disasters as well as individual crises), and the elimination of fees charged by shelters for reuniting nonhuman animals with their humans or surrendering animals to shelters.

Another necessary change is the expansion of a safety net. In a world where the poor are getting much poorer even as the rich are getting much richer, where (in the U.S. in particular) most people are one or two paychecks away from houselessness, and where the social safety net is laughably weak, not to mention composed of a virtually impenetrable bureaucracy, there is little help available for people who need it. As a result of neoliberalism, providing such assistance—what was once the work of the state—is now largely the job, if you can call it that, of private philanthropic organizations. It is not just universal healthcare that will facilitate this goal but also an increase in funding to municipal animal shelters, enabling them to function not in deference to the no-kill desires of private donors but rather in the interests of public health and safety, addressing questions such as what happens if dogs who are known biters are adopted out to households.

Another key change needed is education of humans about dogs. As Veronica pointed out to me, many of the bites and related problems that lead to dogs' being abandoned or surrendered to shelters could be prevented, or at least mitigated, if elementary schools included instruction on reading and understanding dog body language.[7] Such education practices should also be taken up in secondary and higher education, for the recognition of the fact that we all live in a more than human world should be built on attempts to understand what exactly nonhuman animals are trying to say to us.

Challenge Perceptions of Breed

While understandings of breed are often helpful in preparing owners and trainers for the kinds of behaviors (and challenges) to expect from particular dogs—Belgian Malinois folks, I'm looking at you—they are also often a source of confusion.[8] For example, a truly odd moment in my fieldwork came when someone claimed that a particular dog, who could be best described as overwhelmingly enthusiastic and extremely affiliative with humans in particular, was a "pit bull in an Aussie body."[9] The person was trying to convey a sense of the dog's behavior by noting that this behavior defied the expectations of the Australian Shepherd breed. The common equation of breed with behavior is especially troublesome in shelter and rescue settings, where a dog's parentage is rarely known, and identification of breed based on observation is often at odds with DNA analysis. In *Dogs: A New Understanding of Canine Origin, Behavior, and Evolution*, Raymond and Lorna Coppinger recommend that, rather than think of nature versus nurture, we should think of dogs through the synergism of "nature times nurture."[10] In a world increasingly filled with "mutts," conceptions of breed need to be tempered by understandings of what actual dogs do. Rather than claiming that a behavior emerges from a breed-specific proclivity, people in dog worlds need to work to understand dog body language and the role of dog experiences: for example, adequate socialization between three and five months of age. Understandings rooted in assessing dogs' emotions and behaviors as they are presented rather than presumed, coupled with the type of storying put forward by Sharon—the thinking-with a dog who likely had a deprived puppyhood—helpfully challenge an unstable paradigm.

Another constructive breed-related intervention would be to do away with breed-specific legislation (BSL). Rather than trying to understand and manage dog-related public health problems through the lens of breed (such as the poorly defined category of "pit bull"), government agencies need to enact legislation that targets specific problems, such as loose dogs or biting dogs. Follow-through is essential: for example, if a dog with a tendency to cause trouble gets loose, then rather than levying a fine and considering the matter finished, a municipality should take steps to help ensure that the dog does not get loose again. Such measures would have forestalled a number of high-profile attacks by dogs in locales where BSL ended up being instituted.[11] If the problem were recast as one that inheres not in the type of dog, but rather in a particular human-dog form of relating—one that might be aggravated by factors such as poverty—a more just world might emerge.

Support Insiders and Let Them Lead

Many of the animal welfare programs and practices I describe are enacted by white middle-class folks doing "outreach" to communities of color and houseless encampments. In this regard, they uncomfortably replicate colonialist, saviorist dynamics. One program offering free spay-and-neuter services partnered with an all-white biker gang with, from what one interlocutor told me, a history of racist violence. Their day of outreach in an area peopled almost entirely by folks of color was very unsuccessful.[12] Shelter and rescue organizations need to engage with communities to identify and prioritize problems. Well-meaning outsiders need to start heeding and reinforcing community members' own ideas, rather than presupposing that, for example, reducing the number of puppies yields some kind of change for the better. Further, well-meaning outsiders need to follow rather than lead (and I recognize the irony of an academic even writing such a sentence). Real change and better worlds do not come from ideas and approaches proposed by outsiders, particularly when those approaches resemble projects of white supremacy; rather, they come from within. And insiders' voices are not being heard, or not enough.

Shelter and Rescue

Here I detail practices and related interventions oriented specifically toward animal shelters and rescues. Many readers familiar with these spaces will have undoubtedly encountered some of these interventions, but perhaps not all of them. And those unfamiliar with such spaces should note that much of what works well in these institutional settings translates easily to others!

Make Shelters into Actual Shelters

Many municipal shelters operate under the purview of the city's police. Thus many animal control officers are also cops, some of whom may regard members of public as potential perpetrators rather than simply folks in need of help. Police tend to operate as a tool of a repressive racist and colonialist state.[13] Rather than the agents of justice commonly portrayed in law-and-order television dramas, police are much more likely to be the force that supports, say, predatory landlords seeking unjust evictions. Further, police-style approaches are rarely appropriate for problems involving human-animal interactions. For example, fining someone for a loose dog does not fix the problem of a broken fence that the person cannot afford to repair because of medical debt: in fact, the fine exacerbates the problem. The fact that most shelters charge fees for people to surrender animals—that is, to surrender them *to* the shelter, not just to retrieve them from it—is arguably one of the biggest injustices in animal worlds today. Animal shelters need to be removed from the purview of police departments.

More than that, shelters need to become spaces where community members can find help caring for their dogs rather than being labeled as irresponsible when they struggle to do so. If someone has a surgery coming up and no one to care for a dog while they are hospitalized, a shelter should offer assistance. And if a dog is struggling with a behavioral problem such as separation anxiety, a shelter should be able to offer advice from a qualified trainer, rather than the conflicting and often wrong information they are likely to come across on the internet or through television shows such as Cesar Millan's *Dog Whisperer*. If someone is struggling with food insecurity during a bad month, a shelter should be the kind of place where they can get food for their pets, not judgment. Ideally a shelter should provide free veterinary care as well as training advice, both of which can prevent shelter animals from happening in the first place.

Extend Oversight

At present, there is no single body that tracks the data, much less the practices, of animal shelters and rescue organizations. The lack of this kind of oversight has contributed into the deeply problematic and contentious dynamics of no-kill approaches. For instance, if a rescue organization takes a neoliberalist approach focusing solely on "live release" numbers, a dog who ends up being deemed dangerous by a municipality is still counted as a success story from the rescue organization's perspective. What is needed is a body that oversees and holds accountable these various groups, evaluating them not only on the basis of adoption numbers but also with respect to dogs' later lives, and taking account of unsolvable behavioral problems and their impact on public health. In keeping with this approach, shelter and rescue adoptions need to be facilitated long after dogs leave the kennels. Support with behavioral problems, advice for first-time owners, and ongoing dialogues enabling a better understanding of dogs should be a priority for shelters and rescues.

Expand Enrichment!

In many shelter and rescue spaces, the tacit goal is to have enough staff and volunteer support for dogs to go on daily walks. However, walks are not the only or the best stimuli for dogs: for fearful or shy dogs, walks can inadvertently aggravate problem behaviors. As many organizations have already recognized, enrichment needs to be reunderstood to include engaging dogs mentally not only through walks, but also though activities such as extracting food from a kong, working on training with a volunteer, playing "find" with food in boxes, playing other games, chasing bacon-flavored bubbles, and listening while someone reads to them. Further, such approaches shouldn't be regarded only as steps in a structured progression toward desired behaviors. Rather, each day should be, on its own, a good day for a dog.

In this vein, many shelters and rescues have begun to introduce play-groups, enabling residents to play under supervision by humans well versed in dog body language and behavior. Such practices should be expanded, with the caveat here that a dog's willingness to engage in play should not be taken as evidence of its sociability, or lack of it, in other contexts. Many dogs are uninterested in the slobbery bodily engagements of playgroups, for instance, but are fine meeting other dogs while walking off leash on trails. Further, in keeping with this book's thinking, play-groups need to be facilitated in keeping with R+ training techniques, for aversive approaches run the risk of turning a dog off play for life. A recently inaugurated group called the Shelter Playgroup Alliance is one source of advice on such practices.[14]

Train Staff and Volunteers in Behavior and Body Language

I once had the ill fortune to locate, with a neighbor, a pit bull–type dog for whom neither of us had space. I brought him to the local animal shelter in the hopes that his original caretakers might find him. We ended up waiting for roughly an hour, during which time I called around, trying to find other sites that might take him in. At that time I was unfamiliar with the usual procedures employed by rescues and shelters. While we waited, the dog, who earlier in the day had been a model of placidity, lounging on the deck of my apartment while my own dogs barked at him through the window, became fearful. By the time we reached the front counter, he was visibly nervous. When the ACO, a police officer, deliberately loomed over the counter at him and raised his hands menacingly, he barked. I asked the ACO what the dog's chances were, and the man looked at me with suspicion before replying, "With *that* temp test? None, really." The shelter only adopted out "breed ambassadors," he told me, and the dog I was turning in was definitely not one.[15] By "temp test" he was referring to "temperament testing," that is, a snapshot assessment of how dogs might behave outside a shelter. Such tests are quite extensive and are generally not carried out until a dog has been in place for a minimum of three days. Even then, much like a fearful human, dogs will "suppress" some behaviors and exhibit only behaviors that they feel keep them safe, often minimizing what might be termed their real personalities due to the fear and overwhelm of typical shelter environments. To be clear, what this ACO did was be an asshole, not administer a temperament test. He also failed to "see" the dog, whom I called Bruno, in any real way. He clearly had very little knowledge of dog behavior and body language: he was almost bitten by a Chihuahua-type dog whose collar he attempted to grab while Bruno and I were waiting. Bruno may not have been the best of candidates for adoption (although perhaps his owners found him), and the ACO in question was certainly guilty of "breed profiling"—looking for and attempting to elicit "bad" behavior from a pit bull–type dog. But his story also reveals a deeper problem: the ACO was inadequately trained for his job.

Staff and volunteers in shelter and rescue spaces need rigorous, ongoing training in "reading" dogs' bodies accurately. Further, artwork like Lili Chin's should be plastered everywhere in such spaces. Such an approach would not only help prevent a great number of bites and similar problems but also likely facilitate adoption counseling: a person capable of reading a dog's body will know that the exuberantly handsy teenager is likely not a good match for a dog whose body language screams discomfort whenever their harness is put on. Indeed, shelters themselves should be a key locus for the provision of more thorough (or really, in many cases, even basic) education in dog behavior as part of the services they provide to their communities.

Remove Breed from Residents' Information

While removing breed data would likely play havoc with the databases of many shelters and rescues, given how little is often known about shelter animals' history, assertions of breed are more likely to be guesses than anything else. Further, given the complexity of breed itself and the fact that breed does not equal behavior, listing shelter residents' breed is misleading at best. More useful would be information about the dog's behavior and body language as interpreted by a knowledgeable person.

Rethink Adoption Criteria

In dog adoptions, the ideal of "good family homes" is not the one that dogs themselves would construct. Moreover, it reinforces racist, anti-Indigenous, classist, and ableist norms. Real care needs to be taken to rework the criteria that many organizations, particularly rescues, use in determining human candidates' eligibility to adopt. The increasing trend toward "open adoptions" is heartening in this regard. By easing or eliminating requirements such as proof of a landlord's approval or having all family members present at the time of an adoption, open adoptions counter the biases detailed throughout this book. Further, open adoptions have facilitated many wonderful placements that might otherwise have been impossible. In addition, Dot Baisly, the shelter division cochair for the International Association of Animal Behavior Consultants (IAABC), notes that the "reality is that less than ideal outcomes will happen at times, regardless of the restrictions we impose." Some placements simply don't work out. Baisly's assertion is borne out by comparative data showing that policy-free adoptions result in outcomes just as positive as those governed by stringent criteria.[16]

Individual

The following are suggestions for readers interested in engaging the precepts of this book to develop practices and ways of understanding relevant to the relationships of individuals and dogs. Many of the principles and practices presented above apply here as well.

Dig into R+ Approaches

A truism among my interlocutors, as well as the majority of the professionals involved with dog training and behavior today, is that your dog is not interested in running for president.[17] Conceptions of dominance and related ideas about "alpha" behavior are based in research on captive wolves that even the researchers involved have since denounced.[18] Dogs, much like humans, are mostly interested in stability and fitting in well with their social group. Approaches based in the supposed need for "dominance" over a dog are based on inaccurate assumptions and do great and sometimes irreparable harm. For example, if a dog is intent on resource guarding, physical punishment, such as picking her up and shaking her by the scruff of the neck, will often lead her to escalate guarding behaviors out of fear of this punishment. She may end up inflicting a serious (or "high-level") bite and, concomitantly, developing an increased fear of humans. Often no amount of training in other approaches can undo this fear, and the dogs end up being euthanized.[19]

R+ training methods may take time and experimentation, but mistakes in deploying them tend to require simple adjustments rather than the eventual euthanasia of a dog. For example, the main worry with R+ is that the timing of reinforcers might not be accurate: for instance, the dog may not recognize that giving up a prized tennis ball leads to a tasty treat or, more generally, that giving up resources leads to good things. In such instances, the dog may think, instead, that he is being rewarded for sitting or proffering a "look," for example. However, in such cases, a minor change of approach, such as reworking the timing to clarify which specific action is being rewarded, or changing markers—for example, using a clicker instead of a voice cue such as "nic," or vice versa, or using a different reinforcer like a squeaky ball if a dog isn't particularly motivated by food—is often all that is needed.

Adopting R+ approaches can promote and prompt curiosity in dogs themselves. Attunement to and engagement with body language, including one's own as a human and primate, is paramount, as is thinking carefully about how dogs think and how they learn best. Part of this entails taking seriously the responsibility of being at the other end of the leash— that is, sharing the burden of building understanding. Practices of consent are important. Most dogs are intrigued by the possibilities of learning and relating, but enabling them to choose whether to engage and, crucially, to take breaks or even end training sessions is necessary. It is also helpful to end a training session on a good note by soliciting an "easy" cue for a dog and to conclude with a short play session. Luminaries in this field include the ethologist Patricia McConnell, the trainers Leslie McDevitt and Karen Pryor, and the veterinary behaviorist Sophia Yin. Among professional trainers and behaviorists, avoid folks who promote the use of prong collars, choke chains, and e-collars (collars that deliver an electric shock or vibration), and who deploy the language of "balanced training," which is usually code for the mixing of aversive-based and R+ methods. (With deaf dogs, however, vibrating collars are invaluable.) If there is talk of "pack leadership," run the other way. Finally, it is important to remember that a good relationship with a dog, and a good training relationship as part of that, hinges on mutual respect, not some anthropocentric arrangement where a human is dominant.

Learn to Appreciate the Dog(s) You Have, Not the One(s) You Wanted

For many folks, getting a dog involves dreams of going to parks together, having company at gatherings, and snuggling. But many dogs do not share these dreams. For example, dogs who are reactive to other dogs can find dog parks scary places. (In fact, the inability of most humans to accurately read dog-dog interactions, for instance by misreading an initial growl as a sign of aggression rather than a correction, can lead to many human-human as well as dog-dog conflicts in dog parks.) Regardless, it's important to tailor your expectations of your dog(s) to their desires rather than your own dreams. If your dog is leash-reactive but fine with other dogs off leash, it's fine to engage in counterconditioning and desensitization, but you might also consider going to places where dogs can walk off leash (but make sure your dog is excellent at coming when called—that is, he has good "recall"—first!). Much frustration and disappointment can be averted by letting go of goals that your dog does not appear to share.

It's Okay to Want a Dog Who Isn't Traumatized

A central component of saviorist storying is the imperative to adopt a dog clearly in need of "rescue." This is reinforced through widespread shaming of people who do not adopt or do not want to adopt "rescues." But while plenty of dogs up for adoption these days are wonderful and have easily managed behavioral issues, many are simply not suitable for folks who are not well versed in dog behavior, particularly first-time owners. I know that I do not want another dog with the extent of behavioral problems that Annie has, and I should not be shamed for feeling that way. However, as I detail in chapter 4, dogs from official breeders are not guaranteed to be free from behavioral problems. It bears repeating here that Sharon noted to me that in her extensive experience consulting on serious behavioral problems, her clients consisted of roughly half purebreds and half rescues.[20] Getting a puppy is not a sure solution either, as raising puppies and socializing them well involves quite a bit of effort and know-how. All of this said, it is important to push back against the pervasive shaming that extends the neoliberalist impulse of saviorist approaches.

Rethink the Language of "Furbabies"

Rather than conscript dogs into human-specific practices and use terminology that positions them as "family," engage them in ways that attempt to reflect how they might perceive their relationship with you. There is a paucity of language for ways of relating in our social world. Thinking of and casually referring to dogs as one's children does real harm: dogs are not and should not be considered human. Terminology that reflects rather than overcodes the very nonhumanness of dogs nurtures ways of relating more friendly to mutual understanding and does away with the inappropriate expectations. Rather than recycle tired understandings, build new ones!

Multispecies Transformative Justice and Reworlding

In closing, I want to return to my imaginary field note, for while it reveals a world markedly different from that of most human-animal intraactions today, it is emplaced in familiar geographies and larger logics. The many interventions it describes demarcate only momentary interruptions in the logics and discourses, the norms and daily violences, that undergird and make possible particular forms of human-animal intraactions and not others. For example, a world where the Fourth of July poses a problem to both human-animal companionship and animal sheltering is a world that sustains the practices of colonialism. My imagined shelter still occupies stolen land, and the designations of dogs as "at large" or "strays" are shaped by a racist, colonialist, and capitalist nation-state's method of both mapping and producing geographies. As to the question of justice itself, my imagined interaction has no bearing on cases like that of Michael Vick; although the practices I detail through the analytic of interspecies intersectionality may prompt momentary interruptions of calls to, say, "neuter" or "euthanize" dog fighters, they do little to challenge the fact that animal cruelty charges are now a felony in all fifty U.S. states.[21] Those targeted by such laws are often folks who are vulnerable to structural (and, often, material) violences in ways similar to my imaginary woman and her dog.

There are multiple forms of violence at work both in the world that my imaginary field note counters and in the logics and discourses it fails to address. Literal violence, of course, involves physical harm and material neglect. The R+ approaches I describe act as a counter to at least one of these forms of violence. Another form of violence is discursive: that is, violences that happen through discourses, through the language in which ideas are shared and the logics that make ideas thinkable in the first place. One example is the presumptive connectivity through which the clustering of woman of color, pit bull–type dog, and loose dog would likely yield a "bad dog" and "irresponsible" human. Here racial-gendered Otherness conjoins with breed, marking a decidedly dismal, if also familiar, becoming in kind rendered intelligible through a shared presumptive "badness." Discursive violences also act as epistemic violences, violences that work at the level of thinking: that is, violences that mark the joinings of race, gender, and animality as Other in the first place.

Less abstract but deeply connected are structural violences, wherein the conjunction of racial capitalism, ongoing colonialism, and a white supremacist heteropatriarchy make people like my imaginary Filipina woman vulnerable to houselessness in the first place. We might imagine a more detailed scenario where pervasive misogyny and antimigrant bias make it hard for her to find a job, and when she does, she ends up quitting because she cannot handle the climate of sexual harassment. Or perhaps she has had to leave her place of work to care for an elderly family member, whose passing has left her in a financially precarious position but fortunate enough to have inherited a van so that she does not (yet) have to sleep on the street. These scenarios describe varying ways that abstractions and -isms, such as racism, become material, tangible, and real, constraining lives and rendering people vulnerable to more physical and literal violences: they are examples of structural violences. All of these forms of violence are revealed through my analytic of interspecies inter-sectionality, especially as they manifest in specific becomings in kind.

With questions of violences emerge questions of justice. What does justice look like in the dog worlds of this book? My imagining of the shelter as a space of succor, learning, and care draws on an understand-ing of the ways that humans, together with their animals, are margin-alized by and vulnerable to both discursive and structural violences. And yet remaking shelters into spaces of care does not counter the structural injustices and violences that render my imagined woman and her dog houseless in the first place. Nor does it alter the probability that, had the dog been wounded in a fight with another dog at an encampment of houseless folks prior to its escape on the July 4, in addition to being fined and kept separate from her dog, my imaginary woman might well have been charged with animal cruelty. If successful, such a charge would engender a host of additional problems and violences: after she had served time in prison and was permanently separated from her dog, her felony conviction would make finding a job almost impossible. And if her dog was not social with other dogs and ended up staying at the shelter for a prolonged period, his mental health would likely deteriorate, and he would end up like Beth—that is, dead.

In highlighting questions of violence and justice in this manner, I am interested in exploring the kind of justice necessary to produce real change. A punitive sense of justice—the sense of justice that emerges in calls to imprisonment, or the retributive logic wherein dogfighters them-selves are seen as deserving of euthanization—is not a justice that addresses the structural and discursive violences that I identify. And targeting an individual dogfighter with prison time and a felony convic-tion does little to intervene in the culture of dogfighting, including the masculinities that emerge in and through it. Indeed, dogfighters as well as those people likely to be charged with cruelty to and neglect of animals are symptoms of, and really victims of, the cultural work of racial capital-ism, a white cis ableist heteropatriarchy that valorizes "toxic masculini-ties," and ongoing colonialism.

In pointing to these cultural factors, I am invested in a movement and practice that has recently taken hold in legal circles and community work, called *transformative justice*. This approach builds on a related practice, *restorative justice*, which seeks justice through carefully structured and facilitated dialogues between a perpetrator and victim. The goal is not imprisonment but rather an accountability to the victim's needs. It usually entails changes in behavior and actions in conjunction with a recognition and acknowledgment of the harm caused. Transformative justice has a broader reach than restorative justice, which is usually localized through legal remedies and interactions between individuals; transformative justice focuses on larger structural and discursive violences with the goal of preventing interpersonal ones.[22]

What might a specifically multispecies transformative justice look like? What forms and practices might it comprise? In some ways, the scope of this question is otherworldly, for the answer involves the dismantling of racial capitalism, the decolonization of the United States (and other nation-states), the undoing of white cis heteropatriarchy and the ableism and transphobia that feed into it, and the introduction of an episteme wherein "the animal" and the "Other" are not co-constituted. This is why I read speculative fiction. And while these transformations are beyond the scope of this book, I would like to at least evoke the possibility of a different episteme. Given that the episteme that produces man's Others as subhuman, inhuman, and animal subtends the other formations I list, a change to this episteme might very well transform other norms and violences.

Epistemic and discursive change involves what Isabelle Stengers, drawing from the work of Alfred North Whitehead, terms "new abstractions."[23] For Stengers, new abstractions transform the way we perceive, prompting a "leap of the imagination," a "primary glimmering of consciousness [that] reveals *something that matters*."[24] New abstractions are new vectorizations of concrete experience, productions of an "empirically felt variation of the way our experience matters."[25] Further, new abstractions do not necessarily challenge the adequacy of an established matter of fact (such as the greenness of a leaf); rather, they suggest that adequacy itself is a trap, that emergences may be masked in stable facts.[26] The emergent relatings that I identify through queer affiliations in the troublesome worlds of animal shelter and rescue politics are strayings that demarcate new abstractions, alluring understandings that, even as they technically fit within an established social order, also push beyond it. These are bodily and material relatings that, in prompting understandings rooted in the twinned work of sensibility and awareness, yield something different, something new, something radical.

In claiming queer affiliations as new abstractions I refer, of course, to the more promising relatings I describe, not those that delineate shared deviations from a white supremacist heteronormativity. Further, there is no "recipe" for queer affiliations: much as Audre Lorde's invocation of poetry reveals a way of knowing and understanding that cannot be encapsulated into easily transmissible "immutable mobiles," the bodyings and connectivities I highlight are not practices easily encoded into any kind of formula. They transcend both the language and logics of a social order intent on demarcating and isolating intimacy through kinship. And yet these strayings lure us toward different understandings nonetheless: "new" in the myriad ways they counter not only the Cartesian mind/body divide but also the positioning of "the animal." In attending to the material naturecultures of living animals, queer affiliations challenge understandings of animality that, in turn, subtend conceptions of man's Others. Queer affiliations can be seen as becomings that disorder "kind."

Queer affiliations share a move that is both simple and profound: rather than counter the binary logic of man/animal by elevating "the animal" to the level of the human—the humanizing move Glick and others read in the use of the human-specific language of murder and killing with reference to Michael Vick's dogs, and the calls for animals to have "rights"— they dehumanize the human. For example, in my own fretting about how to finish this conclusion and this book, I decided to take off my shoes and scrunch my toes in my dingy carpet—not because I wanted to emulate Bruce Willis in *Die Hard* and the troubled and vulnerable white masculinity his bare feet evoke throughout that film, but because I wanted to emulate what I ask of Annie in our joint labors toward ameliorating her leash reactivity. Just as I push her to think with her body by asking her to stand first on concrete and then on grass in order to stop her circling worries, I wanted to push myself to feel-with and therefore think-with, -in, and -through my body. I pushed myself to think differently so that I might disrupt my own understanding and, hopefully, invite something new, something bodily, something decidedly nonhuman, in. That is, I engaged my body as animal. Countering the human exceptionalism that underpins the binaries of human/animal and man/ Other, the bodily sensibility I describe with this and other queer affiliations joins with an awareness of the violences claimed in the name of "the human," so that what emerges is not the claim trafficked so loosely in "Can't we all just get along?" approaches—namely that "we are all human"—but rather the obverse. Queer affiliations ask us to engage with and relate through a "we" that is animal—that is, a "we" that is not human at all.

Critics of Puar's *assemblages* take issue with a theorization that decenters the subject when so many people have never been subjects in the first place; this claim may well engender similar worries. Yet I also hope that readers might take up this intervention as a means to counter the crafting of man's Others, nonhuman animal or no—that is, as an epistemic disruption that can and should be sustained, one that counters the violences of a human produced through Others who become denigrated in and through categorical kinds. And in arguing for the importance of queer affiliations in moving us toward a deeply sensible awareness, toward a recognition that "we are all animal," I hope that readers identify the beginnings of an intervention desperately needed: a multispecies transformative justice.

Notes

Introduction

I use pseudonyms for all the interlocutors in this book.

1   BADRAP (Bay Area Dog Lovers Responsible about Pit Bulls), https://bad rap.org, accessed January 29, 2020.

2   Mary Franklin Harvin, "Newsome Proposes $50M to Make California a 'No Kill' State for Shelter Animals," KQED News, January 13, 2020.

3   See *Sports Illustrated*, cover, July 27, 1987.

4   See E. M. Swift, "The Pit Bull Friend and Killer," *Sports Illustrated*, July 27, 1987; see also Bronwyn Dickey's fantastic *Pit Bull: The Battle over an American Icon* (New York: Alfred A. Knopf, 2016) for more on these narratives and changes.

5   Malcolm Gladwell, *The Tipping Point: How Little Things Can Make a Big Difference* (New York: Little, Brown, 2000).

6   Steve Hummer, "Vick Burns in Tailgate Effigy at Dome," *Atlanta Journal-Constitution*, September 18, 2011.

7   The trope of the "Vicktim" is prominent in the organization BADRAP's advocacy: BADRAP, "Vick: Still Not Sorry (We Checked)," October 14, 2009, http://badrap-blog.blogspot.com/2009/10/youll-probably-read-this-around -net.html.

8   Megan Glick, "Animal Instincts: Race, Criminality, and the Reversal of the 'Human,'" *American Quarterly* 65, no. 3 (2013): 639–60; see also Christie Keith, "Michael Vick's Unpaid Dues: Why Dog Advocates Aren't Moving On," SFGate, August 25, 2014.

9   For example, see "Meet Leo, Our Michael Vick Dog," Our Pack, www.our pack.org/leo.html, accessed January 22, 2020.

10   See Darren Rovell, "Michael Vick: Rating Those Dogfighting T-Shirts," CNBC, August 6, 2007.

11   David Delaney, "The Space That Race Makes," *Professional Geographer* 54, no. 1 (2002): 6–14.

12 Kimberlé Crenshaw, "Demarginalizing the Intersection of Race and Sex: A Black Feminist Critique of Antidiscrimination Doctrine, Feminist Theory, and Antiracist Politics," *University of Chicago Legal Forum* 1989, no. 1 (1989): 141–43.

13 Crenshaw, "Demarginalizing the Intersection of Race and Sex," 149.

14 Crenshaw, "Demarginalizing the Intersection of Race and Sex," 149.

15 See Jennifer Nash's wonderful summary of this and related moves in her chapter "A Love Letter from a Critic, or Notes on the Intersectionality Wars," in *Black Feminism Reimagined after Intersectionality* (Durham, NC: Duke University Press, 2019), 33–58.

16 Patricia Hill Collins, *Black Feminist Thought: Knowledge, Consciousness, and the Politics of Empowerment* (Boston: Unwin Hyman, 1990), 221–38.

17 Catie Hogan, "I Googled 'Intersectionality' so Now I'm Totally Woke," *McSweeney's*, March 7, 2017.

18 Nash, *Black Feminism Reimagined*, 44, 45.

19 I thank anonymous reviewer A for pointing me to this working of property logic.

20 Nash, *Black Feminism Reimagined*, 49, 56, 35.

21 Jennifer C. Nash, "Re-thinking Intersectionality," *Feminist Review* no. 89 (2008): 11.

22 *Trans** denotes the use of *trans* as a prefix with any number of signifiers; in trans* communities in particular, *trans** can gesture toward transsexual, transgender, and simply trans.

23 I owe this insight to the participants in my Spring 2020 graduate seminar, Theories and Methodologies in Gender, Women, and Sexuality Studies, at Kansas State University.

24 See Jasbir Puar, "I Would Rather Be a Cyborg Than a Goddess: Becoming Intersectional in Assemblage Theory," *Philosophia* 2, no. 1 (2012): 49–66.

25 Gail Mason, *The Spectacle of Violence: Homophobia, Gender, and Knowledge* (New York: Routledge, 2002), 61; Sarah Lamble, "Retelling Racialized Violence, Remaking White Innocence: The Politics of Interlocking Oppressions in Transgender Day of Remembrance," *Sexuality Research and Social Policy* 5, no. 1 (2008): 32.

26 Jasbir Puar and Julie Livingston, "Interspecies," *Social Text* 106 (2011): 3.

27 See Eleanor Klibanoff, "A History of Quarantines, from Bubonic Plague to Typhoid Mary," NPR, January 26, 2020. Also, here I draw from Mel Chen's wonderful analysis in *Animacies: Biopolitics, Racial Mattering, and Queer Affect* (Durham, NC: Duke University Press, 2012), 168–71.

28 Puar, "I Would Rather Be a Cyborg."

29 See Dylan Scott, "Trump's New Fixation on Using a Racist Name for the Coronavirus Is Dangerous," *Vox*, March 18, 2020, www.vox.com/2020/3/18/21185478/coronavirus-usa-trump-chinese-virus.

30 For an example of this critique, see Tyrone Palmer, "'What Feels More Than Feeling?': Theorizing the Unthinkability of Black Affect," *Journal*

of Critical Ethnic Studies 3, no. 2 (2017): 1–3. Palmer points to Brian Massumi's *Parables for the Virtual: Movement, Affect, Sensation* (Durham, NC: Duke University Press, 2002) as a strong example of this type of work.

31 See critiques in A. Breeze Harper, *Sistah Vegan: Black Female Vegans Speak on Food, Identity, Health, and Society* (Brooklyn: Lantern, 2010).

32 Eve Kosofsky Sedgwick, *Tendencies* (Durham NC: Duke University Press, 1993), 5–9.

33 For example, see Emma Whitford, "When Walking While Trans Is a Crime," *The Cut*, January 2018, www.thecut.com/2018/01/when-walking-while -trans-is-a-crime.html.

34 For more on the policing and variations of hair, see "Native American Hairstyles," Native Languages, www.native-languages.org/hair.htm, accessed January 22, 2020.

35 With the term *redemption* I am referencing the *Sports Illustrated* writer Jim Gorant's book *The Lost Dogs: Michael Vick's Dogs and Their Tales of Rescue and Redemption* (New York: Gotham, 2010).

36 Chandan Reddy, "Home, Houses, Nonidentity: Paris Is Burning," in *Burning Down the House: Recycling Domesticity*, ed. Rosemary Marangoly George (New York: Routledge, 1988), 356, 360.

37 Reddy, "Home, Houses, Nonidentity," 361.

38 Cathy Cohen, "Punks, Bulldaggers, and Welfare Queens: The Radical Potential of Queer Politics?" *GLQ* 3 (1997): 437–65.

39 Chen, *Animacies*, 14.

40 The phrasing *multispecies justice* emerges out of ongoing conversations with Donna Haraway, for which I am deeply grateful.

41 Pseudonymous interview with Cynthia, July 2017.

42 "Meat Equals Slavery," PETA, last modified October 14, 2013, www.peta .org/blog/meat-equals-slavery/.

43 Marjorie Spiegel, *The Dreaded Comparison: Human and Animal Slavery* (New York: Mirror, 1997).

44 #Mike for Bachelor Campaign Account (@Maddie_Jones515), Twitter, April 2, 2019, https://twitter.com/Maddie_Jones515/status/111315677 3484146688.

45 Lalo Alcaraz, "Oh My God, This Cruelty Must Stop!," June 7, 2018, www .gocomics.com/laloalcaraz/2018/06/07.

46 In referring to concentration camps I write in accordance with numerous others who position current U.S. detention practices in the context of large-scale humanitarian atrocities; for example, see Masha Gessen, "The Unimaginable Reality of American Concentration Camps," *New Yorker*, June 21, 2019. It should also be noted that most dogs find crating enjoyable when it is practiced properly. For more information about crate training, see Nancy Kerns, "The Benefits of Crate Training Your Dog from an Early Age," *Whole Dog Journal*, last modified March 21, 2019, www.whole

-dog-journal.com/training/crates/the-benefits-of-crate-training-your
-dog-from-an-early-age/.

47 Lori Gruen, "Samuel Dubose, Cecil the Lion and the Ethics of Avowal,"
    Al Jazeera America, July 31, 2015.
48 For example, see Diana Náñez, "Puppies on a Plane: The flight to Idaho
    That Saved 49 Cuddly, Squirming Bundles of Arizona Fur," *AZCentral*,
    April 6, 2016, www.azcentral.com/story/news/local/phoenix-best-reads
    /2016/04/06/puppies-plane-flight-idaho-saved-49-cuddly-squirming
    -bundles-arizona-fur/82540390/.
49 For example, see "Rescue," Adopt a Doggie, https://adoptadoggie.org
    /rescue.php, accessed July 30, 2019.
50 Pseudonymous interview with María, July 2017.

1. Gimme Shelter

1   Author's field notes, May 2013.
2   "Save Them All, No-Kill Movement Timeline: History of Best Friends
    Animal Society." Best Friends, https://bestfriends.org/about/our-story/
    no-kill-timeline, accessed December 17, 2019; Gregory Castle, "A Nod to
    the Innovator of Our Era, the Father of the No-Kill Movement Retires,"
    Best Friends, April 18, 2015, https://bestfriends.org/blogs/2015/04/08
    /a-nod-to-the-innovator-of-our-era-the-father-of-the-no-kill-movement-
    retires.
3   Lynda Foro, "The History of the No Kill Movement," Maddie's Fund, www
    .maddiesfund.org/the-history-of-the-no-kill-movement.htm, accessed
    December 17, 2019; Nathan Winograd, "Books," www.nathanwinograd.
    com/bookstore, accessed December 17, 2019.
4   Foro, "The History of the No Kill Movement."
5   Winograd, "Books."
6   Winograd, "Books."
7   "Pet Statistics: How Many Pets Are in the United States? How Many Ani-
    mals Are in Shelters?," ASPCA, www.aspca.org/animal-homelessness/
    shelter-intake-and-surrender/pet-statistics, accessed December 17, 2019.
    See also Shelter Animals Count, www.shelteranimalscount.org, accessed
    December 17, 2019.
8   For more information, see Maddie's Fund website, www.maddiesfund.
    org/index.htm, accessed December 20, 2019.
9   Pseudonymous interview by author with Jane, July 2017.
10 Pseudonymous interview by author with Nathan, July 2017.
11 Leah Fellows, "Adopt Don't Shop: 8 Reasons Why; They May Surprise
    You," Lu's Labs blog, www.luslabs.org/lus-labs-blog/2018/5/24/adopt-
    dont-shop-8-reasons-why-they-may-surprise-you, accessed December 19,
    2019.

12 For some of these critiques, see Sally Jones, "Adopt, Don't Shop: A Phrase Worth Thousands of Lives," *Canine Journal*, December 7, 2017, www.canine journal.com/adopt-dont-shop.

13 Julia Lane, "AKC Announces Mixed Breed Program: Mutt Lovers Question the New 'Separate but Equal' Designation," *The Bark*, April 2009, updated February 2015, https://thebark.com/content/akc-announces -mixed-breed-program.

14 American Pet Products Association, "Pet Industry Market Size and Ownership Statistics, www.americanpetproducts.org/press_industrytrends .asp, accessed December 18, 2019.

15 See Associated Press, "U.S. Income Inequality at Highest Level in 50 Years, Economic Gap Growing in Heartland," September 26, 2019.

16 "Stand Out from the Pack," Embrace Pet Insurance, www.embracepet insurance.com/employers, accessed December 20, 2019. Seven percent of workplaces now allow pets, according to Naz Beheshti, "Pet-Friendly Workplaces Are a Win-Win for Employee Wellbeing and for Business," *Forbes*, May 22, 2019.

17 Pseudonymous interview with Sara, July 2017.

18 Here I am referencing Spivak's phrasing "white men saving brown women from brown men" in her discussion of British interventions in practices of *sati* in colonial India despite a stated policy of benign neglect. See Gayatri Chakravorty Spivak, *A Critique of Postcolonial Reason: Toward a History of the Vanishing Present* (Cambridge, MA: Harvard University Press, 1999).

19 Pseudonymous interview with Jennifer, July 2017.

20 Pseudonymous interview with Sandra, July 2017.

21 Author's field notes, August 2018.

22 Pseudonymous interview with Jane, July 2017.

23 Nicoledogs, "Why We Need to Talk about Racism, Prejudice and Dog Rescue," Redemption Dogs, August 15, 2017, https://redemptiondogs.com /2017/08/15/racism-animal-rescue-why-we-need-to-talk-about-this.

24 Nicoledogs, "Why We Need to Talk."

25 Nicoledogs, "Why We Need to Talk."

26 "Their Lives Matter," https://theirlivesmatter.org, accessed July 30, 2019; "Black Labs Matter," www.facebook.com/blacklabsmatter, accessed July 30, 2019.

27 "All Paws Matter," www.apmrescue.com, accessed July 30, 2019.

28 Doggie Protective Services, www.dpsrescue.org, accessed January 26, 2020; Child Welfare Information Gateway, "Racial Disproportionality and Disparity in Child Welfare," 2016, www.childwelfare.gov/pubs/issue-briefs /racial-disproportionality.

29 "Saving Deathrow Dogs," Facebook, www.facebook.com/savingdeathrow dogs, accessed December 29, 2019.

30 Dean Spade, "The New Transgender Movement: Race, Poverty, Gender, Policing, and Pinkwashing," *The Laura Flanders Show*, June 23, 2015, www.youtube.com/watch?v=eQJigIBllbU.

31 See Eli Clare, *Exile and Pride: Disability, Queerness, and Liberation* (Boston: South End Press, 1999).

32 *Holiday Film, Saving Up*, Petco commercial, November 14, 2018, www.youtube.com/watch?v=c4_qb2GJACg.

33 Susan Wendell, *The Rejected Body* (New York: Routledge, 1996).

34 See "Walkin' Wheels Dog Wheelchair; Fully Adjustable," Walkin' Pets, www.handicappedpets.com/adjustable-dog-wheelchairs, accessed July 30, 2019.

35 Dominique Mosbergen, "Man Transforms His Home into a Cat Paradise for Maximum Kitty Fun," HuffPost, December 6, 2017.

36 Author's field notes, September 2012.

37 Pseudonymous interview with Rowena, July 2017.

38 For example, see Sarah Wolfe, "Nearly 370 Pit Bulls Seized in Massive Southeast Dog Fighting Bust," Public Radio International, August 27, 2013, www.pri.org/stories/2013-08-27/nearly-370-pit-bulls-seized-massive-southeast-dog-fighting-bust-video.

39 David Delaney, "The Space That Race Makes," *Professional Geographer* 54, no. 1 (2002): 6–14.

40 Author's field notes, September 2012.

41 Pseudonymous interview with Marta, July 2017.

42 See the website My Pit Bull Is Family, www.mypitbullisfamily.org, accessed July 30, 2019.

43 For example, see "Home for the Holidays," Valley Humane Society, https://valleyhumane.org/adoption/home-for-the-holidays, accessed July 30, 2019.

44 For example, see Kristina Marusic, "This Gay Couple Has Rescued More Than 10,000 Dogs," Logo Newnownext, November 15, 2017, www.newnownext.com/ron-danta-and-danny-robertshaw-life-in-the-dog-house/11/2017.

45 Kami Chisholm, dir., *Pride Denied: Homonationalism and the Future of Queer Politics* (San Francisco: Media Education Foundation, 2016).

46 Pseudonymous interview with Teresa, July 2017.

47 Pseudonymous interview with Sharon, July 2017.

48 By "serious bite" I mean a high-level bite according to widely circulated bite scales like the one put forward by Ian Dunbar, "Dr. Ian Dunbar's Dog Bite Scale (Official Authorized Version)," https://apdt.com/wp-content/uploads/2017/01/ian-dunbar-dog-bite-scale.pdf, accessed January 26, 2020.

49 Author's field notes, May 2013.

50 Here I am in dialogue with my friend and colleague Katharine Mershon, who writes beautifully about this dynamic in the field of religious studies.

See Katharine Mershon, "Animal Rescue and Gender," in *Gender: Animals*, ed. Juno Parreñas, 119–32 (New York: MacMillan Reference USA, 2017).

51 For example, the Imagine This company sells a "Who rescued who?" magnet, available at www.chewy.com/imagine-this-company-who-rescued -who/dp/142227, accessed July 30, 2019.

52 Pseudonymous interview with Nathan, July 2017.

53 Pseudonymous interview with Jessica, July 2017.

54 Pseudonymous interview with Jessica, July 2017.

55 Pseudonymous interview with Teresa, July 2017.

56 Most of my interlocutors are invested in setting dogs up in situations where such behaviors do not have an opportunity to manifest in the first place. Encounters like this have generally occurred while assessing dogs with behavioral problems in order to identify the scope of the dogs' reactivity. Pseudonymous interview with María, July 2017.

57 Pseudonymous interview with Teresa, July 2017.

58 Pseudonymous interview with Nathan, July 2017.

59 Pseudonymous interview with Sara, July 2017.

60 Pseudonymous interview with Sara, July 2017.

61 Pseudonymous interview with Veronica, July 2017.

62 Author's field notes, September 2012.

63 Psuedonymous interview with Rowena, July 2017. My discussion with Rowena reflects the nuanced engagement of Julietta Hua and Neel Ahuja with transspecies care in nonprofit chimpanzee sanctuaries, which involves a deeply practical attention to the dynamics of care in the context of an unending captivity. See Julietta Hua and Neel Ahuja, "Chimpanzee Sanctuary: 'Surplus' Life and the Politics of Transspecies Care," *American Quarterly* 65, no. 3 (September 2013): 619–63.

64 Pseudonymous interview with Kayla, July 2017.

65 Pseudonymous interview with Veronica, July 2017.

66 Pseudonymous interview with Kayla, July 2017.

67 Pseudonymous interview with Teresa, July 2017.

68 Author's field notes, June 2013.

69 Pseudonymous interview with Rossella, July 2017.

70 While dog behaviors are context-specific—a sit cue is much more likely to be heeded at home than at the dog park—simply removing the dog from the context of the shelter does not undo the behavior chain that precipitates a bite and does not promise that a dog confronted with circumstances resembling those that informed its earlier fearfulness will alter its response.

71 Pseudonymous interview with Kayla, July 2017.

72 Pseudonymous interview with Veronica, July 2017.

73 Pseudonymous interview with Kayla, July 2017.

74 I am deeply grateful to Katie Batza and the humanities seminar at the University of Kansas for this wonderful insight regarding the connection

between shame and neoliberalism. I am also deeply grateful for extended conversations with Rana Jaleel on this topic.

75   Pseudonymous interview with Naomi, July 2017.

76   Shelter Animals Count, personal correspondence, December 17, 2019.

77   Google Ngram Viewer, https://books.google.com/ngrams/graph?content= animal+rescue&year_start=1900&year_end=2008&corpus=15&smooth ing=3&share=&direct_url=t1%3B%2Canimal%20rescue%3B%2Cc0, accessed July 30, 2019.

78   Pseudonymous interview with Kayla, July 2017.

79   Author's field notes, July 2017.

80   Pseudonymous interview with Sara, July 2017.

81   Pseudonymous interview with Rossella, July 2017.

82   Author's field notes, June 2013.

83   Pseudonymous interview with Jessica, July 2017.

84   I owe this insight to the careful reading and feedback of Rana Jaleel, whose commitments to interrogating the problems of capitalism and neoliberalism add much-needed depth to my own thinking here.

85   Author's field notes, July 24, 2017.

86   See Mark Rifkin, *When Did Indians Become Straight? Kinship, the History of Sexuality, and Native Sovereignty* (New York: Oxford University Press, 2011).

87   See Rifkin, "Romancing Kinship: A Queer Reading of Indian Education and Zitkala-Sa's American Indian Stories," *GLQ* 12, no. 1 (2006): 28; Scott Lauria Morgensen, *Spaces between Us: Queer Settler Colonialism and Indigenous Decolonization* (Minneapolis: University of Minnesota Press, 2011).

88   Rifkin, "Romancing Kinship," 28.

89   Reddy, "Home, Houses, Nonidentity," 360.

90   I owe this insight to anonymous reviewer A.

91   Pseudonymous interview with Rowena, July 2017.

92   Pseudonymous interview with Sharon, July 2017.

93   Pseudonymous interview with Sharon, July 2017.

94   Puig, *Matters of Care: Speculative Ethics in More Than Human Worlds* (Minneapolis: Minnesota University Press, 2017), 71.

95   Brigitte Fielder, "Animal Humanism: Race, Species, and Affective Kinship in Nineteenth-Century Abolitionism," *American Quarterly* 65, no. 3 (2013): 487–514.

96   Pseudonymous interview with María, July 2017.

97   I am particularly grateful to anonymous reviewer A, whose thinking in this regard reshaped my own.

98   Michelle Alexander, *The New Jim Crow: Mass Incarceration in the Age of Colorblindness* (New York: New Press, 2010).

99   Pseudonymous interview with Kayla, July 2017.

2. The Human, the Animal, the Episteme

1 Author's field notes, June 2013.
2 Author's field notes, July 2013.
3 Author's field notes, October 2016.
4 Jakob von Uexküll, "A Stroll through the Worlds of Animals and Men: A Picture Book of Invisible Worlds," 1934, trans. and ed. Claire H. Schiller, in *Instinctive Behavior: The Development of a Modern Concept* (New York: International Universities Press, 1957), 5–80.
5 See Mark Rifkin, *When Did Indians Become Straight?* (New York: Oxford University Press, 2011).
6 Donna Haraway, *When Species Meet* (Minneapolis: University of Minnesota Press, 2008), 37–38.
7 Sylvia Wynter, "Unsettling the Coloniality of Being/Power/Truth/Freedom: Towards the Human, after Man, Its Overrepresentation; An Argument," *CR: The New Centennial Review* 3, no. 3 (2003): 257–337.
8 Wynter, "Unsettling the Coloniality," 290, 263.
9 Anibal Quijano, "Coloniality of Power and Eurocentrism in Latin America," *Nepantla* 1, no. 3 (2000): 555.
10 Wynter, "Unsettling the Coloniality," 297.
11 Quijano, "Coloniality of Power," 555, 533–536.
12 Of course, numerous scholars in addition to Quijano and Wynter explore these dynamics. Among them are Achille Mbembe and Libby Meintjes, who note: "Nature thus remains, in all its majesty, an overwhelming reality compared to which they appear to be *phantoms, unreal and ghostlike*. The savages are, as it were, 'natural' human beings who lack the specifically human character, the specifically human reality, 'so that when European men massacred them they somehow were not aware that they had committed murder'" (emphasis in original). Achille Mbembe and Libby Meintjes, "Necropolitics," *Public Culture* 15, no. 1 (2003): 24.
13 Che Gossett, "Blackness, Animality, and the Unsovereign," Verso blog, September 8, 2015, www.versobooks.com/blogs/2228-che-gossett-blackness-animality-and-the-unsovereign.
14 Wynter, "Unsettling the Coloniality," 305.
15 I put *Caucasians* in quotes here because the term originated in this time as a descriptor of peoples from the Georgian Caucasus but quickly became a referent for a more generalized whiteness. The formation of that whiteness has, of course, undergone numerous transmutations between then and now. See Ladelle McWhorter, "Enemy of the Species," in *Queer Ecologies*, ed. Catriona Mortimer-Sandilands and Bruce Erickson (Bloomington: Indiana University Press, 2010), 81.
16 McWhorter, "Enemy of the Species," 77, 80.

17 For more on Sims, see Brynn Holland, "The 'Father of Modern Gynecology' Performed Shocking Experiments on Slaves: He Was a Medical Trailblazer, but at What Cost?," History.com, August 29, 2017.

18 McWhorter, "Enemy of the Species," 81; Stephen J. Gould, *The Mismeasure of Man* (New York: W. W. Norton,1981).

19 Josiah Nott and George Gliddon, *Types of Mankind* (Philadelphia: Lippincott, Grambo, 1854), 458.

20 Charles Darwin, *The Descent of Man* (New York: American Home Library, 1902), 398.

21 Michael Lundblad, *The Birth of the Jungle: Animality in Progressive-Era U.S. Literature and Culture* (New York: Oxford University Press, 2015).

22 Quijano, "Coloniality of Power," 556.

23 Lugones, "Heterosexualism and the Colonial/Modern Gender System," *Hypatia*, 22, no.1 (2007): 203. Importantly, Lugones notes that "women racialized as inferior" might be transformed into modified versions of "women" through concubinage and similar practices in accordance with the logic of "global, Eurocentered Capitalism," but that the category of "Woman" as it inheres in the "light side" of the gender system remained forever closed to them.

24 For a more detailed account, see Deborah Miranda, "Extermination of the *Joyas*: Gendercide in Spanish California," *GLQ* 16, nos. 1–2 (2010): 253–84.

25 See Sally Markowitz, "Pelvic Politics: Sexual Dimorphism and Racial Difference," *Signs* 26, no. 2 (2001): 389–414.

26 McWhorter, "Enemy of the Species," 83. For more on the history of eugenics, see Nancy Ordover, *American Eugenics: Race, Queer Anatomy, and the Science of Nationalism* (Minneapolis: University of Minnesota Press, 2003).

27 I encourage readers who are interested in tracing out these workings more thoroughly to look into the writings of Bénédicte Boisseron, Claire Jean Kim, Neel Ahuja, Mel Chen, Michael Lundblad, Colin Dayan, Che Gossett, Alexander Weheliye, and Carla Freccero.

28 Claire Jean Kim, *Dangerous Crossings: Race, Species and Nature in a Multicultural Age* (New York: Cambridge University Press, 2015), 51.

29 *Qimmit: A Clash of Two Truths*, dir. Ole Gjerstad and Joelie Sanguya (2012), https://vimeo.com/44819444.

30 Kim, *Dangerous Crossings*, 54–59.

31 Kim, *Dangerous Crossings*, 26–28, 18.

32 Quoted in Gregory Korte and Alan Gomez, "Trump Ramps Up Rhetoric on Undocumented Immigrants: 'These Aren't People. These Are Animals,'" *USA Today*, May 17, 2018.

33 Dan Hassler-Forest, "'The Lion King is a Fascistic Story: No Remake Can Change That," *Washington Post*, July 10, 2019.

34 See Travis M. Andrews, "The Original 'Dumbo' Was Decried as Racist: Here's How Tim Burton's Version Addresses That," *Washington Post*, March 29, 2019.

35   Soul Alchemy, "Save a Pitbull, Euthanize a Dog Fighter," Facebook, January 2, 2020, www.facebook.com/marciaswords/posts/1152285371646054.

36   See Noel Sturgeon, "Penguin Family Values: The Nature of Planetary Environmental Reproductive Justice," in *Queer Ecologies*, ed. Catriona Mortimer-Sandilands and Bruce Erickson (Bloomington: Indiana University Press, 2010), 102–33.

37   Alex Moyle, "Using Dogs as Tools of Racist Repression," *Socialist Worker*, July 17, 2018, https://socialistworker.org/2018/07/17/using-dogs-as-a-tool-of-racist-repression.

38   See "Dakota Access Pipeline Company Attacks Native American Protesters with Dogs and Pepper Spray," *Democracy Now*, September 3, 2016, www.youtube.com/watch?v=kuZcx2zE04k; Mary Lee Grant and Nick Miroff, "U.S. Militia Groups Head to Border, Stirred by Trump's Call to Arms," *Texas Tribune*, November 4, 2018, www.texastribune.org/2018/11/04/us-militia-groups-head-border-stirred-trumps-call-arms.

39   Bénédicte Boisseron, *Afro-Dog* (New York: Columbia University Press, 2018), 71.

40   See Caroline Criado-Perez, *Invisible Women: Exposing Data Bias in a World Designed for Men* (New York: Abrams, 2019).

41   "Color Film Was Designed to Take Pictures of White People, Not People of Color: The Unfortunate History of Racial Bias in Photography (1940–1990)," Open Culture, July 2, 2018, www.openculture.com/2018/07/color-film-was-designed-to-take-pictures-of-white-people-not-people-of-color.html.

42   See Sandra Harding, "Introduction," in *The Feminist Standpoint Theory Reader: Intellectual and Political Controversies*, ed. Sandra Harding (New York: Routledge, 2004); see also Patricia Hill Collins, *Black Feminist Thought: Knowledge, Consciousness, and the Politics of Empowerment* (New York: Routledge, 2000).

43   See Donna Haraway, "Situated Knowledges: The Science Question in Feminism and the Privilege of Partial Perspective," *Feminist Studies* 14, no. 3 (1988): 575–99.

44   Audre Lorde, *Sister Outsider* (Berkeley, CA: Crossing, 1984), 38, cited in Eve Tuck and K. Wayne Yang, "Decolonization Is Not a Metaphor," *Decolonization, Indigeneity, Education, and Society* 1, no. 1 (2012): 1–40. For an additional and profound reading of both Lorde and Zora Neale Hurston, see Lindsey Andrews, "Black Feminism's Minor Empiricism: Hurston, Combahee, and the Experience of Evidence," *Catalyst: Feminism, Theory, Technoscience* 1, no. 1 (2015): 1–38. See also Haraway, "Situated Knowledges."

45   Lorde, *Sister Outsider*, 37.

46   "Audre Lorde," Poetry Foundation, www.poetryfoundation.org/poets/audre-lorde.

47   Quoted in Jeremy Stahl, "'This Is Not Going Well': NBC Producers Look Back on the Concert for Katrina's Kanye Moment," Slate.com, August 27,

2015, quoted in Patrick Shanley, "'SNL': Kanye West Gave Pro-Trump Speech That Didn't Make It to Air," *Hollywood Reporter*, September 30, 2018.

48 Bruno Latour, *Science in Action: How to Follow Scientists and Engineers through Society* (Cambridge, MA: Harvard University Press, 1988).

49 Puig, *Matters of Care*, 58, 59.

50 Puig, "'Nothing Comes without Its World': Thinking with Care," *Sociological Review* 60, no. 2 (2012): 198, 204.

51 For more on "intra-actions," see Karen Barad, *Meeting the Universe Halfway: Quantum Physics and the Entanglement of Matter and Meaning* (Durham, NC: Duke University Press, 2007).

52 Jane Bennett, *Lively Matter: Towards a Political Ecology of Things* (Durham, NC: Duke University Press, 2010), 1, 2.

53 Brian Massumi, "Introduction," in *A Thousand Plateaus*, ed. Gilles Deleuze and Félix Guattari (Minneapolis: University of Minnesota Press, 1987), xvi.

54 Mel Chen, *Animacies: Biopolitics, Racial Mattering, and Queer Affect* (Durham, NC: Duke University Press, 2012), 3.

55 Chen, *Animacies*, 11, 18.

56 Chen, *Animacies*, 14.

57 Chen, *Animacies*, 111.

58 *Oxford English Dictionary*, 2nd ed. (Oxford: Oxford University Press, 2004), s.v. "eugenic."

59 Author's field notes, July 2017.

60 See Eve Kosofsky Sedgwick, "Introduction," in *Touching Feeling: Affect, Pedagogy, Performativity* (Durham, NC: Duke University Press, 2003).

61 Author's field notes, May 2013.

62 See for example Centers for Disease Control, "About Pets and People," www.cdc.gov/healthypets/health-benefits/index.html.

63 *Oxford English Dictionary*, 2nd ed. (Oxford: Oxford University Press, 2004), s.v. "pet."

64 Pseudonymous interview with Cynthia, July 2017.

65 Author's field notes, October 2012.

66 Pseudonymous interview with Yolanda, July 2017.

67 Pseudonymous interview with Nathan, July 2017; Oxford English Dictionary, 2nd ed. (Oxford: Oxford University Press, 2004), s.v. "creepy."

68 Pseudonymous interview with Nathan, July 2017.

69 Pseudonymous interview with Nathan, July 2017.

70 Pseudonymous interview with Nathan, July 2017.

71 Author's field notes, July 2013.

72 Author's field notes, July 2017.

73 Author's field notes, July 2017.

74 Author's field notes, June 2013.

75 Haraway, *When Species Meet*, 336n27.

76 Pseudonymous interview with Nathan, July 2017.

77 Chen, *Animacies*, 99.

78 The concept of *misplaced concreteness* derives from the work of Alfred North Whitehead, which has informed Haraway's scholarship in key ways. For more, see the "Art in Conversation: Donna Haraway with Thyrza Nichols Goodeve," *Brooklyn Rail*, December 2017, https://brooklynrail.org /2017/12/art/DONNA-HARAWAY-with-Thyrza-Nichols-Goodeve.

79 Donna Haraway, *The Companion Species Manifesto* (Chicago: Prickly Paradigm Press, 2003), 1–25.

80 For more on this topic, see Dave Mech, "Wolf News and Information," Dave Mech blog, https://davemech.org/wolf-news-and-information/, accessed July 30, 2019.

81 Many have written on this particular dynamic, but Lauren Berlant's writings in *The Queen of America Goes to Washington City* are particularly salient (Durham, NC: Duke University Press, 1997).

82 Here I am anticipating and attempting to channel Haraway's writings in *When Species Meet* in particular.

83 This example comes from an episode of the rather terrible 1990s television show *Home Improvement*, which has apparently stuck with me these many years.

84 For example, see Marina Kachar, Ewa Sawosz, and André Chwalibog, "Orcas Are Social Mammals," *International Journal of Avian and Wildlife Biology* 3, no. 4 (2018): 291–95.

85 See Robert M. Sapolsky, "Warrior Baboons Give Peace a Chance," *Yes!* (Spring 2011): 34–37.

86 Uexküll, "A Stroll through the Worlds."

87 Giorgio Agamben, *The Open: Man and Animal*, trans. Kevin Attell (Stanford, CA: Stanford University Press, 2002), 40.

88 Uexküll, "A Stroll through the Worlds," 7.

89 Agamben, *The Open*, 46.

90 Vinciane Despret, "Responding Bodies and Partial Affinities in Human-Animal Worlds," *Theory, Culture, and Society* 30, nos. 7–8 (2013): 51–76.

91 Despret, "Responding Bodies and Partial Affinities," 69.

92 Despret, "Responding Bodies and Partial Affinities," 70.

93 Cesar Millan, "Does Your Dog Respect You?," Cesar's Way, November 13, 2015, www.cesarsway.com/does-your-dog-respect-you/.

94 In focusing on R+ approaches I seek to counter the thinking of scholars such as Yi-Fu Tuan, who argues that the "pet" is produced as an entity through the entwining of human dominance and affection. In R+ approaches I locate specific interrelatings that not only work against such anthropocentric positionings but also counter conceptions of training that operate at a level of abstraction, for R+ approaches are produced in and through specific material physical relationships; see Yi-Fu Tuan, *Dominance and Affection: The Making of Pets* (New Haven, CT: Yale University

Press, 1984). The examples I present are relatings more in keeping with what Juno Parreñas, writing about the politics of orangutan rehabilitation in Borneo, terms a "mutual but unequal vulnerability": with a human positioned as holding the leash, but not with the goal of canine submission. See Juno Parreñas, *Decolonizing Extinction* (Durham, NC: Duke University Press, 2018).

95 I detail the specifically scientific stakes of the divide between R+ and aversive methods in "Feminisms, Fuzzy Sciences, and Interspecies Intersectionalities: The Promises and Perils of Contemporary Dog Training," *Catalyst* 3, no. 1 (October 2017): 1–27.

96 See Patricia McConnell, *The Other End of the Leash: Why We Do What We Do around Dogs* (New York: Ballantine, 2002).

97 Some of these interventions are documented in Ben Gilbert's "You Probably Shouldn't Hug Your Dog, Regardless of How Adorable They Are," *Business Insider*, November 21, 2017.

98 See Patricia McConnell, *For the Love of a Dog: Understanding Emotion in You and Your Best Friend* (New York: Ballantine, 2005).

99 McConnell, *The Other End of the Leash*, 56–59.

100 One example of this approach is detailed in "Why You Shouldn't Yell at Your Dog and What to Do Instead," Everyday Dog Mom, www.everydaydogmom .com/why-you-shouldnt-yell-at-your-dog/, accessed January 31, 2020.

101 See McConnell, *The Other End of the Leash*, 2002.

102 The nuances of how and why hand signals and body movements are more effective in training are covered by Stanley Coren in "Are Voice Commands or Hand Signals More Effective for Dogs?" *Psychology Today*, June 29, 2016.

103 Here I draw from Vinciane Despret's thinking on "attunement" in "The Body We Care For: Figures of Anthropo-zoo-genesis," *Body and Society* 10, nos. 2–3: 111–34.

104 See Jean Donaldson, *Culture Clash: A New Way of Understanding the Relationship between Humans and Domestic Dogs* (Berkeley, CA: James & Kenneth, 1996).

105 Stacy Greer, "I'm a Professional Dog Trainer and I Don't Walk My Dogs," Stacy the Trainer, May 13, 2019, https://stacythetrainer.blogspot. com/2019/05/im-professional-dog-trainer-i-dont-walk.html, emphasis removed.

106 Martha Knowles, "Importance of Allowing Your Dog to Sniff," Silent Conversations, May 14, 2018, www.silentconversations.com/importance-of -allowing-your-dog-to-sniff.

107 Knowles, "Importance of Allowing."

108 Uexküll, "A Stroll through the Worlds," 48. I am grateful to Bénédicte Boisseron for locating this particular passage.

109 Saidiya Hartman, *Scenes of Subjection: Terror, Slavery, and Self-Making in Nineteenth-Century America* (New York: Oxford University Press, 1997), 18.

110 Hartman, *Scenes of Subjection*, 19.

111 See, for example, Heidi Nast, "Critical Pet Studies?" *Antipode* 38, no. 5 (2006): 894–906.

112 Anonymous interview, July 21, 2017.

113 N.W.A. is a rap group known for, among other songs, "Fuck tha Police," whose body of work is stridently pro-Black and antiracist. "Fuck tha Police," track 2, *Straight Outta Compton*, Ruthless Records, 1988, compact disc. A movie based on the group is also titled *Straight Outta Compton*, dir. F. Gary Gray (California: Universal Pictures, August 2015).

114 *Mine*, dir. Geralyn Pezanoski (California: Film Movement, March 2009).

115 Nicoledogs, "Why We Need to Talk about Racism," Redemption Dogs, August 15, 2017, https://redemptiondogs.com/2017/08/15/racism-animal -rescue-why-we-need-to-talk-about-this.

116 Manohla Dargis, "Four-Legged Survivors of Hurricane Katrina," *New York Times*, January 14, 2010.

3. Becoming in Kind

1   Rosi Braidotti, *Metamorphoses: Towards a Materialist Theory of Becoming* (Cambridge, MA: Polity, 2002), 118.

2   Donna Haraway, *When Species Meet* (Minneapolis: University of Minnesota Press, 2007), 34, 25.

3   Gilles Deleuze and Félix Guattari, *A Thousand Plateaus* (Minneapolis: University of Minnesota Press, 1987), 238.

4   Deleuze and Guattari, *A Thousand Plateaus*, 240; Haraway, *When Species Meet*, 30.

5   Claire Jean Kim discusses these types of analogies in "Moral Extensionism or Racist Exploitation? The Use of Holocaust and Slavery Analogies in the Animal Liberation Movement," *New Political Science* 33, no. 3 (2011): 311–33.

6   Richard Ryder, "Experiments on Animals," in *Animals, Men, and Morals*, ed. Stanley Godlovitch, Rosalind Godlovitch, and John Harris (New York: Taplinger, 1972); Peter Singer, *Animal Liberation*, 2nd ed. (New York: New York Review of Books, 1990).

7   Malcolm Gladwell, "Troublemakers: What Pit Bulls Can Teach Us about Profiling," *New Yorker*, February 6, 2006.

8   See Marcy Setter's Find-a-Bull test at Pit Bulls on the Web, www.pitbull sontheweb.com/petbull/findpit.html, accessed June 30, 2012.

9   Victoria Voith, Elizabeth Ingram, Katherine Mitsouras, and Kristopher Irizarry, "Comparison of Adoption Agency Breed Identification and DNA Breed Identification of Dogs," *Journal of Applied Animal Welfare Science* 12 (2009): 253–62.

10   Harold Herzog, "Forty-Two Thousand and One Dalmatians: Fads, Social Contagion, and Breed Popularity," *Society and Animals* 14, no. 4 (2006): 383–97.

11 Karen Delise, *The Pit Bull Placebo: The Media, Myths, and Politics of Canine Aggression* (Ramsey, NJ: Anubis, 2007), 20–35; Bénédicte Boisseron, *Afro-Dog: Blackness and the Animal Question* (New York: Columbia University Press, 2018).

12 Delise, *The Pit Bull Placebo*, 48.

13 For locations, see the map of breed-specific legislation provided by Animal Farm Foundation, "Breed Specific Legislation Map," updated monthly, https://animalfarmfoundation.org/community-advocates /bsl-map.

14 Vicki Hearne, *Bandit: The Heart-Warming True Story of One Dog's Rescue from Death Row* (New York: Sky Horse, 2007), 25.

15 Data from "Media Center," National Canine Research Council, www.nation alcanineresearchcouncil.com/media-center/bsl, accessed July 2, 2012.

16 Linda Weiss, "Breed-Specific Legislation in the United States," Animal Legal and Historical Web Center, 2001, www.animallaw.info/articles /aruslweiss2001.htm.

17 Weiss, "Breed-Specific Legislation." The attorney Kenneth M. Phillips points to several cases where the "owners of a pit bull were deemed to be aware of its dangerous propensity to attack without warning, even though it never had done so in the past, thereby supporting a jury's find-ing of civil liability for a dog bite": see "Breed Specific Laws," Dog Bite Law, dogbitelaw.com/breed-specific-laws/breed-specific-laws.html, accessed July 3, 2012.

18 Phillips, "Breed Specific Laws."

19 Colin Dayan, *The Law Is a White Dog: How Legal Rituals Make and Unmake Persons* (Princeton, NJ: Princeton University Press, 2011).

20 Nicolas Riccardi, "Denver's Dogged Outlaws," *Los Angeles Times*, August 2, 2005.

21 The creators of the StubbyDog website are among those who use the phrase *breed-discriminatory legislation* ("12 Reasons to Oppose Breed Discriminatory Legislation," StubbyDog, July 12, 2012, stubbydog. org/2012/07/12-reasons-to-oppose-breed-discriminatory-legislation). The use of the term *canine racism* is widespread; see Karyn Grey, "Breed-Specific Legislation Revisited: Canine Racism or the Answer to Florida's Dog Control Problems?," *Nova Law Review* 27 (Spring 2003): 415–32.

22 Josh Liddy, "Response to Pam Ashley," Sway Love, www.swaylove.org /response-to-pam-ashley, accessed July 23, 2012.

23 Quotation from Tanya Irwin, "Many Shelter Dogs Mislabeled 'Pit Bulls,'" *The Blade*, March 18, 2012, www.toledoblade.com/local/2012/03/18/Many -shelter-dogs-mislabeled-pit-bulls.html.

24 Lisa Capretto, "'Fruitvale Station' Star Michael B. Jordan: 'Black Males, We Are America's Pit Bull,'" *HuffPost*, December 18, 2013, www.huffing tonpost.com/2013/12/18/fruitvale-station-michael-b-jordan_n_4462009 .html.

25 Brian C. Anderson, "Scared of Pit Bulls? You'd Better Be!" *City Journal*, Spring 1999, www.city-journal.org/html/9_2_scared_of_pit.html; Bixby Jones, "Pit Bulls, White Trash, and Ghetto Fabulous A-Holes," The Sandy Tongue blog, April 27, 2012, thesandytongue.wordpress.com/2012/04 /27/794.

26 For example, an Associated Press article from July 24, 2007, "Vick Case Illustrates Pit Bull's Changing Status," includes a subsection titled "Tied into the Hip-Hop Culture" that outlines links between pit bull problems and hip-hop and rap music cultures. Available at www.msnbc.msn.com /id/19937995/ns/us_news/t/vick-case-illustrates-pit-bulls-changing -status.

27 Gina Lombroso-Ferrero, *Criminal Man: According to the Classification of Cesare Lombroso* (New York: G. P. Putnam and Sons, 1911), 11–24; Samuel George Morton, *Crania Americana* (Philadelphia: J. Dobson, 1839).

28 Changes in racial patterns of ownership and breeding in the 1980s are discussed in Hearne's *Bandit* and, with regard to dog men, in *Off the Chain: A Shocking Exposé* on America's Forsaken Breed, dir. Bobby Brown (Allumination Filmworks, 2004).

29 Mel Chen, *Animacies: Biopolitics, Racial Mattering, and Queer Affect* (Durham, NC: Duke University Press, 2012), 14.

30 Steve Hummer, "Vick Burns in Tailgate Effigy at Dome," *Atlanta Journal-Constitution*, September 18, 2011.

31 NBC Sports documents the graffiti in "Mural of Michael Vick Depicts Him Choking a Puppy Wearing a Cowboys Jersey," NBC Sports, August 27, 2009; Lisa Richards deploys the image of Vick in chains image in "Excusing Michael Vick's Animal Abuse as Reaction to Slavery and Segregation," Lisa Richards: Rock N' Roll Politics, January 4, 2011, sports.yahoo.com /nfl/blog/shutdown_corner/post/Philly-graffiti-artist-wants-Vick-to -treat-Cowbo?urn=nfl,185585, accessed July 7, 2012.

32 Typical of these arguments are assertions that those who engage in street-level fights are less responsible than earlier dog men; for example, their failure to weed out "man eaters" allegedly results in more incidents of dogs biting humans than previously, when such dogs were assiduously put down. See, for one example, "What Is You [sic] Opinion on Dog Fighting," Yahoo Answers, answers.yahoo.com/question/index?qid=200803181 80257AAVT6Pq, accessed January 30, 2013.

33 Glen Elder, Jennifer Wolch, and Jody Emel, "Race, Place, and the Bounds of Humanity," *Society and Animals* 6, no. 2 (1998): 198.

34 Elder, Wolch, and Emel, "Race, Place, and the Bounds of Humanity," 194.

35 Jim Gorant, *The Lost Dogs: Michael Vick's Dogs and Their Tales of Rescue and Redemption* (New York: Gotham, 2010), 10.

36 Achille Mbembe remarks on this dynamic in *On the Postcolony* (Berkeley: University of California Press, 2001), 26–28.

37 Quoted in Gorant, *Lost Dogs*, 109.

38 Megan Glick, "Animal Instincts: Race, Criminality, and the Reversal of the 'Human,'" *American Quarterly* 65, no. 3 (2013): 640.

39 Glick, "Animal Instincts," 641; "Remarks by President Trump at a California Sanctuary State Roundtable," White House, May 16, 2018, www.white house.gov/briefings-statements/remarks-president-trump-california -sanctuary-state-roundtable/.

40 Glick, "Animal Instincts," 656.

41 Kim, *Dangerous Crossings*, 254–255.

42 Kim, *Dangerous Crossings*, 255, 275–78.

43 I attended a seminar on illegal animal fighting in which a USDA agent gave details of a bust where three successive contests were staged inside a building operated by the USDA and its informants. The dogs involved in the contest, government agents or no, were all put down. Humane Society of the United States and Oakland Animal Shelter, Oakland Police Department, July 8–9, 2010.

44 Susan McCarthy, "A Better Life for Michael Vick's Pit Bulls: BAD RAP Lends a Helping Hand," *The Bark*, July–August 2008, https://thebark.com /content/better-life-michael-vicks-pit-bulls.

45 Bay Area Dog Lovers Responsible about Pit Bulls (BADRAP) was one of two rescue groups involved in evaluating the Vick dogs. The video "See Them Now" was posted on the BADRAP website, www.badrap.org/rescue /vick/now.html, accessed February 1, 2011.

46 Gorant, *Lost Dogs*, 148, 212, 227.

47 Lauren Berlant, *The Queen of America Goes to Washington City: Essays on Sex and Citizenship* (Durham, NC: Duke University Press, 1997), 5.

48 The Canine Good Citizen is a program run by the AKC. The test involves ten elements, including accepting a friendly stranger and supervised separation. See "What is CGC?," American Kennel Club, www.akc.org/events /cgc/program.cfm, accessed July 27, 2012.

49 Berlant, *Queen of America*, 6.

50 The novelist and scholar Toni Morrison analyzes this tendency extensively in *Playing in the Dark: Whiteness and the Literary Imagination* (New York: Random House, 1992).

51 These descriptions are easy to find; one of the more prominent is that of the Villalobos Rescue Center, also featured in the television show on Animal Planet, *Pit Bulls and Parolees*, www.vrcpitbull.net/dog, accessed July 3, 2012.

52 Julie Kink, "Gentle Pit Bull Ruby Working to Erase Breed Stereotype," *St. Croix Valley Press*, November 27, 2009, www.presspubs.com/st_croix /news/article_7d40b429-aa49-5740-add4-1035a36f51df.html.

53 Joanne Brokaw, "Leo, One of the Michael Vick Dogs, Passes Away," Patheos blog, December 18, 2011, www.patheos.com/blogs/heavenlycreatures /2011/12/leo-one-of-the-michael-vick-dogs-passes-away.

54 Gorant, *Lost Dogs*, 148.

55 Ken Foster, *The Dogs Who Found Me* (Guilford, CT: Lyons, 2006), 11.

56 Quoted in Foster, *The Dogs Who Found Me*, book jacket.

57 Catalina Stirling, "Jasmine's Story," www.jasmineshouse.org/who-we-are /jasmines-story, accessed January 27, 2013.

58 David Delany, "The Space That Race Makes," *Professional Geographer* 54, no. 1 (2002): 6–14. I delve into understandings of home in light of histories of race and gender more thoroughly in chapter 4.

59 *Redlining* is a term for the practice of denying services such as bank loans and insurance to residents of primarily nonwhite communities. *Blockbusting* refers to a practice whereby large numbers of properties in a neighborhood are purchased through the fomentation of fears that people of color and poor people are taking over the area, with the goal of reselling those properties at a higher price.

60 These details come from the Save Lennox website, http://savelennox.com, accessed April 1, 2013. DNA tests indicated that Lennox was an American Bulldog and Labrador Retriever mix.

61 "Pit Bull–Type Dog Lennox Put Down, Council Confirms," *BBC News*, July 11, 2012.

62 Agence France-Presse, "Belfast Euthanizes 'Illegal' Pit-Bull Lennox despite International Campaign," Raw Story, July 11, 2012, www.rawstory.com /rs/2012/07/11 /belfast-euthanizes-illegal-pit-bull-lennox-despite-inter national-campaign/.

63 This image has since been taken down but is viewable at the Save Lennox website, http://savelennox.com, accessed March 24, 2014.

64 "Heartbreak as Death Row Dog Lennox Destroyed by Belfast City Council," *Belfast Telegraph Digital*, July 11, 2012; Karlene Turkington, "Raising Awareness for Racially Profiling Dogs such as Lennox," *Opelika Observer*, April 6, 2012, https://opelikaobserver.com/raising-awareness-for-racially -profiling-dogs-such-as-lennox/.

65 "This Could Be YOUR Family, Please Help Fight This Injustice," My Pit Bull Is Family Facebook group, www.facebook.com/MyPitBullisFamily.

66 Many of these images appear on the I Am Lennox Facebook page, www .facebook.com/WeRLennox, accessed March 24, 2014.

67 Robin J. DiAngelo, *White Fragility: Why It's So Hard for White People to Talk about Racism* (Boston: Beacon Press, 2018), 56–57.

68 Angela Davis, *Women, Race, and Class* (New York: Random House, 1983).

69 Davis, *Women, Race, and Class*, 101, 108.

70 "The Color of Justice," Constitutional Rights Foundation, www.crf-usa .org/brown-v-board-50th-anniversary/the-color-of-justice.html, accessed June 30, 2019.

71 Ibid Ibn Safir, "Meet Dog Park Diane: White Woman Calls Police to Dog Park after Black Man's Dog Humps Hers," The Root, February 28, 2019, www.theroot.com/meet-dog-park-diane-white-dog-owner-calls-police -after-1832975830.

72 Marc Bekoff, "Why Dogs Hump: There Isn't a Single Reason behind This Normal Behavior," *Psychology Today*, September 1, 2012, www.psychology today.com/us/blog/animal-emotions/201209/why-dogs-hump.

73 Many rescuers also experience a sense of stigma from owning a "breed ambassador," observing that "you've got to work harder . . . you are being scrutinized and watched every minute of the day." Quoted in Hilary Twining, Arnold Arluke, and Gary Patronek, "Managing the Stigma of Outlaw Breeds: A Case Study of Pit Bull Owners," *Society and Animals* 8, no. 1 (2000): 26.

74 See Hanna Gibson, "Detailed Discussion of Dog Fighting," Animal Legal and Historical Center, 2005, www.animallaw.info/article/detailed -discussion-dog-fighting.

75 My access to this archive was made possible by the generosity of my friend and colleague Jere Alexander.

76 Ed Faron and Chris Faron, *The Complete Gamedog: A Guide to Breeding and Raising the American Pit Bull Terrier* (Charlotte, NC: Walsworth, 1995), 86.

77 Faron and Faron, *The Complete Gamedog*, 55.

78 Quoted in Faron and Faron, *The Complete Gamedog*, 75. *Ch* is short for champion, a dog who has won three fights.

79 Faron and Faron, *The Complete Gamedog*, 63. The term *grand champion* indicates a dog who has won five fights.

80 Bobby Hall, *Bullyson and His Sons* (Charlotte, NC: Walsworth, 1986), 85, 73.

81 Rhonda D. Evans and Craig J. Forsyth, "The Social Milieu of Dog Men and Dog Fights," *Deviant Behavior: An Interdisciplinary Journal* 19 (1998): 61.

82 Faron and Faron, *The Complete Gamedog*, 11, 12.

83 Vick made this statement during an interview with Piers Morgan, quoted by Jonathan Tannenwald, "Michael Vick Admits: 'I Let Money Change Me,'" *Philadelphia Inquirer*, July 17, 2012.

84 The experiment was done by Robert Rosenthal. See Rosenthal, *Experimenter Effects in Behavioral Research* (New York: Appleton-Century-Crofts, 1966). Rosenthal's own interest was in demonstrating experimental bias.

85 Vinciane Despret, "The Body We Care For: Figures of Anthropo-zoo-genesis," *Body and Society* 10, no. 2 (2004): 122.

86 Quoted in Despret, "The Body We Care For," 122.

87 Haraway, *When Species Meet*, 16.

88 Hall, *Bullyson and His Sons*, 191.

89 L. B. Hanna, *The American Pit Bull Terrier and His Master* (Elsted Marsh, UK: Beech, 1926) ,84; Faron and Faron, *The Complete Gamedog*, 54.

90 Jessica Dolce, "How I Failed as a Dog Rescuer: Lessons from a Sanctuary," Notes from a Dog Walker blog, July 21, 2012, notesfromadogwalker. com/2012/07/21/how-i-failed-as-a-rescuer-lessons-from-a-sanctuary.

91 Donna Haraway, "enlightenment@science_wars.com: A Personal Reflection on Love and War," *Social Text* 50 (Spring 1997): 123.

92 John Berger, *Why Look at Animals?* (New York: Penguin, 2009).

93 Jonathan Burt touches on the ambivalences of these representations in *Animals in Film* (London: Reaktion, 2002).

94 In making this proposal, I am also in conversation with Val Plumwood, who proposes "interlocking oppressions" as a way to think through the relationship among race, species, gender, and other categories of difference. See Plumwood, *Feminism and the Mastery of Nature* (London: Routledge, 1993).

95 This move echoes Elizabeth Povinelli's argument in "Notes on Gridlock: Genealogy, Intimacy, Sexuality," *Public Culture* 14, no. 1 (2002): 215–38, in which she proposes an interruption of the ties among sex, kinship, and intimacy as a way to get at a more promising queer politics.

96 Sheila Pell, "Downtown Dogs," *The Bark*, March–April 2008, 60.

97 Richard Tuttlemondo, "About," Petsmart Charities, www.petsmartcharities.org/resources/resources-documents/downtown-dog.pdf, accessed July 23, 2012.

98 Tuttlemondo, "About."

99 Susan McHugh wonderfully documents the extensive history of connections between nonbreed dogs seen as "mutts" and "mongrels" and folks living on the edges of societies, such as Ireland's Travellers and folks who live outside homes in the United States. See "Mutts," in *Dog* (London: Reaktion), 127–70.

4. Queer Imaginings and Affiliative Possibilities

1 Mel Chen, *Animacies: Biopolitics, Racial Mattering, and Queer Affect* (Durham, NC: Duke University Press: 2012), 104.

2 Eve Kosofsky Sedgwick, *Tendencies* (Durham NC: Duke University Press, 1993), 9.

3 Gayatri Gopinath, "Nostalgia, Desire, Diaspora: South Asian Sexualities in Motion," *Positions* 5, no. 2 (1997): 485.

4 See Donna Haraway, "Anthropocene, Capitalocene, Plantationocene, Chthulucene: Making Kin," *Environmental Humanities* 6 (2015): 159–65.

5 See Mark Rifkin, *When Did Indians Become Straight?*(New York: Oxford University Press, 2011); Roderick Ferguson, "The Nightmares of the Heteronormative," *Cultural Values* 4, no. 4 (2000): 419–44; Diane Lewis, "Anthropology and Colonialism," *Current Anthropology* 14, no. 5 (1973): 581–602.

6 For example, see Margo DeMello, "'Bunderground Railroad' Saves Hundreds of Rabbits from Euthanasia," Dodo, March 4, 2014, www.thedodo.com/it-takes-a-village-451691556.html.

7 See Lauren Berlant and Michael Warner, "Sex in Public," *Critical Inquiry* 24, no. 2 (1998): 547–66.

8 I reference here several interactions I witnessed at the annual meeting of the Society for Social Studies of Science in Pasadena, California, October 20–22, 2005.

9   Many thanks to Kansas State University undergraduate Kayla Clark for this wonderful turn of phrase.

10 Discussed in Kristen Warfield, "Shelter 'Marries' Bonded Dogs So People Will Have to Adopt Them Together," Dodo, February 22, 2019, www.the dodo.com/close-to-home/shelter-dog-wedding-jack-diane.

11 For example, former U.S. presidential hopeful Ben Carson noted in 2013, "Well, my thoughts are that marriage is between a man and a woman. It's a well-established, fundamental pillar of society and no group, be they gays, be they NAMBLA, be they people who believe in bestiality, it doesn't matter what they are, they don't get to change the definition." Quoted in "Ben Carson: Compares Same-Sex Marriage to Bestiality," Human Rights Campaign, www.hrc.org/2016RepublicanFacts/ben-carson, accessed July 14, 2019.

12 *Adorable Dog Commercials by Subaru*, YouTube, March 28, 2018, www .youtube.com/watch?v=8hYItcm_daM.

13 For more on Subaru's coded advertising, see Alex Mayyasi and Priceo-nomics, "How Subarus Came to Be Seen as Cars for Lesbians," *Atlantic*, June 22, 2016.

14 Winston Giseke, "The Beagle Effect: How Saving Puppies Enriched these LGBT People," *The Advocate*, March 5, 2012, www.advocate.com/news /daily-news/2012/03/05/beagle-effect-how-saving-puppies-enriched-these-lgbt-people. While the article discusses beagles rescued from labo-ratories, pit bulls also feature prominently in movements oriented toward the prevention of the use of dogs in animal testing: see Sue Coe's *Pit's Letter* (New York: Four Walls Eight Windows, 2000).

15 *Our Pride Video!* BADRAP, June 27, 2011, www.facebook.com/BADRAP. org/posts/172314092832426.

16 "Dog Doesn't Consider Itself Part of Family," *The Onion*, March 14, 2014, www.theonion.com/articles/ dog-doesnt-consider-itself-part-of-family,35532.

17 Gail Mason, *The Spectacle of Violence: Homophobia, Gender, and Knowledge* (New York: Routledge, 2002), 61; Sarah Lamble, "Retelling Racialized Vio-lence, Remaking White Innocence: The Politics of Interlocking Oppres-sions in Transgender Day of Remembrance," *Sexuality Research and Social Policy* 5, no. 1 (2008): 32.

18 For example, see Nazia Parveen, "Birmingham School Stops LGBT Lessons after Parents Protest," *Guardian*, March 4, 2019.

19 Cathy Cohen, "Punks, Bulldaggers, and Welfare Queens: The Radical Potential of Queer Politics?" *GLQ* 3 (1997): 437–65.

20 For example, see Kidi Tafesse, "What the 'Mississippi Appendectomy' Says about the Regard of the State towards the Agency of Black Women's Bodies," Movement for Black Women's Lives, May 1, 2019, https://black womenintheblackfreedomstruggle.voices.wooster.edu/2019/05/01/what

-the-mississippi-appendectomy-says-about-the-regard-of-the-state-towards-the-agency-of-black-womens-bodies.

21 Lisa Duggan is widely credited with originating the concept of homo-normativity; see "The New Homonormativity: The Sexual Politics of Neo-liberalism," in *Materializing Democracy: Towards a New Cultural Politics*, ed. Russ Castranovo and Dana Nelson (Durham, NC: Duke University Press, 2002), 175–94.

22 Marlon Bailey, Priya Kandaswamy, and Mattie Udora Richardson, "Is Gay Marriage Racist?," in *That's Revolting!: Queer Strategies for Resisting Assimilation*, ed. Mattilda Bernstein Sycamore (New York: Soft Skull Press, 2008), 113.

23 Bailey, Kandaswamy, and Richardson, "Is Gay Marriage Racist?," 116.

24 For example, see "LGBT Homelessness," National Coalition to End Homelessness, https://nationalhomeless.org/issues/lgbt, accessed July 31, 2019.

25 David Eng, *The Feeling of Kinship: Queer Liberalism and the Racialization of Intimacy* (Durham, NC: Duke University Press, 2010), 43.

26 For a comprehensive overview, see Cedric Robinson, *Cedric J. Robinson: On Racial Capitalism, Black Internationalism, and Cultures of Resistance*, ed. H. L. T. Quan (London: Pluto, 2019).

27 Eng, *The Feeling of Kinship*,10, 47.

28 Eng, *The Feeling of Kinship*, 38; Siobhan Somerville, "Queer Loving," *GLQ* 11, no. 3 (2005): 347–49.

29 Kami Chisholm, dir., *Pride Denied: Homonationalism and the Future of Queer Politics* (San Francisco: Media Education Foundation, 2016).

30 For one take on pinkwashing, see "The Rise of Pride Marketing and the Curse of 'Pinkwashing,'" The Conversation, August 26, 2014, https://theconversation.com/the-rise-of-pride-marketing-and-the-curse-of-pink-washing-30925.

31 See "Weekend Read: The First Pride Was a Riot," Southern Poverty Law Center, June 22, 2019, www.splcenter.org/news/2019/06/22/weekend-read-first-pride-was-riot.

32 Roderick Ferguson, *Aberrations in Black: Toward a Queer of Color Critique* (Minneapolis, MN: University of Minnesota Press, 2004), 4.

33 "About," Trans Day of Visibility, http://tdov.org/about, accessed June 16, 2019.

34 Eric Stanley, "Anti-trans Optics: Recognition, Opacity, and the Image of Force," *South Atlantic Quarterly* 116, no. 3 (July 2017): 612–20. While "clocking" holds a colloquial meaning denoting the act of noticing something as aberrant or out of place, Stanley's usage, reflects its more particularized deployment in contemporary U.S. popular culture.

35 Jacques Derrida, *The Animal That Therefore I Am* (New York: Fordham University Press, 2008).

36 Emmanuel Levinas, "The Paradox of Morality," in *The Provocation of Levinas*, ed. Robert Bernasconi and David Wood (New York: Routledge, 1988), 169.

37 David Clark, "On Being 'The Last Kantian in Nazi Germany': Dwelling with Animals after Levinas," in *Animal Acts*, ed. Jennifer Ham and Matthew Senior (New York: Routledge, 1997), 56.

38 Matthew Calarco contends that Levinas holds a "classical . . . view of the animal," who is "blind and deaf to the call of the Other" in *Zoographies: The Question of the Animal from Heidegger to Derrida* (New York: Columbia University Press, 2008), 56. See also Donna Haraway, *When Species Meet* (Minneapolis: University of Minnesota Press, 2008), 19–23.

39 See Alexandra Horowitz, *Inside of a Dog* (New York: Scribner, 2009), 259–82.

40 See Randy Kidd, "The Canine Sense of Smell," *The Whole Dog Journal*, October 14 2004 (updated April 23, 2019), www.whole-dog-journal.com /health/the-canine-sense-of-smell.

41 Horowitz, *Inside of a Dog*, 73–75.

42 Author's field notes, April 2013.

43 See Mara Velez, "The Shelter Playgroup Alliance," *IAABC Journal*, https:// winter2019.iaabcjournal.org/shelter-playgroup-alliance, accessed July 31, 2019.

44 See Horowitz, *Inside of a Dog*, 196–205.

45 Author's field notes, May 2013.

46 Pseudonymous interview with Cindy, July 2017.

47 Mel Chen, *Animacies: Biopolitics, Racial Mattering, and Queer Affect* (Durham, NC: Duke University Press, 2012), 104, 11.

48 Michel Foucault, "The Social Triumph of the Sexual Will," in *Ethics: Subjectivity and Truth*, ed. Paul Rabinow (New York: New Press, 1994), 158. For a nuanced critique of whiteness in Foucault's thinking, see Marlon Ross, "Beyond the Closet as a Raceless Paradigm," in *Black Queer Studies: A Critical Anthology*, ed. E. Patrick Johnson and Mae G. Henderson (Durham, NC: Duke University Press, 2005).

49 Elizabeth Povinelli, "Notes on Gridlock," *Public Culture* 14, no. 1 (2002): 216.

50 For a more complete rendering of this approach, see Grisha Stewart, *Behavior Adjustment Training 2.0: New Practical Techniques for Fear, Frustration, and Aggression* (Wenatchee, WA: Dogwise, 2016).

51 In referencing consent in feminist discussions, I invoke a very broad conceptualization of the term. Consent, while certainly germane to discussions of what can be termed a pervasive, heteropatriarchal "rape culture," is also crucial in other contexts: for example, in making sure that adults ask children for permission before engaging in bodily contacts such as hugs. See Hazel/Cedar Troost, "Reclaiming Touch: Rape Culture, Explicit Verbal Consent, and Body Sovereignty," in *Yes Means Yes! Visions of Female*

Sexual Power and a World without Rape, ed. Jaclyn Friedman and Jessica Valenti (Berkeley: Seal Press, 2008).

52 Suzanne Dubnicka, "Consent and Dog Training," All the Dogs, February 12, 2019, https://allthedogstraining.com/consent-and-dog-training.

53 Audre Lorde, "Uses of the Erotic: The Erotic as Power," in *Sister Outsider* (New York: Ten Speed Press, [1984] 2007), 89.

54 Lorde, *Uses of the Erotic*, 88.

55 Karen Pryor, *Don't Shoot the Dog: How to Improve Yourself and Others through Behavioral Training* (New York: Simon & Schuster, 1984).

56 For example, see Kelsie McKenzie, "10 Signs of a Backyard Breeder," It's Dog or Nothing, April 7, 2014, https://itsdogornothing.com/10-signs -of-a-backyard-breeder.

57 Jenna Stregowski, "Signs of a Bad Breeder or Backyard Breeder," The Spruce Pets, September 26, 2019, www.thesprucepets.com/signs-of-a -bad-breeder-1117328; The Kennel Club, "Managing Inbreeding and Genetic Diversity," The Kennel Club blog, https://www.thekennelclub .org.uk/health/for-breeders/inbreeding-and-genetic-diversity/managing -inbreeding-and-genetic-diversity, accessed June 1, 2020; Irene Sommerfeld-Stur, "Infertility and Inbreeding: How Veterinarians Should Tell Breeders What They Do Not Want to Hear," *World Small Animal Veterinary Association World Congress Proceedings*, 2006, www.vin.com/apputil/content /defaultadv1.aspx?pId=11223&id=3859259&print=1. See Donna Haraway, *The Companion Species Manifesto* (Chicago: Prickly Paradigm Press, 2003), for an extensive discussion of efforts to track a seizure disorder in lineages of Australian Shepherds and commentary on the difficulties of introducing similar initiatives in other breed lines.

58 Pseudonymous interview with Sara, July 2017.

59 Pseudonymous interview with Sharon, July 2017.

60 Pseudonymous interview with Nathan, July 2017.

61 Michelle Murphy, *The Economization of Life* (Durham, NC: Duke University Press, 2017).

62 Rachel Walden, "Reproductive Justice Concerns Surround Long-Acting Contraception Methods," Our Bodies Ourselves blog, June 13, 2014, www .ourbodiesourselves.org/2014/06/reproductive-justice-concerns-long -acting-contraception.

63 Author's field notes, June 2017.

64 Author's field notes, July 2008; Haraway, *Companion Species Manifesto*, 81–87.

65 u/RhubarbRaptor, "[Discussion] Reputable Mutt Breeders?," www.reddit .com/r/dogs/comments/czq630/discussion_reputable_mutt_breeders/, accessed June 2, 2020.

66 See American Kennel Club, "AKC's Guide to Responsible Dog Breeding," The American Kennel Club blog, www.akc.org/breeder-programs/breeder -education/akcs-guide-responsible-dog-breeding, accessed June 5, 2020.

67 Adrienne Farricelli, "Four Facts about Hybrid Dogs Unethical Breeders Don't Want You to Know," PetHelp.com, May 24, 2019, https://pethelpful.com/dogs/The-Truth-about-Hybrid-Vigor-in-Dogs-Breeders-Dont-Want-You-to-Know.

68 Alison Kafer, *Feminist, Queer, Crip* (Bloomington: Indiana University Press, 2013), 11.

69 For more extensive discussion of and critique of Millan's approach, see Lynne Peeples, "Critics Challenge 'Dog Whisperer' Methods," Live Science, November 12, 2009, www.livescience.com/5846-critics-challenge-dog-whisperer-methods.html.

70 Author's field notes, June 2013.

71 Pseudonymous interview with Veronica, July 2017.

72 Author's field notes, June 2013.

73 Pseudonymous interview with Rowena, July 2017.

74 Pseudonymous interview with Yolanda, July 2017.

Conclusion

1 I borrow the language of "imagining otherwise" from the 2018 National Women's Studies Association conference title, "Just Imagining: Imagining Justice," Atlanta, GA, November 8–11, 2018.

2 For an accessible discussion of Foucault and *discourse*, see "Michel Foucault," Stanford Encyclopedia of Philosophy, April 2, 2003, revised May 22, 2018, https://plato.stanford.edu/entries/foucault/.

3 For example, see Lina D., "15 Unusual Animal Friendships That Will Melt Your Heart," Bored Panda, www.boredpanda.com/unusual-animal-friendships-interspecies/?utm_source=google&utm_medium=organic&utm_campaign=organic, accessed January 28, 2020. I am also referring to the question famously asked by Rodney King, the Black motorist whose beating by Los Angeles police officers was caught on film and led to mass unrest across the United States in 1992.

4 Mizuho Nakamura, Navneet Dhand, Bethany J. Wilson, Melissa J. Starling, and Paul D. McGreevy, "Picture Perfect Pups: How Do Attributes of Photographs of Dogs in Online Rescue Profiles Affect Adoption Speed?" *Animals* 10, no. 1 (2020): 152.

5 For example, see Lauren Artino and Erin Couch, "'One of the Worst We Have Seen': About 50 Neglected Animals, 2 Dead Dogs Found in Apparent Hoarding Situation in Bethel," Fox 19, January 5, 2020, www.fox19.com/2020/01/06/one-worst-we-have-seen-around-neglected-animals-found-hoarding-situation-bethel-home/.

6 For one excellent entry on this topic, see Leslie Irvine's *My Dog Always Eats First: Homeless People and Their Animals* (Boulder, CO: Lynne Rienner, 2013).

7   Pseudonymous interview with Veronica, July 2017.
8   For those who are not fortunate enough to have Belgian Malinois owners
     in their social spheres, such dogs are often characterized as high drive,
     high energy, and fairly disinterested in and even hostile toward unfamil-
     iar humans. They are used widely in police work as well as drug enforce-
     ment in the U.S. and elsewhere.
9   Author's field notes, August 10, 2013.
10   Raymond Coppinger and Lorna Coppinger, *Dogs: A New Understanding
     of Canine Origin, Behavior, and Evolution* (Chicago: University of Chicago
     Press, 2001), 30.
11   Here I reference the cases discussed by Malcolm Gladwell in particular in
     "Troublemakers: What Pit Bulls Can Teach Us about Profiling," *New Yorker*,
     February 6, 2006.
12   Pseudonymous interview with Jane, July 2017.
13   For readers interested in the connections between police and racism,
     transphobia, homophobia, and colonialism, David Correia and Tyler
     Wall's *Police: A Field Guide* (New York: Verso, 2018), is a good place to start.
14   See Mara Velez, "The Shelter Playgroup Alliance," *IAABC Journal*, https://
     winter2019.iaabcjournal.org/shelter-playgroup-alliance/, accessed July 31,
     2019.
15   Author's field notes, September 10, 2013.
16   See Jessica Pierce, "Open Adoptions in Shelters Help Animals and People:
     A View from the Inside on What Open Adoptions Are and How They Can
     Help Animals," *Psychology Today*, February 26, 2019.
17   Here I am drawing on the language of Trish King, a professional behav-
     iorist and trainer who also teaches humans; for more, see "About," Canine
     Behavior Associates, www.canine-behavior-associates.com/about-1/about
     -trish/, accessed January 29, 2020.
18   See for example L. David Mech, "Biographical Material," Dave Mech blog,
     http://davemech.org/biographical-material/, accessed January 29, 2020.
19   I am thinking in particular of a case described by the ethologist Patricia
     McConnell, whose chapter "The Truth about Dominance" in her wonder-
     ful book *The Other End of the Leash* (New York: Ballantine, 2002) details
     not only this case but also the larger philosophy I sketch out here.
20   Pseudonymous interview with Sharon, July 2017.
21   See "Felony Animal Cruelty Laws in All 50 States," National Humane
     Education Society, www.nhes.org/felony-animal-cruelty-laws-in-all-50
     -states/, accessed January 30, 2020.
22   Readers interested in the history and theory of both restorative and
     transformative justice should see Anthony J. Nocella II, "An Overview of
     the History and Theory of Transformative Justice," *Peace and Conflict
     Review* 6, no. 1: 1–10. For a take on accountability that builds on these
     understandings, see the disability studies scholar and activist Mia Mingus's

"How to Give a Good Apology, Part 1: The Four Parts of Accountability," December 18, 2019, https://leavingevidence.wordpress.com/2019/12/18/how-to-give-a-good-apology-part-1-the-four-parts-of-accountability.

23 See Isabelle Stengers, *Cosmopolitics I* (Minneapolis: University of Minnesota Press, 2010).

24 Isabelle Stengers, "A Constructivist Reading of Process and Reality," unpublished manuscript; Alfred North Whitehead, *Modes of Thought* (New York: Free Press, 1938; rept. MacMillan 1968), 116.

25 Stengers, "A Constructivist Reading," 3.

26 Stengers, "A Constructivist Reading," 2.

Index

affect, 14, 73–75; and becomings, 102, 122–24; and bodyings, 166; and knowledge politics, 20, 57; and like-race logics, 114–16; and love, 121, 131; and queerness and racialization, 74–75; and saviorist storying, 47–50; and sensibility, 57; and temporality, 158–59; and understanding dogs, 76–79, 83–84, 89, 94

affiliation, 57, 129–30, 151; and animal rescue and sheltering, 164; and bodyings, 153; and dog behavior, 128–29, 144, 147–48, 162; and dog breeding, 157–58; and intimacy without relatedness, 144, 146; queerness of, 129–32; refusals of, 161–64; and relatedness without kinship, 144; and temporality, 158–59

American Kennel Club, 3, 104, 112, 158

American Pit Bull Terrier, 3, 104–5, 135

animal: construction of "the," 14, 85, 141, 166, 187–88

animal rescue, 3–6, 25; and ableism, 32–33; and accountability, 178; and adoption criteria, 26; and affiliations, 164; and assumptions of abuse, 36–37; and becoming in kind, 125; and dog selection, 26; and friction with purebred, 27; and geographies, 33–36; and inappropriate placements, 44–46; increase in numbers of, 47; and ontology, 36–38; policy changes for, 176–77, 180–81; and pulling from shelters, 25–26; and racialization, 29–32, 34; as retailers, 47–48; and socioeconomic status, 33; and structural violence, 100; and Vick dogs, 6–7, 16–17; whiteness of, 29. *See also* animal shelter

animal sanctuaries, 41–43, 123, 162, 173–74; and no-kill movement, 24

animal shelter, 4, 25, 173; and accountability, 178; and adoption criteria, 26; and affiliations, 163, 164; and dog-dog playgroups, 4; keeping dogs out of, 174–75; and knowledge claims, 56, 97; and neoliberalism, 46–47; and no-kill movement, 5, 26; and open-admission policies, 4, 25, 163; policy changes for, 177–81; and prison references, 31–32; queer affiliations in, 159, 163; and rescues' pulling dogs, 25–26; telos of, 36–37; and transphobia, 36. *See also* animal rescue

interspecies intersectionality, 7–20, 22–23, 156, 172; and accountability, 48; and becoming in kind, 101–3, 125–27; and colonialism, 49–50; and disruptions, 167–69, 171–73, 185–86; and empathy, 94; interruptions of, 51–54; and knowledge claims, 57–59; and knowledge politics, 39–41, 45–46; and neoliberalism, 47; and no kill, 44–46; and racialization, 41; and saviorist storying, 29, 37–39, 43, 183; and sensibility, 89; and temporality, 42. *See also* intersectionality

intimacy without relatedness, 144–46, 148, 164–65

Jacobson's nose, 142–43
Jordan, Michael B., 107

Kafer, Alison, 158–59
Kandaswamy, Priya, 136
Kennebac Valley Humane Society, 133
Kim, Claire Jean, 64–66, 110
kinship, 16–17; and dog men, 120–21; norms of, 19, 35, 111–12; 130–40; relatedness without, 144–49; strayings from, 102, 126–27, 165. *See also* relatedness without kinship
Knowles, Martha, 93

Lamble, Sarah, 11–12, 135
Latour, Bruno, 71
Lawrence v. Texas, 132, 137
Lennox, 114–19
Levinas, Emmanuel, 141
like-race logic, 20–22, 97, 103, 106–8, 114–16, 131; in LGBTQ advocacy, 138
Livingston, Julie, 12
Lombroso, Cesare, 107
Lorde, Audre, 9, 70–71, 84, 152–53, 166, 188
Louis-Leclerc, Georges, 61

love: and becoming in kind, 120–25; and houselessness, 127; and intimacy without relatedness, 146; and knowledge politics, 94; and LGBTQ advocacy, 130–35; of Michael Vick for dogs, 122; and pit bull politics, 113–14; and positive reinforcement training, 152–53, 165–66; and saviorist storying, 79; and Vick dogs, 111
Loving v. Virginia, 138
Lugones, María, 63–64
Lundblad, Michael, 63

Martin, Trayvon, 115–16
marriage, 138, 152; of dogs, 133–34; gay marriage, 111, 130, 134, 136–40; and temporality, 159
Mason, Gail, 11–12, 135
Massumi, Brian, 73
Mbembe, Achille, 109–10
McConnell, Patricia, 90–92, 182
McDevitt, Leslie, 182
McWhorter, Ladelle, 61–64
Mech, L. David, 85–86
Millan, Cesar, 160, 178
Mine (film), 98–100
Morton, Samuel, 61–62, 107
Mowat, Farley, 88
multispecies justice, 19, 54, 172, 184, 187–89
Murphy, Michelle, 156–57
mutts, 38, 157–58, 160, 167–69, 176

Nash, Jennifer, 9–11
necropolitics, 109–10
neoliberalism, 29, 46–49, 52, 175, 178, 184
new materialisms, 73. *See also* Chen, Mel; posthuman
no-kill movement, 5, 17, 24–28, 36, 38–39, 42–48, 173, 175, 178; and temporality, 43–46
Nott, Josiah, 61–62

Obama, Barack, 66
Obergefell v. Hodges, 138
Onion, The, 135
open-admission animal shelter, 4–5, 25–26, 48, 163. *See also* animal shelter

Pacelle, Wayne, 109
pet industry, 28
Pezanoski, Geralyn, 98–100
pinkwashing, 138–39
pit bull, 3–6, 19, 78–79, 127, 175; and backyard breeding, 154; and badness, 163, 171, 179–80, 185; and becoming in kind, 101–4, 125–26; and BSL 5–6; and category problems, 104–6, 175–76; and dog men, 120–23; and geography, 114; and LGBTQ advocacy, 134–39; and love, 113–14; owned by Michael Vick, 6–7, 111–13; and policing, 168, 170; and politics, 147, 172; and racialization, 6–7, 13–15, 22, 66, 106–7, 114–18; and rescue politics, 47, 113; and saviorist storying, 40
police: in animal sheltering and control, 139, 168, 177–85; and homonormativity, 139; and massacre of sled dogs, 65; and racism, 107, 117–18, 137; and use of dogs, 67
positive reinforcement training, 59, 132, 160, 179, 181–83; and bodyings, 149–53, 165–66, 169; and love, 152–53, 165–66; versus aversive training, 90–92
posthuman, 15, 73. *See also* new materialisms
Povinelli, Elizabeth, 148, 164
Pride Denied (film), 36, 138
Pryor, Karen, 153, 182
Puar, Jasbir, 12, 189
Puig de la Bellacasa, María, 51, 56, 71–73, 75, 84, 89, 94–95. *See also* thinking-with
purebred dogs, 26–27, 155–58

Qimmit: A Clash of Two Truths (film), 65
queer affiliations, 19–22, 129–32, 144, 148, 158–59, 169; and bodyings, 153–54; and dog breeding, 156–58; and logics, 165–69; promises of, 143, 149, 165–66, 171, 187–89; and refusals, 164; and strayings, 143–44, 161, 164, 187–89; and temporality, 158–59
queer-forward, 171–72
queer of color theorizing, 11, 17, 130, 135–40, 151, 154, 169
queer theory: and affiliations, 129–32; and family, 16–17, 130–39; and home, 16–17; and intimacy, 148; and like-race logic, 138; and love, 130–35; and norms, 16; and queer of color interventions, 135–40, 151, 154, 169; and refusals of relating, 161–64; and temporality, 158–61, 166–67. *See also* queer affiliations; queer of color theorizing
Quijano, Anibal, 60–63

racial capitalism, 63, 137, 151, 158, 185–87
racialization: and *assemblage*, 14–15; and COVID–19, 14–15; and family, 17–18, 34, 49–53, 65, 96, 112, 140; and geography, 7, 12–13, 16–17, 20; and homes, 17–18, 34–35, 49–53, 65, 96; and like-race logic, 20–22, 97, 103, 106–8, 114–16, 131; and pit bulls, 6–7, 12–13, 20, 13–15, 22, 66, 106–7, 114–18; and the posthuman, 14–15. *See also* like-race logic
Rattay, Nicole, 113
Reddy, Chandan, 17, 50
Redemption Dogs blog, 30–31, 99
refusals in relating, 161, 163–64
relatedness without kinship, 144, 146–49, 164–65

restorative justice, 126, 187
Richardson, Mattie Udora, 136
Robinson, Cedric, 137
Rowling, J. K., 66

saviorist storying, 17–18, 23, 37–42,
183; and accountability, 43–48;
and affect, 41–42, 48–49; as affective production, 47–50; and colonialism, 49–50; interruptions of
50–54; and love, 79; and no kill,
38–39, 173; and racialization, 39–
41; and shaming, 45–47, 183–84;
and temporality, 41–42
Schenkel, Rudolph, 85
Sedgwick, Eve Kosofsky, 16, 129–30
sensibility, 15, 18–19, 22, 60, 76, 81,
84–85; and affect, 57; and affiliation, 129–30; and awareness, 97–
100; and bodyings, 149–53; disruptions effected by, 97–100; of dogs,
142–43; and geography, 92–93; and
knowledge politics, 57–60, 84–85,
88–89; lack of, 82–83, 89–90, 96–
97, 139, 163; limitations of, 95–96,
167; and positive reinforcement
training, 89–96, 153–54; promise
of, 188–89; and recognition, 165–
66; and relatings, 147–48; in relation to common sense, 81; and
sniffing, 93–94, 165; and temporality, 91–92, 158–59, 165; and
visibility, 141–43, 147. See also
insensibility
Shelter Animals Count, 24
Shelter Playgroup Alliance, 145,
179
Sheridan, Phillip, 64
Sims, J. Marion, 61
species: and dog bites, 67; and ethol-
ogy, 88; and knowledge claims, 59;
and polygenism, 13–14, 61–64; and
Umwelt, 87
Spivak, Gayatri, 29

Standing Rock Sioux Tribe, 67
standpoint theories, 59, 67–75, 89,
97. See also feminist standpoint
theories
Stengers, Isabelle, 123, 187
strayings, 143–44, 154, 164; from
family norms, 127, 143, 145–49,
153, 156–57, 165–7; from homes,
127, 143, 147–49, 153, 156–57, 167;
importance of, 169; from kinship
norms, 102, 126–27, 165; of queer
affiliations, 143–44, 154–61, 164,
167–69, 187–88
Strum, Shirley, 88
Subaru, 133–34

temperament testing, 179–80
temporality 166–67; and affect, 158–
59; and affiliation, 158–59; and dog
perceptions, 91–92; and no kill, 43–
46; and queer theorizing, 35, 158–
61, 166–67; and saviorist storyings, 41–42; and thinking-with, 75;
and valorization of death, 159–61,
167. See also death-value timing
thinking-with, 51–53, 56–58, 98–100,
173, 176; and becoming in kind,
127; and positive reinforcement
training, 188; and sensibility,
84–85, 129, 143; and strayings,
143. See also Puig de la Bellacasa,
María
toxic masculinity, 186
transformative justice, 184, 186–89
Trump, Donald, 66, 71, 109
Tudor, Earl, 121, 124
Tuttlemondo, Richard, 126–27
Types of Mankind, 62fig.

Umwelt, 57, 86–88, 91–92, 94–95,
141–43

Vick, Michael, 6–7, 66, 107, 185;
and becoming in kind, 109; dogs

Feminist Technosciences
Rebecca Herzig and Banu Subramaniam, *Series Editors*

Figuring the Population Bomb: Gender and Demography in the Mid-Twentieth Century, by Carole R. McCann

Risky Bodies & Techno-Intimacy: Reflections on Sexuality, Media, Science, Finance, by Geeta Patel

Reinventing Hoodia: Peoples, Plants, and Patents in South Africa, by Laura A. Foster

Queer Feminist Science Studies: A Reader, edited by Cyd Cipolla, Kristina Gupta, David A. Rubin, and Angela Willey

Gender before Birth: Sex Selection in a Transnational Context, by Rajani Bhatia

Molecular Feminisms: Biology, Becomings, and Life in the Lab, by Deboleena Roy

Holy Science: The Biopolitics of Hindu Nationalism, by Banu Subramaniam

Bad Dog: Pit Bull Politics and Multispecies Justice, by Harlan Weaver